# THE
# HOUSES
## OF
# ST. AUGUSTINE

(Notes on the Architecture from 1565 to 1821)

By

Albert Manucy

The St. Augustine Historical Society

St. Augustine, Florida

1978

*Copyright 1962 and 1978*

*By the St. Augustine Historical Society*

*Library of Congress Catalog No. 65-67871*

*Rose Printing Company*

*Tallahassee, Florida*

# ACKNOWLEDGMENT

SINCE my first exposure to it at the University years ago, architectural history has intrigued me. So have the old houses of St. Augustine. The two interests, given time, inevitably produced this book.

But this kind of study cannot be done singlehandedly. I am indebted to many people.

The sponsorship of the St. Augustine Historical Society made the project possible. It is part of the research program outlined by the Board of Directors. Especially helpful were the research notes, sketches, photographs and other aids contributed by the Society's President, J. Tyler Van Campen, and John Carver Harris and Mrs. Doris Coleman Wiles of the staff.

To other associates of the Society, John W. Griffin, William B. Griffen, and Dr. Charles W. Arnade, we owe much of the chapter on the history of housing. Bartolo Crichlow Jr. provided a number of measured drawings essential to the study. Others were obtained from the Historic American Buildings Survey of the National Park Service, and from the files of the St. Augustine Historical Society.

We are grateful to the National Park Service for encouragement and specifically to our colleagues Jean C. Harrington, John W. Griffin and C. Ray Vinten for their suggestions. Charles E. Peterson, Supervising Architect of the Historic American Buildings Survey, reviewed the manuscript and illustrations against his broad knowledge of architectural history. And Frederik C. Gjessing was especially helpful with his intimate knowledge of West Indian colonial construction.

Luis Rafael Arana, National Park Service historian, not only furnished documentary information but served as arbiter on Spanish word usage. To his wife, Eugenia, we are indebted for the painstaking task of preparing the typescripts.

Dr. Hale G. Smith of Florida State University made his St. Augustine archeological findings available and showed his interest in many other ways. For specific data on thatch, thanks are due Mrs. Matthew W. Stirling of Washington, D. C., Richard H. Stewart of the National Geographic Society, and Robert Halgrim of The Edison Home, Fort Myers, Florida. For profitable discussions about the structural details of historic buildings, we are indebted to William F. (Billy) Sánchez, Fred Stone, Harry Mangus and Karl Masters of St. Augustine; and to George Watson, consultant of the St. Augustine Historical Restoration and Preservation Commission.

To the latter Commission, and especially to its Director, Earle W. Newton, thanks are due for encouragement and for aid in developing the final ink drawings. From my pencil sketches Professor Henry C. Edwards of the University of Florida supervised the production of the ink renderings, most of which are the work of Bruce Balk, gifted student in the University's Department of Architecture.

Though the list cannot be complete, those who have given us comments (or in some cases, tacit reviews) and other aid and interest must be mentioned. They include Turpin Bannister, Dean of the College of Fine and Applied Arts, the University of Florida; and also of the University, Dr. John M. Goggin and William Stewart and Blair Reeves; Samuel G. Stoney and Adolphus N. Manucy of Charleston; Walter Hartridge of Savannah; Professor George Kubler of Yale University; Dr. Helen Hornbeck Tanner of Michigan; F. A. Hollingsworth, A.I.A., Hon. David R. Dunham and W. J. Winter of the St. Augustine Historical Society; and my wife Clara and our family, who have patiently endured my preoccupation.

ALBERT MANUCY

*June, 1962*

Since 1962, this book has contributed to the awakening of interest in St. Augustine architecture. Historic houses have undergone restorative work; researches at archeological sites have led to reconstructions; and these successes have even brought about the creation of new structures in the unique St. Augustine style.

The first edition of the book is out of print. The St. Augustine Historical Society, which over the past century has properly assumed a leadership role in matters historical, determined that a new printing was needed in continuing explanation and support of St. Augustine's architectural heritage. Inasmuch as ongoing researches confirm the basics expressed in the 1962 text, this writer happily concurred.

A.M.
October 1978

# CONTENTS

Acknowledgment .................................. 3

The St. Augustine Look ........................... 7

A History of Housing ............................ 14

Design and Materials ............................ 48

Sources ......................................... 134

Notes ........................................... 144

Glossary ........................................ 152

Index ........................................... 167

1. THE ST. AUGUSTINE LOOK

# THE ST. AUGUSTINE LOOK

Ever since Spanish times, St. Augustine has been a "quaint" town. Nobody has ever taken the trouble to find out why. The St. Augustine Look has been researched from impressionistic writings rather than from the matter-of-fact records of the tax assessor; from art photographs in place of house measurements; from genealogy, not the house plan; and from the romance of antiquity instead of prosaic construction details.

This book attempts a systematic examination of St. Augustine colonial architecture. Actually, our objective is threefold: (1) to summarize the history of housing to 1821, (2) set forth architectural characteristics, and (3) define constructional terms and practices.

Such an approach suggests that historical information is a major objective. Indeed, architecture's contribution to historical knowledge is measureless. Architecture manifests the resources of a community, the economic condition, talent, and needs of the people, their tastes, and often their ideals. And while it is sensitive to stress and change, at the same time it is often durable enough to preserve the very record of change. Structural search reveals many facts not to be found in written records.

But if architecture is physical evidence of history, certainly history makes a tremendous impact upon architecture. Events in the life of a community are generally the reason for distinctive construction. Thus if you will understand architecture, you must also know history.

ST. AUGUSTINE began in 1565 as a Spanish military base. That is essentially what it remained for almost 250 eventful years. Drake of England burned the settlement in 1586, freebooters sacked it in 1668, South Carolinians besieged and burned it in 1702, and British troops bombarded it in 1740.

Its role as a little military outpost on a wilderness frontier did not justify monumental architecture. As the fort here is small and uncomplicated in contrast to towering defenses at more strategic harbors, so are the houses unpretentious.

Understandably, details about houses before 1700 are hard to get. Homes were mainly wood and thatch. In the humid subtropical climate, these impermanent materials failed to stand before the onslaught of mold and insect, fire and storm. Finally the era of early housing came to an abrupt end when British firebrands touched tinder-dry thatch in 1702. The record says only 20 or 30 houses "of no value" escaped the holocaust.

The renascence after 1702 brought, perhaps for the first time, many substantial houses, spacious and comfortable. Whether the plans were "modern" or traditional, roomy or cramped, one-story or two, extant examples show that the builders had learned how to fit their structures to the climate.

In 1763 the fortunes of a distant war gave this town (along with the rest of Spanish Florida) to Great Britain, and King George's subjects lived here for 20 years. Theirs was a culture foreign to the Spanish. They destroyed dozens of common little homes, remodeled many of the better ones, and built scores of small timber-frame houses for a flood of refugees from the Revolution to the north. Then, like the Spanish before them, they departed, victims of a treaty which gave Florida back to Spain.

The Spanish return (1783) began a new period of turbulence. The Iberian grasp on Florida, never truly firm, relaxed utterly as the nation tried to cope with Napoleon in Europe and a new spirit of independence amongst her colonies in the Americas. Yet in spite of unsettled conditions, after 1790 a number of substantial homes, the parish church and even one or two significant public structures were built. Several examples of this late stage in the colonial architecture are left. The era ended with the cession of Florida to the United States in 1821.

Diverse cultural influences were at hand much earlier, however. First of all was the Stone Age civilization of Florida which faced the colonists as they strode into the utterly unfamiliar wilderness. True, the settlers were all Spaniards; but the new citizens were bringing traditions as varied and distinctive as the many provinces of the homeland. Through the years, other people came. Most were Spanish citizens, but again their origins differed: Spain, the Canary Islands, Mexico, Cuba and other Hispanic-American colonies. Through all, Indian influence continued; and there were generally a few Britishers around, some of them Irish enough to live compatibly with the Spaniards. After 1690 increasing numbers of Negro slaves from the Carolina plantations found freedom and welcome at St. Augustine.

Thus, quite in contrast to the homogenous communities of New England or Virginia, St. Augustine had heterogenous populations exerting many cultural influences, generally in conditions of poverty. Those houses which survived catastrophe underwent a sort of continuous development, in which countless structural additions were made and few taken away.

Although the town population was varied, in some ways it was fairly stable. Except for cataclysmic events such as the great fires or the mass immigration of the British, the demand for housing did not exceed supply. There was also plenty of land and no need to crowd row houses along the streets. It was a military town, though not one of transcendent importance. Government money kept the economy going. With very little trade, industry, farming or ranching, opportunities were meager. In consequence, a man's requirements were few — shelter for the family, a few fruit trees, perhaps a small garden.

So a great many factors have influenced the houses of St. Augustine. The frontier conditions and poverty of the early settlement inhibited construction. Then the catastrophe of 1702 swept away the old town and brought remarkable opportunity. As at no other time, good materials and capable craftsmen were on hand (trained through long years of construction on the stone fort), together with a noticeable improvement in the economy, and new defenses that promised security the city had never had before. The nature of the materials, the national tradition of the people, and the workman's skill were fundamental influences on the buildings. Almost equally important was the climate. Add to these the continuity of the years and the impacts of the cultures which followed the Iberian at St. Augustine: the architectural picture becomes kaleidoscopic and most intriguing — but confused. To ameliorate some of the confusion we have tried to search out and set forth salient characteristics of house construction.

Even more important than the events are the people. It needs to be stressed that there was sudden and almost total population change — not once, but twice — as Spaniard and Briton took turns living there. Another significant element was the large group of Mediterranean colonists who arrived during the British regime. The town also achieved a considerable population of Negro slaves, freemen, and American frontiersmen. In the late years it was a community of many peoples.

## THE DWELLINGS

Our searching has been done in Spanish and English documents, pertinent maps and prints, photographs of old buildings, excavated sites and structures, and in and about standing historic houses. The house of the common man seems to have a special kind of impermanence, as any homeowner can tell you. Time lets man keep (for a while) only structures of unusual worth or beauty. In St. Augustine, timber and tabby have almost disappeared. Thatch has long been gone. Out of some 300 houses standing in 1821, only a tenth are left — mostly stone houses of the 1700's. Probably these are the better houses, not representative of the total architecture.

2. CHARLOTTE STREET ABOUT 1860

Nor can all these houses be satisfactorily dated. Since the fort is the only building that survived the 1702 fire, no house predates 1703.

Pinpointing a house date is a hard job. Documents date public and church property but are seldom concerned with private dwellings. For the later buildings, tax or testamentary records sometimes help; but for early houses even these basic records are scarce. When records are absent, architectural analysis and archeological search are the only recourse, valuable both in standing houses and in excavated ruins. Careful search may bring much lost information to light, such as surprisingly vivid traces of even the poor man's house.

The St. Augustine house is a distinctive house. Its distinction comes from a combination of features, no one of which is unique. It is a house comfortable and often roomy, especially in the late examples.

There are three basic house plans. One, because of a special feature which makes it ideal for the east coast climate, can properly be called the "St. Augustine plan." The feature is a loggia, or sometimes a sheltered porch, opening onto the yard in a way that anticipates the so-called "Florida room" of the 20th century. The porch or loggia admitted the winter sun but excluded the cold winds. In the summer it let in the breeze and tempered the sun. Yet it cannot be shown that the "St. Augustine plan" is indigenous. The probability is that the elements stemmed from Spain through the West Indies.

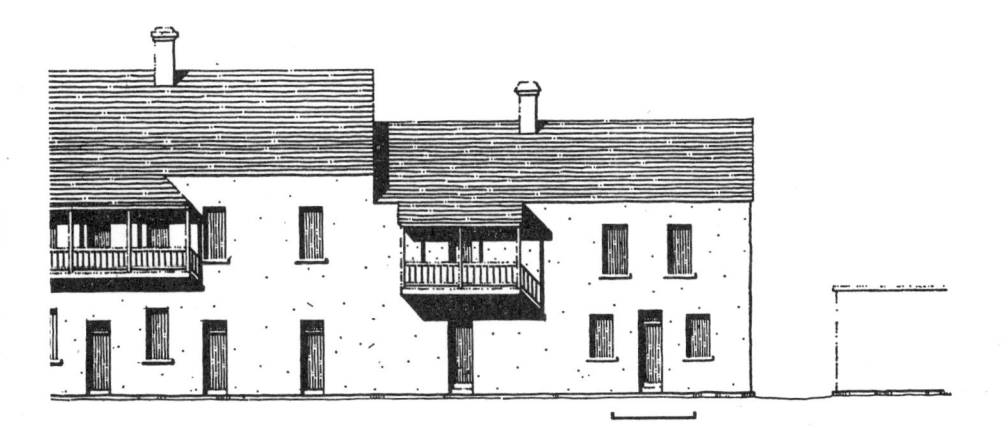

With this plan, the main entrance to the house was through the loggia or the porch, which faced a side yard. A gate in the fence gave access to the street. In fact, the fence gate was the usual way to enter Spanish domiciles, no matter what the floor plan. Doors opening directly into the house from the street came after 1763.

Native materials were thatch, wood, tabby and shellstone, or a combination of these. Fire and other hazards made stone and tabby the most acceptable, and using such coarse materials invariably gave buildings a massive appearance. Smooth plaster to waterproof the masonry further emphasized severe simplicity.

The façades are 1-, 1½- and 2-story, well-proportioned, generally with large openings. Inside shutters and *rejas* were the rule until 1763; afterwards outside shutters and glazed sash came into vogue. Street balconies were common. So were porches and loggias, usually on the yard rather than the street. Chimneys were uncommon before 1763. Privacy-giving high fences were part of the street façade. Roofs were both flat and pitched, the flat ones made of tabby and the pitched ones of thatch or shingle.

\* \* \* \*

This much and little more we know. Spelled out into dimensions and materials and design it gives us the specifications for an informal architecture well suited to the land and the people in colonial times.

Of what use is such knowledge?

To the historian this is factual, tangible data, casting light upon the past. Because of it, he can teach a better history lesson.

The architect finds that it deepens the well of resources from which he can draw solutions for his specialized problems. Perhaps it also increases the layman's interest in the heritage of his country.

But for St. Augustine this knowledge is supremely significant.

For now we know why the St. Augustine look, though it resembles the Spanish, has character of its own. It is a distinctive architecture and an authentic tradition for us to hold. And this is important . . .

> For tradition is not a barren pride in a dead glory. Tradition is something that provides refreshment for the spirit; it is something that gives us deep assurance and a sense of destiny, and a determination to hold fast to the great things that have been done through valor and imagination by those who have gone before us.[1]

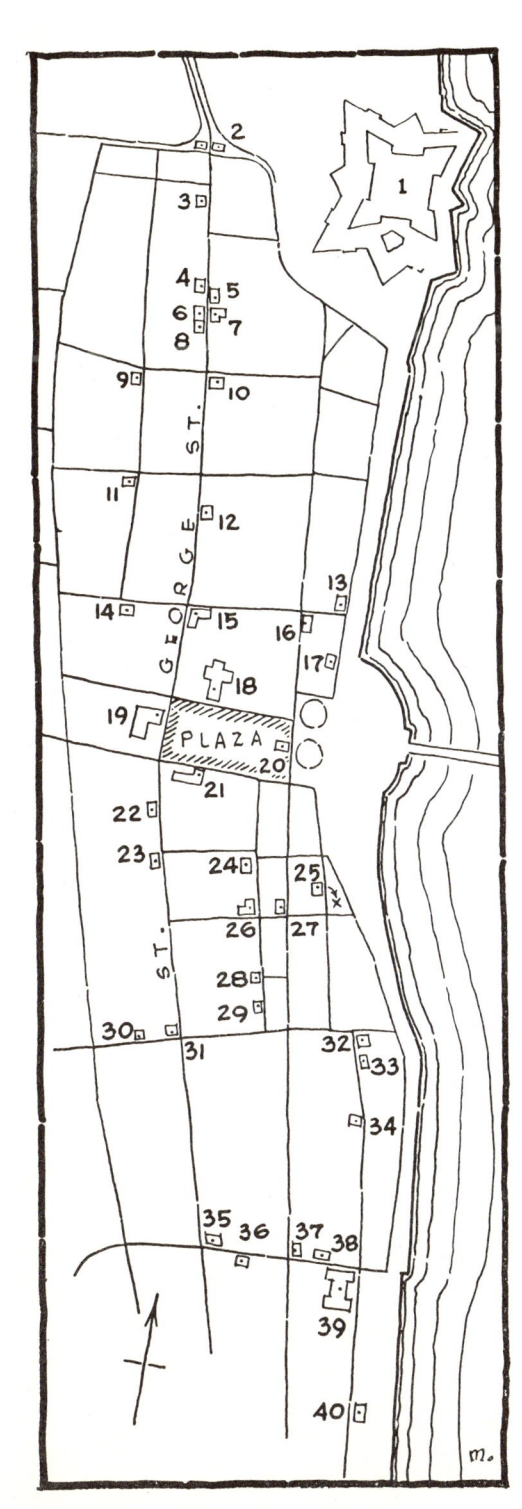

## 3. COLONIAL BUILDINGS IN ST. AUGUSTINE

Although most of these buildings have undergone changes required by successive occupants, each retains significant structural elements dating from colonial times.

1. Castillo de San Marcos
2. City Gate
3. 14 St. George
4. 46 St. George
5. 39 St. George
6. 52 St. George
7. 43 St. George
8. 54 St. George
9. 42 Spanish
10. 65 St. George
11. 62 Spanish
12. 105 St. George
13. 42 Avenida Menendez (foundations only)
14. 57 Treasury
15. 143 St. George
16. 101 Charlotte
17. 46 Avenida Menéndez (a 19th c. reconstruction)
18. Cathedral of St. Augustine
19. Governor's House
20. Market—1824
21. Trinity Episcopal Church—1825
22. 214 St. George
23. 224 St. George
24. 12 Avilés
25. 16 Marine—re-erected
26. 20 Avilés
27. 20 Charlotte
28. 32 Avilés
29. 36 Avilés
30. 46 Bridge
31. 250 St. George
32. 43 Marine
33. 45 Marine
34. 56 Marine
35. 279 St. George
36. 31 St Francis
37. 22 St. Francis
38. 14 St. Francis (Oldest House)
39. St. Francis Barracks
40. King's Bakery

13

# A HISTORY OF HOUSING

## THE BEGINNINGS (1565-1599)

ST. AUGUSTINE's first houses were the huts of an Indian village. For St. Augustine came into being at the Timucua community called Seloy.

Pedro Menéndez de Avilés, the Spanish leader, had sent a vanguard ashore on September 6, 1565, to build a fort. The friendly Timucua chief offered the big communal house to the newcomers, who quickly fortified it with an entrenchment. Don Pedro landed with the rest of his people September 8 and established the settlement in formal ceremony.

St. Augustine was only one of the chain of colonies in Don Pedro's plan, but none of the others survived the years. St. Augustine too battled storm and attack, hunger and fear, and even lived through a change of site in 1572 (from one side of Matanzas Bay to the other), as well as periodic proposals to abandon it altogether.

Once the dream of a thriving province faded, the town slipped into its role of military outpost. The garrison seldom exceeded 150 men, and they were soldiers with no wish to carve farms out of the wilderness. You could hardly blame them. In the 1500's the St. Augustine peninsula was a forest of oak and pine, with palmettos to grub out wherever you wanted to plant.

There were only about a dozen farmers and their wives. Each man was allotted a small plot — just about as much as he could work with the hoe. (In early days it was the only tool he had.) Like the Indians, the men sowed corn and squash. An old record says they spent half the day coaxing the land to grow the corn and the other half grinding the grain into meal for bread. Without the seafood so plentiful in these waters, the people would have starved. Fish, shellfish, cornmeal, beans and squash were the staples.

Even chicken tasted like fish, complained the settlers, due to the fiddler-crab diet the resourceful fowls scratched out along the bay. Wild cats and bear ate the cattle and hogs.[2]

Perhaps the low point came in 1577, when the men of the settlement numbered but 80, and Indian attacks had driven them and their families inside the fort. The town itself was "all destroyed, the houses torn down."[3]

When Sir Francis Drake came in 1586, however, the settlement had been rebuilt and the garrison somewhat increased. Sir Francis happened upon St. Augustine quite by accident on his way back to England from the Caribbean. To the consternation of the Spanish, the first shot from the enemy cannon struck through the flag flying above the fort. In the face of Drake's 20-odd vessels, the entire population fled to the wilderness after firing a few token shots at the invaders. The English sacked and burned the community, "a little town or village without walls, built of wooden houses, as the plot doth plainly show."[4]

The "plot" or plan represents a number of small rectangular houses with pitched roofs, neatly laid out in blocks near the bay and a fair distance south of the wooden fort. The Latin legend on the plan states that St. Augustine was built of wood and was soon reduced to ashes. Also mentioned were "delightful gardens" and "fertile soil." This is fine testimony to the perseverance of the toiling farmer, but you should remember that after the long months of their voyage the Englishmen were perhaps unduly appreciative of greenery.

Like the phoenix, St. Augustine rose again from the ashes, but it was with the same impermanence as before:

> All the house walls are built of wood [*madera*] and the roofs of palm [*palma*], with some of the main ones of board [*tabla*] . . . The Spaniards make the walls of their houses out of cypress [*savino*] because it does not rot when in the ground.[5]

4. DETAIL FROM MAP OF ST. AUGUSTINE ABOUT 1593

A map of the period clearly shows vertical board walls and thatched roofs (Fig. 4). The records indicate some 120 houses and a population of about 700.[6]

Fire came again in 1599, devastating much of the town, including the Franciscan friary. And a storm drove the sea over the land, destroying other houses and even part of the fort. These disasters at the end of the century, typical of St. Augustine's early misfortunes, underline the presence of flimsy board and thatch buildings.[7]

Masonry was not altogether absent from Florida, however. At Santa Elena (Port Royal, S. C.) the colonists made oyster-shell lime and used it to construct *azoteas* (flat roofs) on their wattle and daub huts, and also to whitewash the walls. The Santa Elenans remained in Florida when their settlement was abandoned in 1587.[8]

In pre-Portland cement days, lime was the universal bonding agent in masonry. It was made by calcining limestone or seashells. Mixed with sand, it formed the mortar used to lay up brick or stone. With sand plus an aggregate such as pebbles or shell, it was *tapia* or tabby, a versatile material much like modern concrete and suitable for walls, roofs and floors. There were lime formulas for rough work, fine work, plasters, whitewashes and so on.[9]

As the Santa Elena record shows, the technique of making lime was known to the Florida colonials. Plenty of raw material was at hand, especially in the great shell middens of old Indian village sites conveniently beside the waterways.

A few years earlier (1580), Governor Pedro Menéndez Marqués had officially reported the discovery of stone nearby:

... I went to an Indian town four leagues from this [St. Augustine] ... I found an abundance of stone near the sea ... I will endeavor to have some of it brought here ...[10]

He had, of course, found the shellstone which the Spanish called *coquina*, large deposits of which were on Anastasia Island.

But the first positively recorded masonry construction at St. Augustine appears to have been a stone powder magazine built at the fort by order of Governor Méndez Canzo between 1596 and 1598. The Governor was enthusiastic; he resolved to build a whole new fort of stone. But in spite of this optimist, it was decided that "the foundations were not strong enough ... because in digging one cubit beneath the surface one finds sand and water." In 1602 Canzo admitted that no work had been done on the dream fort. But, he said, "Much stone for building has been prepared."[11]

Nevertheless the documents mention only board and thatch on into the 1600's: 1602 — the houses are only palm thatch, in constant danger of fire; 1604 — the burned friary is being built again in wood since stone is scarce; 1605 — the governor furnishes 300 boards for the friary.[12]

# PRECARIOUS PERMANENCE (1600-1702)

Civic progress had been made, however, even if the architecture was unimpressive. A palm thatch hospital — the first hospital[13] in this land — had been in existence since 1597, the year Governor Gonzalo Méndez de Canzo had arrived, bringing many kinds of seeds — including the Granada orange — to plant in his new province. "This land produces," the Governor soon reported. "There is in great plenty many kinds of fruits and vegetables — figs, pomegranates, beans, sweet potatoes, citron," and so many others that he could not name them all.[14] The corn harvest increased greatly and a horse-powered mill was built to grind the corn, freeing the people from doing this time-consuming drudgery by hand.

Governor Méndez de Canzo also laid out the town plaza, built the first public market, set up an official system of weights and measures, and did many other things to put the town on a substantial footing. It is small wonder that when some of the king's advisers urged the abandonment of St. Augustine as a useless expense, this optimistic Governor pointed out the value of the settlement as a haven for shipwrecked people (1500 castaways in 20 years), a center for Christianizing the Indians, and a base for exploration. After the English colony at Jamestown took root a few years later, there was no longer any doubt about the need for Spain to keep St. Augustine.

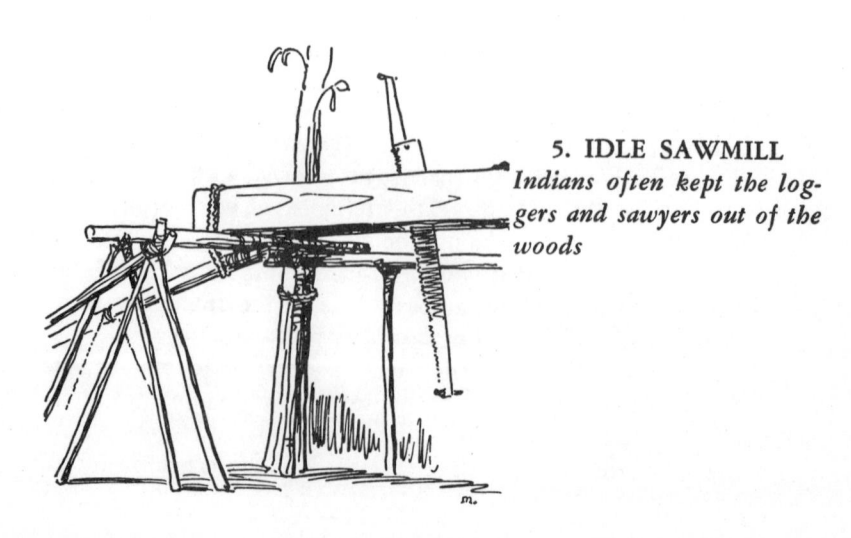

5. IDLE SAWMILL
*Indians often kept the loggers and sawyers out of the woods*

**6. THE STONE QUARRY OPENED IN 1671**

But housing improvements were negligible. And if there were no floods or fires, then time took its toll. A 1655 report suggested bringing in a crew of slave stonecutters,

> for because the old houses are made of wood, they are almost impossible to repair. Today most of them are in ruins due to the lack of Indians to bring material for repair; and there is no hope of improvement.[15]

A few years later, construction of the stone fort got underway at last. The town had been sacked in 1668 by pirates, who boasted they would come back to make St. Augustine their home port. Since the corsairs left without putting the place to the torch, the Spaniards were prone to believe them; and the hue and cry which reached the ears of the crown brought a new Governor with authority to build a strong fort. The newcomer was Manuel de Cendoya. On the way to Florida he got money from Mexico and men from Cuba, including an engineer, masons and limeburners. In 1671 quarries were opened on Anastasia Island. On the mainland near the fort site, kilns were built and began turning oyster shells into lime. The first stone of Castillo de San Marcos was laid on November 9, 1672.[16]

The fort was under construction over a 25-year period. During most of that time it seems to have demanded all the energies of its builders because, despite the imported artisans skilled in masonry (and the local workmen who were learning the new skills), the records are slow to show that startling improvements took place in domestic architecture. For example, in 1675 the visiting Bishop Calderón remarked that the houses were "wood with board walls" and therefore no protection against heat or cold.[17] According to Governor Salazar,

> Most of the houses they build are flimsy and without much room, since they are merely boards with palm-thatch roofs.[18]

From this disparagement we surmise that the Governor's new house was sturdy and roomy, but there is no indication that he built in masonry. Since at the time (1680) he was retiring from office to live at St. Augustine, this house was no doubt his personal property rather than an official residence.

During Salazar's tenure a masonry magazine much like a house had been built in the fort (Fig. 7). It showed what could be done. The one-story structure had plastered stone walls reinforced with timber frame, a barrel-tile roof, and tabby floors. But again in 1683 wooden construction for even the important buildings was certified by reports that stressed the threat of pirate torches.[19]

Important changes did come, however, about 1690.

There were three old houses belonging to the crown: one for the Governor, another for the Treasurer, and the third for the Accountant. The buildings were rotten and Governor Diego de Quiroga wanted them rebuilt in stone. To this the crown agreed, if the fort was finished.

**7. STONE BUILDING OF 1675**

*This was a tile-roofed magazine at the fort*

The Governor's House was a 2-story wooden structure with stone foundations. The presence of stonework in this old house shows that masonry, though perhaps unusual, was not unknown to an earlier generation.

Further, the three houses were roofed with shingles, said to be "customary in this presidio." The inference is that shingles and stonework came along after 1672 with the men and money of the fort-building project.

Thus by 1690 St. Augustine was on the verge of its "stone age." People had seen the great raft loads of coquina from the quarries and watched the stone-cutters and masons. Stonemasonry was no longer a mystery. The citizens asked for stone to build new houses and Governor Quiroga endorsed the request: it would be "practical and beneficial . . . to introduce stone buildings because of the repeated fires caused by wooden ones." Since the quarries had more than enough stone for government buildings, the Governor began to sell off the broken stone to the townsfolk.[20]

Nevertheless, progress was slow. It does not appear that the people actually bought much stone. For when Jonathan Dickinson, the shipwrecked Quaker, passed through St. Augustine in 1696, he said most of the houses were old and not half of them were occupied. As for the three royal houses abuilding of stone, the work was only partly done. The masonry walls of the Governor's House were up before the enemy came in 1702, but the house for the Treasurer was still under construction and in wood, not stone. On the third building, there is no information.[21]

By 1700 then, there was very little masonry in St. Augustine except the massive fort. Some stone was in the Governor's House, but the only other stone structure thus far mentioned is the mission of Nombre de Dios, north of the city.[22] Even such important places as the hermitage of Nuestra Señora de la Soledad, which was the parish church for many years, were of wood. So was the infirmary next door. Unfortunately the high altar of the hermitage was too close to the infirmary kitchen,

> where it is necessary to light a fire at all hours to prepare the medications for the sick. Since the buildings of the place are all made of wood, the church and the altar and images are excessively damaged [by the smoke] . . . But this can be easily remedied by your majesty's ordering that the entire area where the church and chapel touch the side of the said infirmary, be made of stone. This will be small work and less cost, because it is only one wall which must serve as a shield so the smoke will not drift into the church from the hospital.[23]

# THE RENASCENCE (1703-1763)

If the 1690's gave promise to the people of St. Augustine, the events of 1702 were bitter disappointment indeed.

By the turn of the century the town had grown to about 500 families. There were close to 1,500 people, including the garrison bachelors, the Indians and Negroes.

And in Europe the grandson of the French king succeeded to the throne of Spain. Britain, mindful of this increase in French power, readied for war which came in 1702. In America the Carolina colonists professed to see a dangerous French-Spanish coalition at St. Augustine and, forehandedly planning how to divide the plunder and slaves, moved on Florida by land and sea. Eight hundred strong they were, and had no trouble taking the empty town. The entire Spanish population had moved into the fort.

Against the citadel siege operations began. The Spanish undertook countermeasures. Especially were they concerned with houses the English could use for cover near the fort. One balconied house in particular belonging to Adjutant Joseph Rodríguez Meléndez was "the strongest, newest and highest"; from here the enemy shot two of the fort defenders.[24]

The Spanish commander ordered the destruction of all cover within a musket shot of the fort (Fig. 8). In carrying out these orders, garrison sallies burned or otherwise razed the properties of

**8. DEFENSE AREA**

*During the 1702 siege the Spanish destroyed all their own houses within musket shot of the fort*

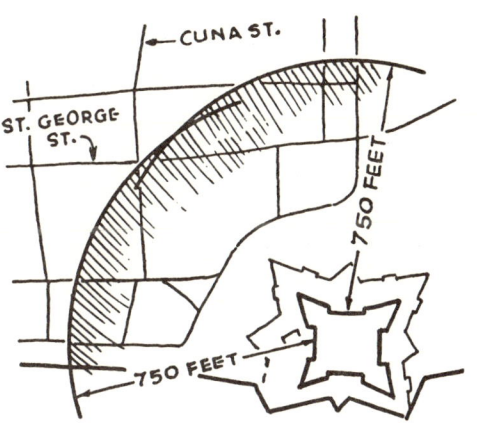

31 people, in a quadrant extending about 750 feet from the fort walls — all the area bounded by St. George and Cuna streets.[25]

On the day after Christmas the siege was finally lifted. But as they left, the invaders set fire to the town,

> the houses of which for the most part were of thatch and boards [wrote the Governor]. In a short while some were burned and the fire spread to others, but with the discharge of the fort artillery the fire diminished and some escaped.[26]

Indeed very few were spared. One report tells us that the
> British applied themselves to destroying the city, which they did with such vigor that only the hospital and some 20 damaged houses remained. All the others were burned, especially the parochial church, the convent of St. Francis, the mission of Nombre de Dios . . . and six other missions. Not a sign of them was left since they were built of wood . . .[27]

Another further confirms the cataclysmic loss:
> [The enemy] laid waste the entire city by fire. They did not spare the principal church, the convent and church of San Francisco, or the royal houses of Governor, Royal Accountant and Treasurer, so that the houses left were few indeed. Only the hermitage of Nuestra Señora de la Soledad was left, for even the hermitage of Nuestra Señora de la Leche was reduced to ashes . . .[28]

And though la Soledad had escaped the worst, it was nevertheless badly damaged. In all the city only "about 20 houses of no value" were left.[29]

23

**BEFORE 1702
TABBY & STONE**

**AFTER 1702
STONE**

LATER REBUILT ON SAME WALL LINE

DESTROYED c. 1702

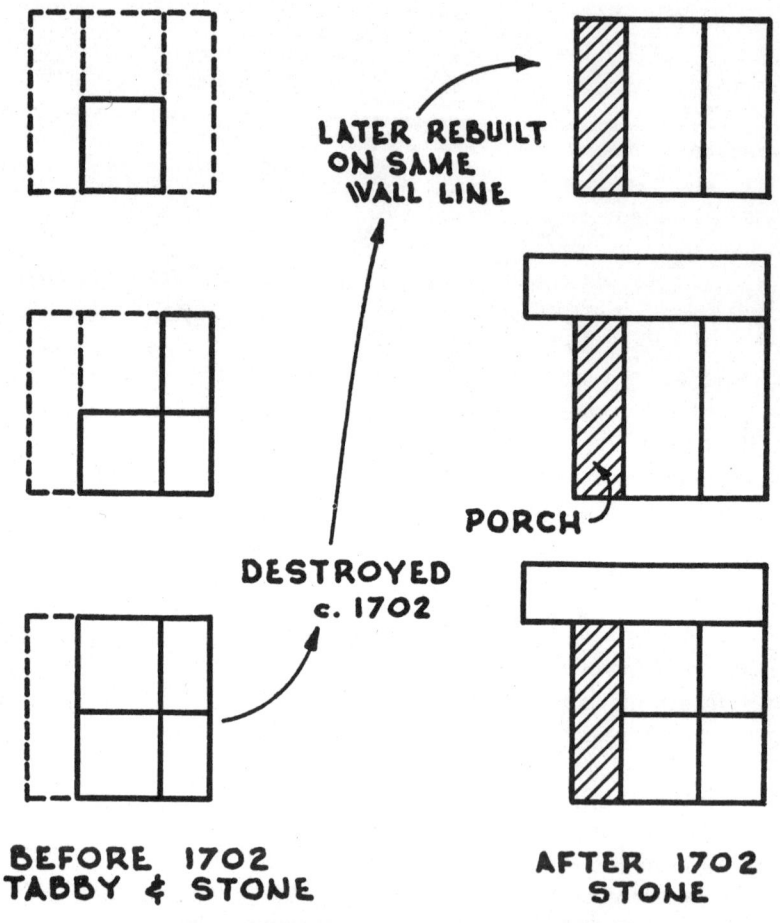

PORCH

9. EVOLUTION OF A SPANISH HOUSE

A half dozen other eye-witness statements say the same. The town was virtually destroyed. Confirmation also comes from the long list of claims submitted to their government by citizens who had suffered loss. The list contains 149 entries, some for two or more structures.

The first 31 entries on the list are the houses destroyed by Spanish troops to protect the approaches to the fort. Among them is the house of Adjutant Joseph Rodríguez Meléndez, mentioned earlier.

Out of the 149 entries on the claims list, there are only 14 mentions of building materials, such as "wood," "boards and thatch" and "boards and shingles." Since all 14 instances occur in the first fifth of the list, it seems likely that the scribe decided such data were superfluous. No masonry was mentioned.[30]

The surviving 20 houses "of no value" were probably near la Soledad hermitage, which was on the west side of St. George Street, between Bridge Street and Green Lane.[31]

Recovery took many years. The housing boom, promised after completion of the fort had freed artisans and materials, was smothered in the destitution that followed the torches of the Carolinians. Neither was the war over; although the Britishers had been repulsed, hostile Indians were a constant danger. Defenses had to be repaired and strengthened.

Stone pulled from the fire-blackened walls of the Governor's House went into a new guardhouse on the plaza (Fig. 10). A heavy palisade to block access to the city by land was completed in 1706. Before this there was no security except in the fort itself. But even the essential defense work was done under trying, dangerous conditions. Matters got so bad that the Governor wrote Spain to hold up money for reconstruction because there was "no way to get the materials needed for construction; the enemy had made it impossible."[32] Even the troop of horse to guard the men who went into the woods to cut timber suffered "constant killings and hostilities" from the Indians. This was the situation as late as 1709.[33]

If new lumber was hard to get for the royal houses, it was impossible for the "man in the street." (The people were actually "living in the street in scanty straw shelters.")[34] However, the presence of scorched and re-used ceiling joists in one existing house[35] suggests that some owners were able to salvage at least a few useful materials from the ruins.

10. THE MAIN GUARD HOUSE IN 1764

**11. THE GOVERNOR'S HOUSE IN 1764**

The "straw shelters" were still plentiful in 1712. The Franciscans complained they were living "in some wretched huts that scarce protect us from bad weather," instead of in a decent friary.[36] Other domiciles were hardly more substantial, if we may judge from the home of Don Joseph Benedit Horruytiner:

> the houses of his residence and their lot [are] all enclosed by a wooden fence. The bedroom and parlor have a stone wall on the north side and palm thatch kitchen).[37]

One wonders what happened to the *south* wall.

The Governor's House (Fig. 11) seems to have been completed at last by 1713, when on a festive occasion the Governor and his wife tossed silver coins from its balconies to the crowd in the street and patio.[38]

The beneficent official was Don Francisco de Córcoles, who had come to Florida in 1706. To him was due much of the credit for reconstruction work. Testimonials citing his efforts recalled the times when "everyone was in wretched condition, two or three families living in a single house because they did not have the means for building." He had "ordered wood cut for houses, buying palm thatch for the people so as to put roofs on and fences around them." Additionally, during his regime many houses of stone and tabby were erected. In short, by 1715 the city was "very much along and well populated."[39]

The year 1715 was by no means the end of the building boom. A fiscal report of the period suggests the very considerable numbers of men and sums of money involved:

> From May 5, 1717, when the quarrying of stone and building of lime kilns were begun ... [for a certain construction project], until March 7, 1718, the sum of 2,142 pesos and 5 reales was spent in payment to the overseers, master workmen and laborers, and for renting horses ...

>For work done on the said projects and laying foundations, 5,417 pesos and 6½ reales in payment in various certificates of the workmen, overseers and laborers.[40]

The renascence that followed 1702 had three phases: 1) emergency housing of thatch, canvas, or other available materials; 2) new and permanent homes built by those who had the resources and abilities to do so; 3) government aid enabling the householder to regain or surpass his pre-1702 status. The latter assistance touched almost every family in St. Augustine, because the Governor used government personnel to obtain the materials that people needed for building. Financial aid in response to citizens' claims, though slow in coming, was also of great importance.

Quite likely the government also furnished technical help in the person of one or more construction experts. These could range from royal engineer or construction superintendent to master builders in the various trades.

Artisans are by nature conservative in their trades, apprentices being taught by their masters that there is only one way to do a job — the right way. The old construction techniques would be perpetuated through men with a fine tradition of workmanship, many of them builders with long careers under Spain's notable royal engineers. Countering the traditional, perhaps, would be the ideas of a few "moderns" — for though St. Augustine was isolated, some of its people were occasional visitors to New Spain, Cuba, or the homeland; and the upheaval of 1702 had brought in a number of new men. At the very least, new people brought their own provincial preferences. Destruction of the old St. Augustine gave remarkable opportunity to citizens of the new era. Hence the very real question: How much did the houses of the renascence resemble the pre-1702 houses?

The fact is that most of the "new" St. Augustine houses reveal the austere kitchen-and-bedroom plan of the old tradition. The people who built such houses were poor people, much more concerned with food, clothing and a shelter over their heads than with the niceties of architectural style. Yet, the renascence also brought, perhaps for the first time, many substantial houses, spacious and comfortable. Whether the plans were "modern" or traditional, roomy or cramped, one-story or two, there is positive evidence that the builders had learned how to fit their structures to the peculiar needs of presidio life in the Florida east coast climate.

# PEN PICTURES

During the 1730's the establishment of the British colony of Georgia gave urgent emphasis to St. Augustine's role as an outpost in Spain's international system of defense. One local addition, for instance, was the erection of barracks near the plaza for troops brought from Havana. The town underwent considerable development during the preparations for the War of Jenkins' Ear.

The British besiegers who came in 1740 were unable to penetrate the improved defenses. The town emerged from the ordeal with only minor damage from bombardment. An English spy reported:

> I believe there is about 300 Houses in it, and 3 Churches all built of stone. I am told that the Churches is finely adorned within but make a mean appearance without as does the Houses, the Stone they are built of is soft substance being a Number of Small sea Shells Conjeald together.[41]

To a casual witness, plastered walls would mean that all masonry buildings were "stone." A lot of them were stone — the coquina (shellstone) cut from the quarries on Anastasia Island. Others, however, were built of a coarse tabby made of lime and sand with oyster shell aggregate. This concrete was sometimes called "oyster-shell stone" *(piedra de ostión)*. More and more houses were built of this material for the common folk, so that tabby became the majority material.[42]

In 1763 the English came peaceably to St. Augustine, having at last won it from Spain by diplomatic advantage. British observers found the Spanish tradition curiously different from their own, so they remarked many details which would have been too familiar for mention by Spanish writers.

Dr. William Stork, writing to promote immigration, described the houses as

> built of free-stone, commonly two stories high, two rooms upon a floor, with large windows and balconies; before the entry of most of the houses runs a portico of stone arches [Fig. 49]; the roofs are commonly flat. The Spaniards consulted convenience more than taste in their buildings . . .[43]

Many of the houses "especially in the suburbs," he noted, were built of wood or palmetto leaves.

William Gerard de Brahm, government surveyor, gave a most positive picture; one would think that all houses were as like as peas in a pod:

**12. BALCONIES ON ST. GEORGE — A "PRINCIPAL" STREET**

All houses are built of Masonry; their entrances are shaded by Piazzas supported by Tuskan Pillars or Pillasters against the South Sun [Fig. 49]. The houses have to the East windows projecting 16 or 18 inches into the street, very wide and proportionately high [Fig. 42]. On the West side their Windows are commonly very small, and no Opening of any kind to the North, on which side they have double walls 6 or 8 feet asunder, forming a kind of Gallery, which answers for Cellars and Pantries. Before most of the entrances were arbours of vines, producing plenty and very good grapes [Fig. 77]. No house had any Chimney for a Fire-place.[44]

13. "A TABBY WALK WITH SEATS OF THE SAME"

John Bartram, the Quaker botanist, provides a welcome amount of detail:[45]

> The town is pleasantly situated, but without regularity; the streets very narrow, about 15 foot. The principal street 22, many 12. The lanes crossing the streets near right angles, 6 or 8. [See Figs. 1, 2, 19.] The houses both stands and is built as irregular. For as the inhabitants consisted of officers of the garrison, governor, and some civil magistrates and clergy and some merchants, these built themselves good houses after the Spanish fashion, all or most with pleasant covered balconies, supported with double beams fastened in the wall at convenient distance. The upper beam projects over the under one a foot or more, which is a good support. [See Figs. 12, 50-52.] On the back side of the house or yard, where the chief entrance is (for few but the grand houses, except taverns, had street doors, and these led mostly through a common passage to the court and kitchens; every court yard had its draw well) [Fig. 78] there is generally a terraced[46] walk, with seats of the same 18 inches high next the house wall, to sit down upon when weary of walking [Fig. 13]. The walks about 9 foot wide, with a staircase at one end to the chambers; the steps easy, all terraced [Fig. 55]. A row of pillars or arches [Figs. 48-49] generally supports a roof continuing from the common roof to the body of the house, if it be a shingled roof. These best houses is generally built of hewn shell stone, as is most of those that is flat roofed and terraced on the top, with stone battlements, which have pipes, mostly of burnt clay, let through the wall and projecting a foot or more to carry off the water [Fig. 62].
>
> As they had no chimneys, so they had no glass windows, but the best houses had large windows next the street, all bannistered and projecting a foot or more from the house wall. Some had 3 and some 5 rows, one above another, each about two foot long and one inch and half or 2 square, set in the cross pieces of the frame at 2, 3 or 4 inches distance, which was fastened by cross end pieces into the frame of the window and supported by a step of stone at the bottom [Fig. 42]. All these windows had strong shutters within side, many of which had a little one in each [Fig. 44], and many windows had a lattice with holes one inch square, reaching half way or more up the window [Fig. 43]. But now the English officers is making great alteration. The sun and light now begins to shine through glass and many chimneys is peeping above the roofs of the houses.

But most of the common Spanish houses was built of oyster shells and mortar, as well as garden and yard walls. They raised them by setting two boards on edge as wide as they intend the wall, then poured in lime-shell mortar mixed with sand, in which they pounded oyster shells as close as possible [Fig. 14]. And when that part was set, they raised the planks, and so on till they had raised the wall as high as wanted.[47] This was strong enough to sup-

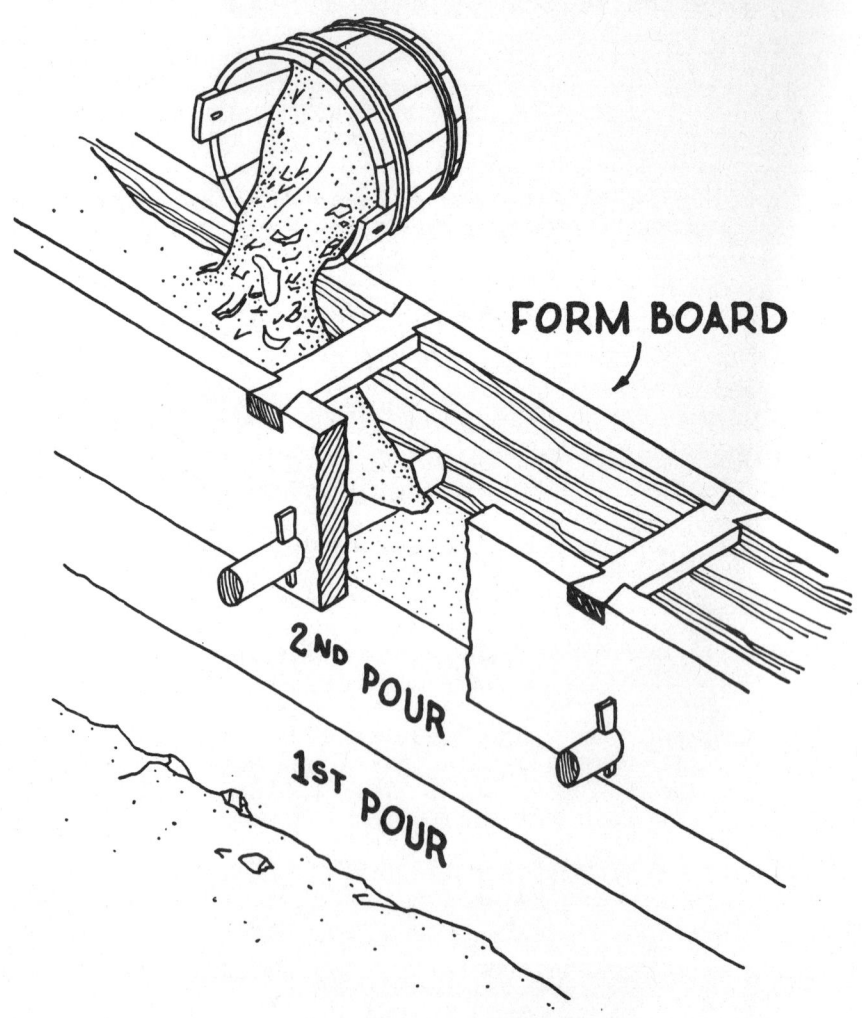

14. BUILDING A TABBY WALL

**15. A CHARCOAL BRAZIER**

*"No house had any chimney," said Bartram. Actually there were a few fireplaces, but most of the Spanish houses were heated by charcoal in metal-lined braziers*

port a terraced chamber floor and palmetto thatched roof, which was very tight. But as most of these was built by the common soldiers and poor people at different times, as they could get money to enlarge them, the new and old walls is apt to wind and crack so that the soldiers can easily pull them to pieces for their wood to burn, which is scarce here. These last mentioned houses had also their little bannistered and latticed windows, and some had a hole through the roof to let out the smoke when they cooked their victuals, a little of which served them and that very mean . . .

Many bannisters of the back windows next the yard or garden don't project out from the wall as the front windows, which often do a foot beyond the wall, so that it's very convenient sitting within the window, observing unseen what passeth in the street. But they observed no general model, but everyone built according to his ability or fancy.

Bartram mentioned three construction materials: stone, tabby, and wood. According to others, *all* houses were masonry. Fortunately there is a precise record in the 1764 map prepared as the Spanish left. The map key names three basic materials: *piedra* (stone), *ripio* (tabby), and *madera* (wood). Of a total of 342 houses, 124 (36%) were stone, 140 (41%) were tabby, and the other 78 (23%) wood.[48]

# BRITISH CHANGES (1764-1783)

The rapid and total departure of the Spaniards, and their replacement by a people of different culture meant that the houses of St. Augustine suddenly underwent unusual and powerful stresses.

The first of the foreigners to come were the soldiers and a small coterie of government employees to set up the colonial administration. Not far behind were the tradesmen who supplied the needs of the regiment. Generous land grant policies attracted a number of planters, some of whom acquired and maintained property in town.

Inevitably many picturesque and verminous domiciles were lost. Bartram remarked that King George's soldiers pulled down "about half the town" to make firewood, which was scarce. He added that destruction was easy, since these poor houses, even the masonry ones, were merely year-by-year accumulations of winding and cracking, jerry-built rooms. But many other buildings were soon put to good use.[49]

James Cameron, a soldier who had served at the siege of Havana, found himself at St. Augustine in 1763 with the Second Battalion of the Royal Scots. He and wife Ann bought a pair of houses on Charlotte Street. One was "a good Stone House well Shingled." The other was smaller, with a thatch roof. Cameron had chimneys and fireplaces installed and enjoyed his house well enough until he lost his life with the Florida Rangers in a Georgia campaign just before the end of the Revolution. In view of the housing press at this time, Ann relinquished the property and moved into a new little one-room board house given her by a friend.[50]

The friend was Dorothy Moore. She and her husband John had also come to St. Augustine at the beginning of the British regime. John was a victualler and innkeeper who came to own considerable property. His first purchase was an "unfinished Stone House built after the Spanish Manner with 3 rooms upon a floor, 2 Stories high." It had a shingle roof, but no floor. There was a flat-roofed, detached kitchen. John finished the house and enlarged it to 7 rooms and a "Garret fit for an Assembly." The addition had stone walls, was properly floored and plastered and whitewashed on the inside, and served as the parlor and dining room of the inn. Out in the yard, John built a large frame kitchen, complete with chimney and oven. The Spanish kitchen was converted into a store. Lime and orange trees were growing and a good-sized garden "Raised a Sufficiency of Roots for the large family."

A few years later John Moore bought a second lot and put up another inn. This was a 2-story, 6-room frame house with a balcony. It must have been painted red, because it was called the "New Red House . . . for the Accommodation of Gentlemen" and had all the requisite outbuildings, such as kitchen, 5-horse stable, privies and high board fence.[51]

Benjamin Lord came to St. Augustine in 1778 as Surveyor General for East Florida. He bought a lot with two buildings upon it, one of them an old Spanish house. This he repaired by plastering the walls, mending the roof and floors, glazing the windows and painting. The other structure was converted to a kitchen, a store and a shed.[52]

Out of the turbulent times of the Revolution, a new generation of huts arose. St. Augustine under the Union Jack was a refuge for hundreds of Loyalists fleeing their hotheaded cousins in Georgia or Carolina. One was John Mills, a Tory justice of the peace and notary public from Charleston. He reached St. Augustine in 1782 and built a small frame house and kitchen on Lt. Governor Moultrie's property near the fort. He, like most of the others, departed in 1784 at the end of the British reign.[53]

So these examples are fairly typical of the various things that happened to housing. Cameron, the soldier, bought a Spanish house and put in a chimney. Moore, the grocer and host, converted an unfinished Spanish house into an inn and later built a garish new one. Ben Lord, the surveyor, took an old house and renovated it to suit his taste. Refugee John Mills put up a shack on another man's land.

Clearly the architectural changes accomplished during this period, whether repair, adaptation, alteration or new construction, were practical ones. They were made either for economic reasons — that is, to enable the new citizen to make a living — or to introduce conveniences or standards of housing without which he did not feel "at home."

In the latter case, what were some of the factors? Was English architectural influence imported directly from London? Who were the builders? Where did they come from?

As usual, there are no simple answers. For an example, let us look at the little house built near the fort for John Mills, the loyalist refugee. The description is meager: a house 16 x 22 feet with a kitchen and a clapboard fence.[54] But there are several clues from which reliable information can be deduced.

John Mills was from Charleston. During the establishment of Savannah some years earlier, James Oglethorpe had prevailed upon Governor Bull of South Carolina to send "two houses frames and boards of saw'd cypress" from Charleston to Savannah.[55] Obviously the purpose was to instruct in American practicalities some of the carpenters newly come from England. Obviously, too, these were *typical* small houses.

It follows that the Charleston prototype (we use the term loosely) had some influence upon houses in the colonial vanguard. In Georgia the Carolina house thus became the "common freeholders' house," a frame structure about 16 x 24 feet, sheathed with unplaned, feather-edge boards, roofed with shingles and floored with undressed planks.[56]

In fact, the minimum standard had already been written into the specifications for Savannah: each freeholder was required to build "one House of brick, or framed, square timber work . . . at least Twenty four feet in length, upon Sixteen in breadth, and eight feet in height."[57] Inclusion of this specification did not mean that the sponsors of Georgia were introducing something new. Rather, they were spelling out sound and contemporary English practice as applied to a special problem. The practice itself was deeply rooted in medieval tradition. Even the house size (16 x 24 feet) had evolved from a centuries-old unit of measure based upon the amount of space a yeoman needed to house his ox team.[58]

Actually the dimensions of a dwelling were always a little bit less than the given standard, so the 16 x 22-foot size of John Mills' house is acceptable as evidence of a typical "minimum" house, dozens of which had been built in South Carolina and Georgia. The type is well illustrated in Peter Gordon's 1734 view of Savannah. It was not, of course, limited to the minimum 16 x 24-foot size. After all, a man and his family would grow.[59]

The matter of carrying architecture from one colony to another was nothing new. In early days, perhaps, Charleston owed more to the Caribbean than it did to London; and this affinity for things tropical may have been a reason why so many Carolinians made their way to Florida when trouble started.

The transport of buildings by sea is readily documented. The frame of the soldiers' barracks was prefabricated in New York and erected at St. Augustine in 1771. This was a 3-story, E-shaped structure with porches round about and a cupola adorned by a weathercock. William Curtis, a shop-keeper, took down his Charleston house and brought it to St. Augustine in 1782. Here he sold it, complete with doors, sashes and shutters, and built a new 1½-story house. Others, when they left St. Augustine, dismantled their houses for shipment to new fields of interest, usually in the West Indies.[60]

A number of the British citizens were self-reliant men perfectly capable of accomplishing their own construction projects. Robert Robinson, a butcher who made extensive repairs and alterations to his property, claimed that "the Work was Chiefly done by him and a Negroe of his own, but that he sometimes hired a Negroe Carpenter." Those who had slaves trained for construction work certainly used them or hired them out to others. But there were also British artisans such as James Scotland, carpenter, David Yeats, a tiler, and John Tully, a "stone builder" (mason).[61]

And there was William Watson, called a house carpenter.

Watson, a mature journeyman, had come to Florida from England in 1766, and stayed until after the change of sovereignty. He purchased and renovated old houses. In some cases he built new ones, then sold at a profit. He must have been a man with better than average imagination, for he is credited with having converted a 20 x 80-foot range of stables into a proper dwelling. That he was no ordinary carpenter is also shown by his ownership of a large tract up North River, from which 20 Negroes kept him supplied with lumber and shingles.

Will Watson, who owned £25 of "Books of Architecture & others," was far more than a master carpenter. He and others like him were the architects of their day. Unluckily, after Will left St. Augustine, a shipwreck cost him all his books and tools and most of his personal property. He and his wife found themselves back in London, grown old, and faced with making a new start in life.[62]

The following table documents some typical changes the English made in the physical appearance of St. Augustine. This is, of course, only a small part of the picture. At the height of the British boom (1783), several thousand people lived in St. Augustine. For numbers of them, there was no housing at all. Hastily built huts of palm thatch, springing up wherever immigrants could beg or borrow land, must have given the town the same impermanent look it had after the catastrophe of 1702.[63]

## Examples of British Changes[64]

| PROPERTY DESCRIPTION | REPAIRS, ALTERATIONS, ADDITIONS |
|---|---|
| [Spanish] house, stone, small, shingle roof; good condition. (1763) | Added chimneys. |
| Unfinished Spanish house, stone, 2-story, shingle roof; built "after the Spanish manner," 3 rooms per floor, not floored or boarded. Detached stone kitchen, 16' x 20', flat roof. (1764) | Converted to inn. Added large parlour, dining room, garret, of stone, making 4 rooms on ground floor (10' x 14', 18' x 24', and two 16' x 16'); shingle roof, floors, plaster, glass, inside whitewash. Added cellar of stone, with small frame bedroom adjoining. Added large frame kitchen, oven, chimney. Added 5' clapboard fence. (c. 1765) |
| [Spanish?] house, "stone and lime," large, 2-story, 2 rooms per floor, "tenantable." Outbuildings. Stone well, "excellent" water. (1770) | Improved. |
| [Spanish?] house, "stone and lime," "half as large," 2-story, ground story used as kitchen. Fence. Garden, orange trees. (1770) | Lodging room built over kitchen. |
| [Spanish?] house, stone gable ends, wooden middle, 40' front x 18', 1½-story, shingle roof, glass. Fence, 8', stone in front, clapboard elsewhere. (1777) | Converted a wall to a kitchen. Added full length piazza with room at end. Built frame store, 12' x 50', shingle roof. New clapboard fence, 6½'. |
| "Old Spanish" house, 31' (front) x 38'. Another building. No fence. (1778) | Repaired house roofs, floors, wall plaster; glazed and painted. Converted other building to kitchen and store, built adjoining shed. Fenced. |
| [Spanish] house, stone, square, flat roof, 6 rooms each floor; out of repair, one room fallen. (1778) | Converted to gable roof; rebuilt fallen room, added chamber over; repaired back door and 2 windows; added chimney. Added frame stable with tile roof, oven, slaughterhouse, well, fence. |
| [Spanish] house, stone, 1-story, no glass. Small frame kitchen. (1778) | Repairs: floored large room, made and glazed 5 new windows, put in new doors and locks; added "Look out" at end of house. Added stone chimney to kitchen. Built frame storehouse, "not well finished." Built 6-horse frame stable. |
| "Old Spanish" house, stone, 18' x 34', 2-story, 2 rooms with closet per floor, shingle roof, "recent complete repair." Detached kitchen. New board fence. (1778) | |

| PROPERTY DESCRIPTION | REPAIRS, ALTERATIONS, ADDITIONS |
|---|---|
| [Spanish?] house, stone, 50' front x 20', 2-story and garrets, shingle roof, glass; "very good." (1781) | Repaired kitchen. Added open shed stable and board fence. |
| [Spanish] house, stone, 16' x 36' x 16' high, in ruins. (1782) | Rebuilt house. |
| [Spanish] house, stone, 16' x 30' x 16' high. No outhouses. Rotten clapboard fence. (1782) | Repairs: shingles, glass, back room floor. Added fowl house, hog house and "a necessary of rough boards and roofed with the same." Built 8' clapboard fence. |
| British house, weatherboarded frame, 20' x 35', 2-story, front balcony, shingle roof, sashed and glazed, paneled doors, plastered and whitewashed. Kitchen, frame, shingle roof, not glazed. Board stable for 4 or 5 horses. (1773) | Called "the New Red House for the accommodation of gentlemen with all necessary outhouses." (1786) |
| [British] "range of stables," stone back, open front, 2 years old. (1779) | Converted to dwelling, 20' x 80', 1-story, 7 rooms. (1779) |
| [British] house, stone, 2 years old. (1779) | |
| British house, frame, 16' x 43', 1-story, 2 rooms and kitchen, shingle roof, glass, 2 brick chimneys; not lined, but papered upon canvas. (1780) | Dismantled for move to Bahamas, but lost. (1784) |
| [British] house, stone and frame, 20' x 32' x 18' high, 2-story, 2 rooms per floor, short shingle roof, glass, part lined, new. (c. 1780) | |
| [British?] back store, frame, 18' x 10' high, 1-story, short shingle roof. (c. 1780) | |
| [British] stables for above two houses, one for 3 horses, one for 4. (c. 1780) | |
| [British?] house, frame, 14' x 20', 1-story and garret, shingle roof, glazed. (1780) | Added stone chimney, rough frame kitchen, and 6' clapboard fence. Converted kitchen into store. |
| British "log house," 16' x 24', for 7 Negro slaves. (1782) | |
| British house, boarded, small 1-room, clapboard roof. (1782) | |

| PROPERTY DESCRIPTION | REPAIRS, ALTERATIONS, ADDITIONS |
|---|---|
| British house, frame, 16' x 18', 1½-story, 2 rooms per floor, shingle roof, glass. Old fence. (1782) | |
| British tavern, frame, 16' x 20', 3 good rooms on ground floor, "compleat barr" and 2 large rooms above, shingle roof; "low but not large." Stable; Necessary House; enclosed yard. (1782) | Stable converted to kitchen. |
| British house, frame covered with feather-edge boards, 14' x 24', 1-story, 2 rooms, cypress, shingle roof, floored; unfinished, no glass, no chimney. Small temporary clapboard kitchen. Clapboard partition fence for garden. (1782) | |

Despite the British innovations, St. Augustine was not fundamentally changed. The Friary, though converted into a barracks by the English, retained much of its original character. As for other buildings,

> The houses are built quite after the Spanish fashion, with flat roofs and few windows . . . [a German observer recorded. He went on to say that] here and there the English have houses with more windows, especially on the street side . . . Almost every house has its little garden, of which splendid lemon and orange trees are not the least ornaments.[65]

**16. ST. FRANCIS BARRACKS**
*Until 1763 it was the Franciscan friary*

## SPANISH MINORITY (1784-1821)

When the British flag left Florida, with it went the vast majority of the citizens, unwilling to give allegiance to Spain. The decision in many cases meant sacrificing properties, often at a quarter of the value. For there was no mass immigration into newly-Spanish Florida; the market could hardly have been worse. Aside from the few newcomers, less than 50 among British men of substance elected to stay on; obviously they could pick and choose property at their own price.

Under these circumstances, numerous sellers had to do the same as other St. Augustinians had done in 1763. They left their properties with an agent, the sales proceeds to be remitted when purchasers were found. In proven hardship cases, the British government allotted compensation. Much of the property was worthless, however. The year of the Spanish return the government engineer rated 39 percent (110 out of 277) of the houses as uninhabitable.[66]

The largest market for real estate was probably among the colonists imported from the Mediterranean some years earlier. They had been settled at New Smyrna as plantation workers, but with the failure of that project, St. Augustine had become their home. Now these Minorcans, Italians and Greeks were the bridge between departure of the British and return of the Spanish. They formed a large part of the population and garrison throughout the stormy years of the second occupation by Spain, and stayed on to become citizens of the United States in 1821.[67]

"They have shown no great desire to engage in the grubbing of waste lands, preferring to make a living in the town," noted one observer. "Although almost all of them left their country in the extremest poverty, the greater part have here risen to good circumstances through their industry and frugality qualities they are said to possess in a high degree."[68]

People of such reputation would naturally seize the advantage of a buyer's market. Many of the old Spanish houses became homes for these quiet people and were thus cared for down through the years. According to an English traveler,

> Their cottages, which were in the narrow streets nearest the water, were, to a certain degree, picturesque; festooned with nets and roses, shaded by orange trees; and hung round with cages of nonpareils, and other singing birds . . .[69]

**17. THE MANUCY HOUSE**
*It was a yellow house on the northeast corner of
St. George and Cuna Streets*

A number of the Minorcans (as the Mediterranean people came to be called) were granted land just north of the city in 1807. For military reasons this approach to the town defenses had to be kept clear and farming was a good way to do it. However, housing upon the land was severely restricted. Each grantee could have but a single palm-thatched hut 9 x 12 x 10 feet high. It had to be located right beside the road so that "one man may be enough to set fire to all at one run."[70]

The return of Spanish rule in 1784 was no homecoming of the families which had left Florida a generation ago. Some Floridians indeed came back. But St. Augustine would never again be a truly *Spanish* town. For of the thousand or so people here, fewer than 100 were Spaniards. (Most of these were either native-born Floridians or Canary Islanders.) The Minorcan-Greek-Italian group numbered around 450. About 300 Britons and 500 slaves were also in the province, a good many of them living in town. Negro, Britisher, Minorcan, Greek, Italian, Spaniard, Canary Islander and *Floridano* — This was a diverse population indeed!

It was hardly a prosperous community, however. The machinery of government was kept moving and a garrison was maintained, thanks to a subsidy granted by the crown. As in earlier times, high officials could live comfortably; minor employees and soldiers generally had food and clothing; but for people not on the government payroll life was apt to be difficult. Supplying the needs of them all was the privilege of Panton, Leslie and Company, traders who had done well during British times and now held a monopoly of Indian trade. In East Florida such trade actually amounted to very little. But thanks to Leslie, who lived at St. Augustine and enjoyed the governor's confidence, the Company had a virtual monopoly of *all* trade; there was little room — and few goods — for the small merchant. In those days, not much could be offered as return cargo for the Yankee vessels that flew the Spanish flag and scraped over the shallow bar with shipments of flour, salt meat and dry goods.

If there was no fortune to be made in commerce, one had to turn to fishing, building or farming. The cry of "mullet on the beach" was a heartening sound then, as it is now; and many sought communion with the waters in order to fatten the larder. A few achieved professional proficiency and undertook to supply the needs of the garrison and the community.

Others turned to the building trades. At New Smyrna, the Minorcan-Greek-Italian group had bound themselves to work several years in return for grants of land when their indentures expired. When the project failed, the colonists came to St. Augustine. With them they brought 10 years of Florida experience, earned as they carved the New Smyrna community out of the wilderness. All were used to hard work. Many were skilled workmen. So while elsewhere construction might be the province of the slave artisan, at St. Augustine numerous builders were freemen from the Mediterranean. These proud old names are on today's rosters of the building trades as evidence that craftsmanship has been handed down from father to son.

Agriculture was a necessary occupation for many, but produced wealth for only a few. These fortunate ones were generally people of means even before they came to Florida. Otherwise they could not have acquired the extensive properties — land, slaves, housing and equipment — essential for the successful ranch or plantation. Hence a well-to-do planter could afford a town house at St. Augustine, as well as his comfortable domicile in the country.[71]

As in earlier times, large houses and extended family systems were the only forms of wealth. An interesting illustration is the so-called "Avero complex" on northern St. George Street, which seems to have flowered during the renascence after 1702. Events triggered by the marriages of the several Avero girls (possibly because their mama wanted them living close by) brought several adjacent properties into this family. The ownership survived the British interim and the properties became more valuable through the years.[72]

Quite naturally, the buildings on such properties grew larger. John Bartram once remarked that many St. Augustine houses were constructed room by room "as they could get money to enlarge them." Homeowners have always been notorious property-improvers.

New houses in colonial times were not built in a continuous operation. In the first place, production of materials took time — time to quarry and cut the stone; time to "burn" lime, slake and cure it; to fell trees and pit-saw the boards; to split and dress the shingles and laths, do the millwork and make the nails and hardware. Putting up the house was also a long process. Shell-lime mortar hardened slowly. Joinery, using few nails, was tedious and complicated. Artisans could be expected to relieve the monotony with hunting and fishing at the first opportunity — as do their descendants today.

Construction details were undergoing change. The old houses, erected by Spanish builders, conformed to Spanish building practice. After 1763, British workmen introduced their own methods. The Minorcans, Greeks and Italians may have learned their trades in the traditions of their own countries, but they had also been influenced by their British bosses; now they were subject to Spanish influence. Add the effect of American contacts, and it is plain to see that building practices after 1783 were bound to differ from both the Spanish and English traditions of earlier generations. (See Fig. 35.)

The influence of citizens from the United States grew steadily stronger. Florida was opened to foreign immigration a few years after the Spanish came back, and commercially the provinces soon became a dependency of the United States. True, there were later restrictions, intended to control the burgeoning of U. S. enterprise. But they were far from effective. Spain became involved in wars following the French Revolution. As the long struggle continued in Europe, Spain's American empire was falling to pieces. In Florida, the government was not strong enough to keep out the frontiersmen, adventurers and troublemakers.

Fortunately, St. Augustine was a garrison town with the security that comes from disciplined soldiery. By the end of the Spanish regime (1821), the town had grown to about 2,000 people and another 2,000 lived in East Florida plantations. Half of this population, even in town, were slaves.[73]

So despite the turbulence, St. Augustine built a number of significant structures. Government money paid for decorative pylons at the north entrance to the city, a new powder magazine beyond the south limits of the settlement and, with the aid of gifts from the communicants, a new parish church which was later to become the Cathedral of St. Augustine.

The church and the magazine were designed by Mariano de la Rocque, the king's engineer at St. Augustine. Rocque did numerous other things, including the remodeling of a pair of old houses into a customs-and-counting house (Fig. 40). The edifice contained an apartment and offices for the royal accountant, as well as a suitable strong room for customs use.

House construction ranged from small to large and traditional to "modern," because the owners themselves were of various classes and backgrounds from government official to planter, merchant, artisan and soldier. Homes which have survived are not pretentious, but good taste and quality workmanship are clearly present. Costly architecture was not to be expected; Florida was not yet an abode for the wealthy.

A home somewhat representative of the era is the town house long associated with the Fatio family. Built in the early 1800's, it plainly shows the influence of Spaniard, Englishman and American — as well as a growing family which caused rather drastic enlargement.

Builders put up either timber-frame or stone houses. Occasionally they combined the materials. Tabby walls, however, were out of favor. The tabulation of houses made in 1788 by the royal engineer enumerated 133 houses of wood *(madera),* 114 stone *(mampostería)* and only 19 tabby *(ostión).* Probably the latter were survivors of the tabby houses so numerous before 1763. Most of the wooden buildings were recent makeshifts from hectic Tory times. Over 100 of them were mere shacks.[74]

If we may judge from extant masonry examples, the houses of the 1783-1821 period were similar to, yet quite different from, Spanish construction of the earlier regime. The difference has been

18. TREASURY STREET AT CHARLOTTE ABOUT 1850

minimized by the modernizations endured by all houses from time to time — modernizations which also brought the structures closer to the traditions of the U. S. journeyman.

Be that as it may, the buildings of the second Spanish period were just about the last of characteristic St. Augustine architecture. As more and more U. S. citizens came to Florida, they brought their own ideals of housing and perhaps a certain impatience with the old buildings of another culture. Yet not all rejected the Spanish way, because the face of the little town was pleasant and distinctive. This is the way William Cullen Bryant described St. Augustine as colonial times ended:

> At length we emerged upon a shrubby plain, and finally came in sight of this oldest city of the United States, seated among its trees on a sandy swell of land where it has stood for three hundred years. I was struck with its ancient and homely [*i.e.,* "homey"] aspect, even at a distance. . . . We drove into a green square . . . and thence through the narrow streets of the city to our hotel. I have called the streets narrow. In few places they are wide enough to allow two carriages to pass abreast. . . . The old houses, built of a kind of stone which is seemingly a pure concretion of small shells, overhang the streets with their wooden balconies, and the gardens between the houses are fenced on the side of the street with high walls of stone. Peeping over these walls you see branches of the pomegranate and of the orange tree, now fragrant with flowers, and, rising yet higher, the leaning boughs of the fig, with its broad luxuriant leaves.[75]

The banner of Spain came down in 1821 and many of her nationals left St. Augustine. Their departure was not really important, because for a long time now, they had been only a minority. Yet the influence of Iberia would last for generations. Despite nondescript modernizations, the inflexible old city plan with its narrow shady streets would keep the St. Augustine look from total disintegration. The aspect of the architecture had come from sound and practical construction; it would not be changed in a hurry. The stability of a slow-growing population (for there was no massive migration) was likewise a factor; it meant long use and good care for the old buildings, and little need for new ones.

At long last St. Augustine had become a community where people lived, not because the job was here, but because they liked the place. It was home.

# DESIGN AND MATERIALS

## FLOOR PLANS

THE REMARKABLE MAP of 1788, made by Engineer Mariano de la Rocque for tax purposes, records the floor plans of almost 400 buildings in the town of St. Augustine, including some 280 dwellings.[76] Study of the house plans reveals that they are basically of three different types (Fig. 20.).

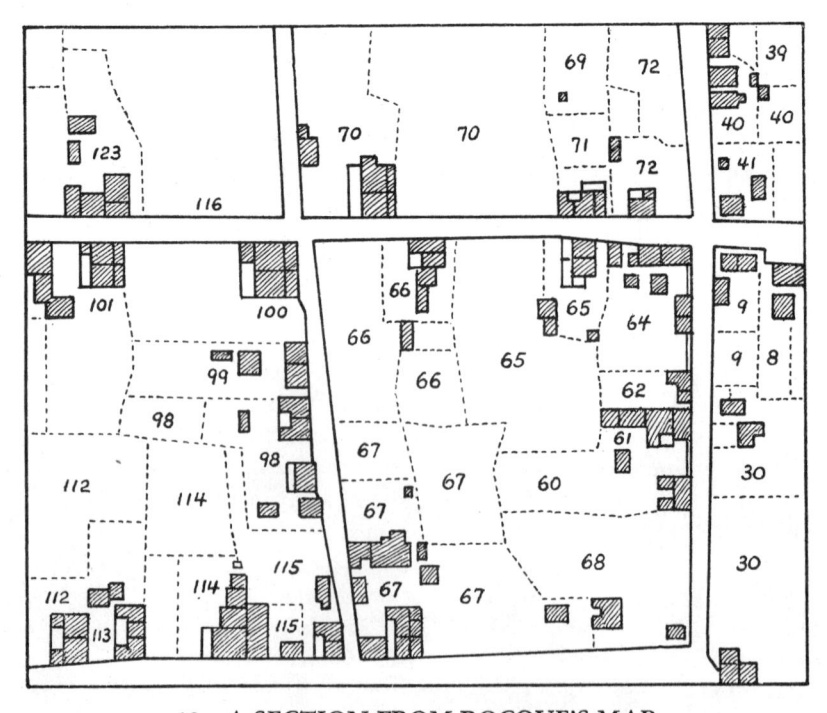

19. A SECTION FROM ROCQUE'S MAP
*This facsimile shows the detail — house plan, outbuildings, property and fence lines — found on the royal engineer's map of 1788.*

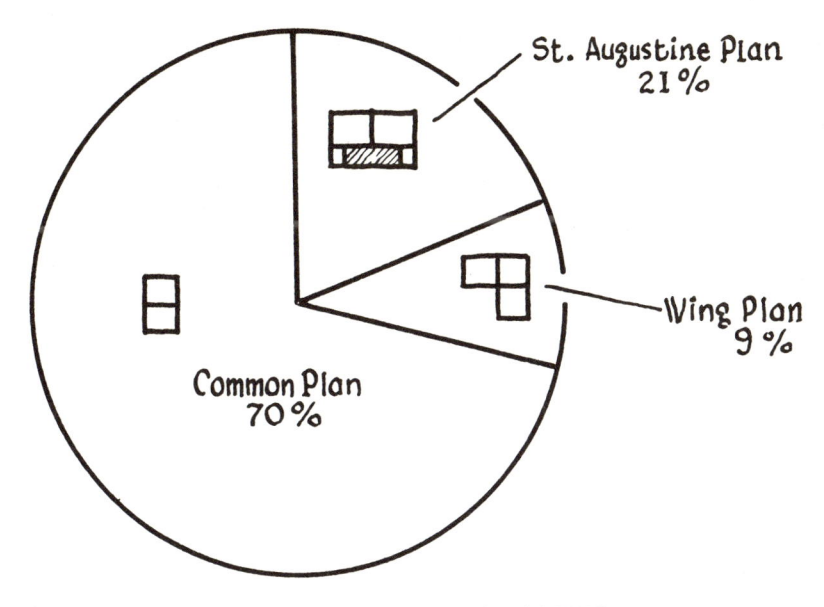

20. THE THREE PLAN TYPES

The following table shows the relative frequency of the plan types and subtypes of the 1788 map. The count includes only buildings identifiable as dwellings.

## Popularity of Floor Plan Types (1788)

| Basic Plan | Sub-Type | Number | Percent |
|---|---|---|---|
| COMMON PLAN | 1-room | 78 | 28 |
|  | 2-room | 99 | 35 |
|  | 3 or more | 22 | 7 |
| ST. AUGUSTINE PLAN | loggia | 32 | 11 |
|  | porch | 28 | 10 |
| WING PLAN | L-shape | 17 | 6 |
|  | U-shape | 6 | 2 |
|  | H-shape | 3 | 1 |

**BASIC PLAN**

## The Common Plan

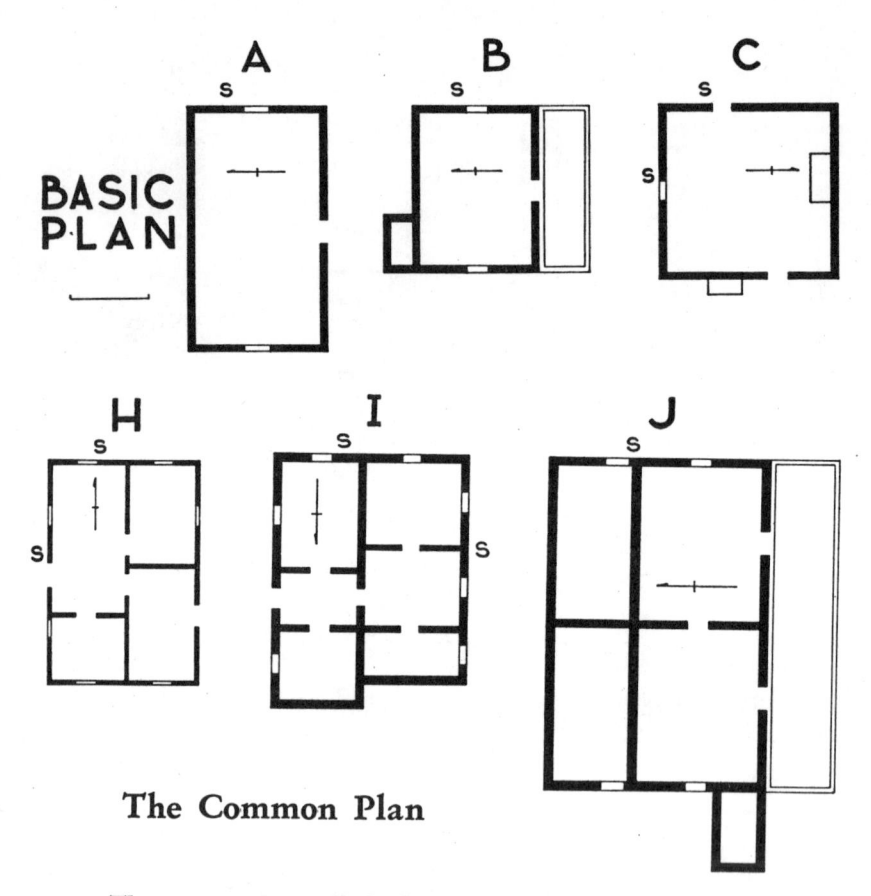

The one- or two-celled plan (Fig. 21) is so widely used all over the world that we should be surprised only if it were *not* found in St. Augustine. Because of its universality, and because the dwelling built upon this plan was the "common Spanish house," it is proper to call it *the common plan*. Actually, most of those shown on the 1788 map are probably of British rather than Spanish origin. But in plan there would be little difference between John's frame shack and Juan's tabby hut.

The prototype is the rectangular one-room cottage of the medieval laborer, a shelter that provided only the necessities — a roof to keep off the rain, walls to stop the wind, a hearth for cooking, and perhaps stairs or a ladder to a sleeping loft. If primitive, it was also practical, especially on the frontier.

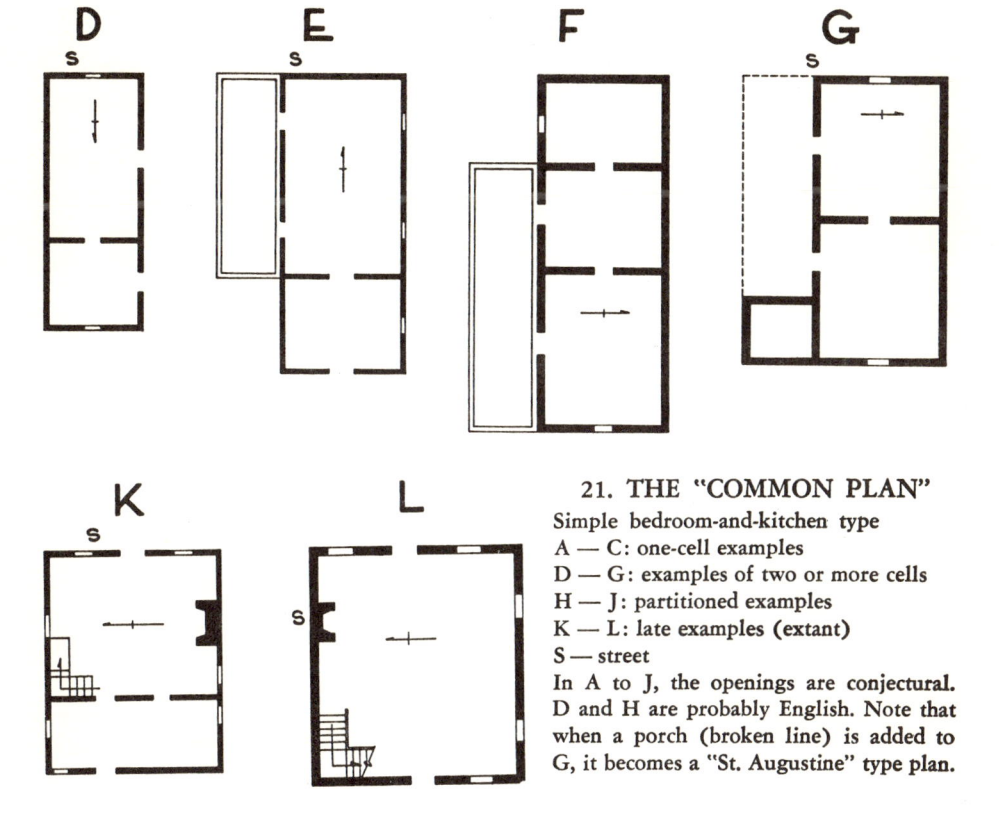

**21. THE "COMMON PLAN"**
Simple bedroom-and-kitchen type
A — C: one-cell examples
D — G: examples of two or more cells
H — J: partitioned examples
K — L: late examples (extant)
S — street
In A to J, the openings are conjectural. D and H are probably English. Note that when a porch (broken line) is added to G, it becomes a "St. Augustine" type plan.

In St. Augustine, the rooms of the plan were fairly spacious. One-room buildings chosen at random show a variety of dimensions (all approximate, of course, due to the small scale of the map):

| | | | | |
|---|---|---|---|---|
| 12'x12' | 14'x16' | 15'x20' | 16'x20' | 12'x22' |
| 14'x30' | 15'x22' | 16'x26' | 15'x25' | 16'x35' |

In two-room dwellings, the rooms tended to be a bit smaller. Again, these are random samples:

| 1st Room | 2nd Room |
|---|---|
| 8'x13' | 8'x13' |
| 12'x18' | 12'x18' |
| 12'x22' | 12'x10' |
| 14'x12' | 14'x20' |
| 16'x20' | 16'x20' |
| 18'x28' | 18'x17' |

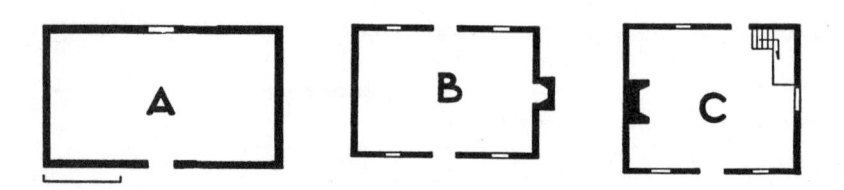

22. "COMMON PLAN" HOUSES

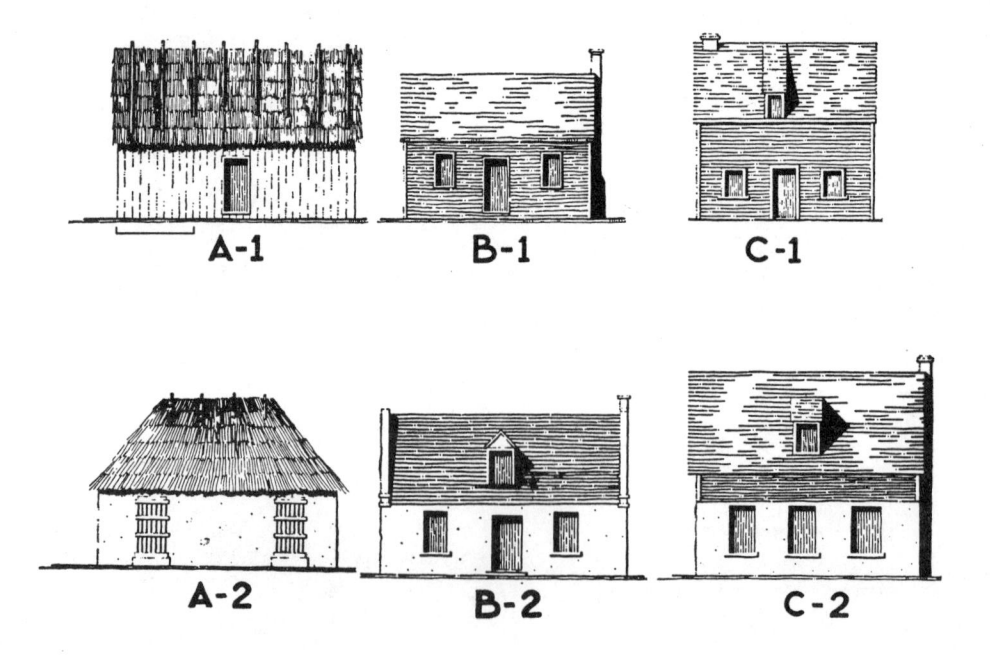

Many of the common houses (Fig. 22), simple as they were, had porches or balconies, and detached kitchens. For although the one- or two-cell plan is identified with the poor man (who was in the majority), an ambitious fellow's house grew with his fortunes —especially if he were married. And the floor plan was readily ca-

52

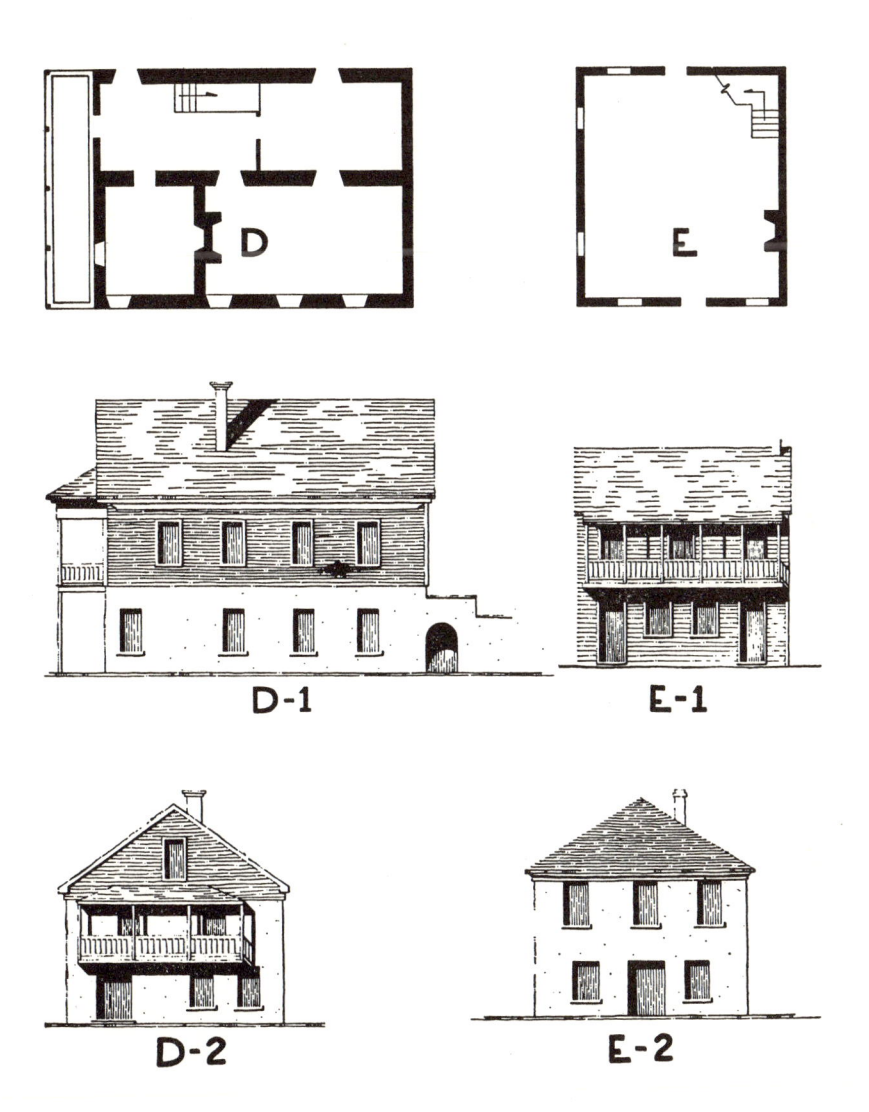

pable of expansion. Perhaps the easiest method was to add rooms in single file, so that the old roof lines might be extended right over the new work. However, examination of the Oldest House, the Llambias House, and the Arrivas House has shown that in these instances the original small houses were enlarged in practically all directions. (Fig. 23).

53

23. AN EVOLUTION FROM COMMON TO ST. AUGUSTINE PLAN

## The St. Augustine Plan

The second type I call *the St. Augustine plan* (Fig. 24) because very clearly it met local needs.

It is essentially a simple rectangle of from two to four rather spacious rooms, with a loggia or a porch, and often a street balcony.

Actually, this plan is found in two forms. The more popular one has a loggia (open-sided room) as an integral part of the plan, centered on the side. The other version substitutes a sheltered porch for the loggia. In both cases, the main entrance was through either the loggia or porch, which opened onto the yard.

Random examples show typical dimensions for this plan:

| Overall Size (Feet) | Main Room (Feet) |
|---|---|
| 24x36 | 16x16 |
| 28x42 | 16x20 |
| 28x43 | 18x20 |
| 30x36 | 18x18 |
| 32x32 | 16x16 |
| 32x42 | 16x18 |
| 45x42 | 25x22 |

The plan was almost invariably oriented with the open areas facing south or east, so that in summer the prevailing southeast airs ventilated the large rooms and made the porches wonderfully pleasant; the sun was overhead and the shade was cool. Thick masonry walls insulated against heat. But when winter came and the sun dropped toward the south horizon, sunlight crept into the loggias and porches, flooding them with light and warmth. The massive walls held out the cold, and the house bulk protected the open areas from the frigid northwest wind. A sheltered porch or a loggia, snuggled between walls that broke the chill breeze and reflected the sunlight, was comfortable on all except the coldest days.

Certainly this built-in comfort was the main reason for the popularity of the plan. We do not know the total number built before 1763, but at least 37 lasted long enough to be recorded on the 1788 map. In addition, most of the two dozen or so "better" homes erected during the British period are in plan very similar to this St. Augustine type.

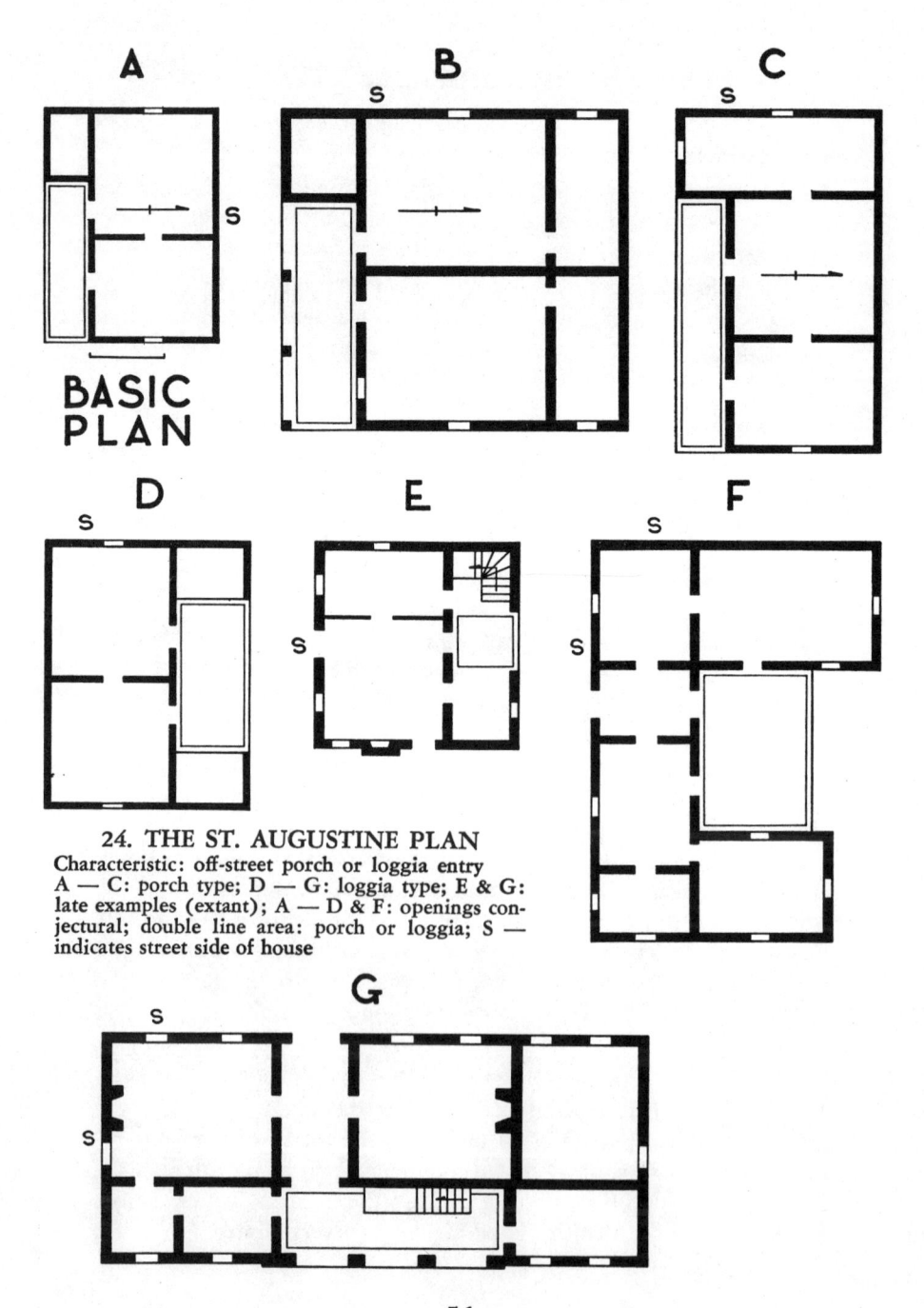

**24. THE ST. AUGUSTINE PLAN**
Characteristic: off-street porch or loggia entry
A — C: porch type; D — G: loggia type; E & G: late examples (extant); A — D & F: openings conjectural; double line area: porch or loggia; S — indicates street side of house

## 25. ST. AUGUSTINE PLAN HOUSES
"A" is in part a conjectural restoration

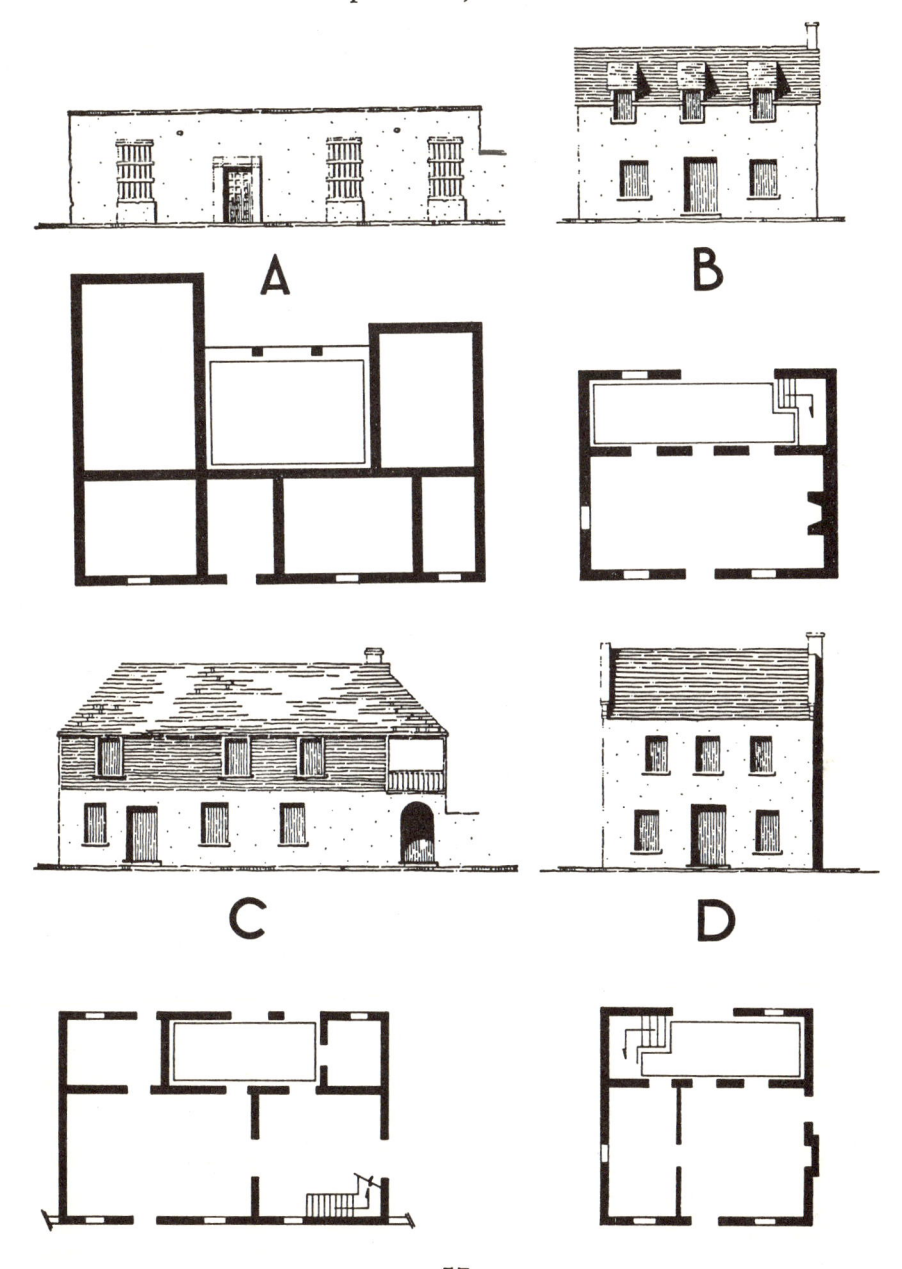

## The Wing Plan

Judged by its frequency, the wing plan (Fig. 26) was the least popular of the three types. It is characterized by a main structure of two or more rooms, plus a substantial wing or two which makes the plan an L, U, or H. In its better aspects, with attractive arcades or galleries around a patio, it was a somewhat pretentious layout for the residence of a government official or a prominent family. An extant example is the Treasurer's House, although it has lost a wing and gained a story since Spanish times. Do not, however, leap to the conclusion that all wing plans came full-drawn from the drafting board of the royal architect. Wings could be — and were — added to less ostentatious structures, provided a man had the wherewithal to do it.

## Carry-over Plans

For the earlier years we have no information about plans except what can be guessed from painfully meager contemporary descriptions, or from later buildings seemingly built in the old tradition. The one- or two-cell hut or house was prevalent during the 18th century and certainly during early times as well. Of other types we have no reliable knowledge. However, from two important maps we can deduce a great deal.

When the Spanish left Florida in 1763-1764, Juan Joseph Elixio de la Puente prepared a map of all real estate in St. Augustine.[77] Unfortunately, his data are much less detailed than Rocque's of 1788. But close comparison shows that better than half the dwellings on the 1788 map can be identified beyond reasonable doubt (identical sites and structural materials) with houses on the 1764 map. The majority of these carry-over buildings were masonry. Their floor plans probably did not undergo drastic change. Hence the type plans of 1788, with few exceptions, must have originated during the renascence of 1703-1763.

The following table summarizes the information on carry-overs:

### Known House Carry-Overs 1764-1788

| Type of Plan | Number |
| --- | --- |
| Common | 94 |
| St. Augustine | 37 |
| Wing | 16 |

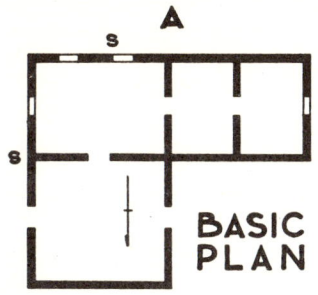

## 26. THE WING PLAN

Characteristic: one or more wings
A: openings conjectural; B: this is probably a "St. Augustine" plan to which wing was added. Broken line denotes old loggia. C: the east wing is conjectural reconstruction. Double line area: gallery or arcade; S — indicates street side of house

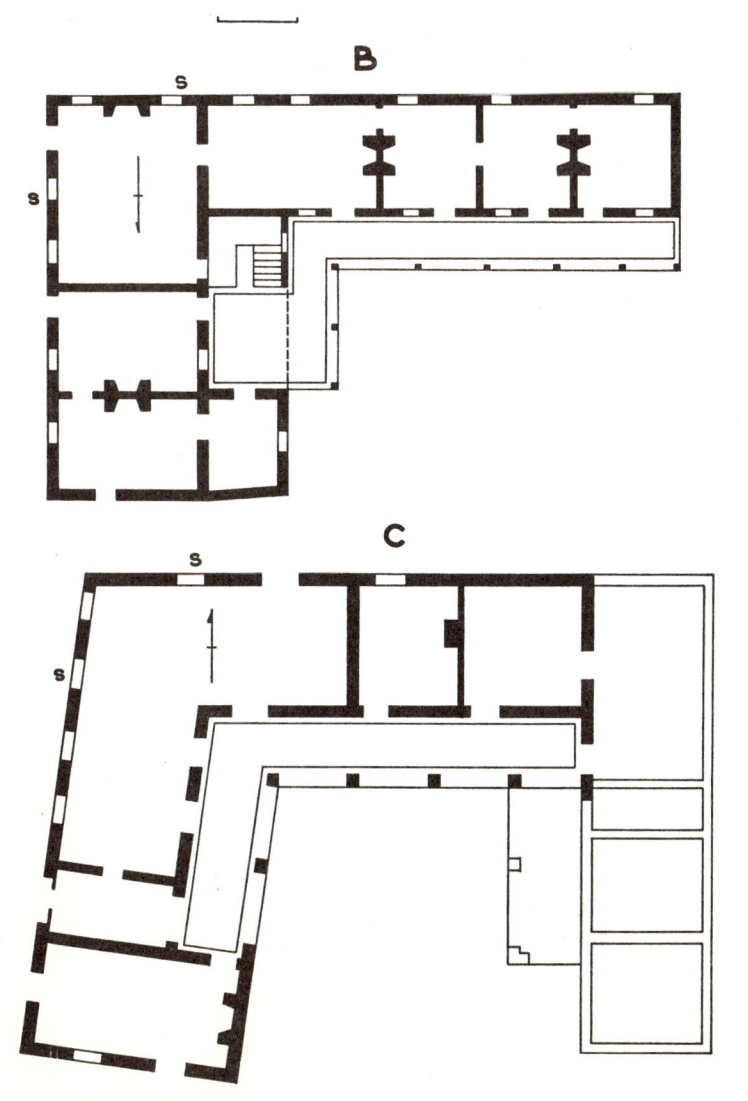

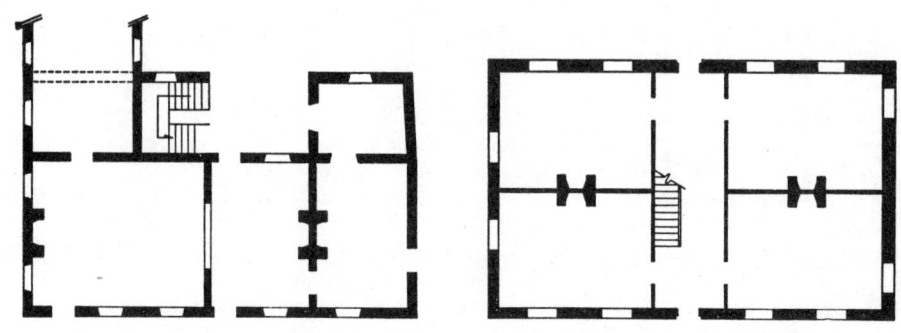

**27. THE ST. AUGUSTINE PLAN (LEFT) COMPARED WITH AN AMERICAN HALL PLAN**

Thus the 1788 map has given us the floor plans for 147 pre-1764 structures.

The ratio of plan types did not change appreciably, despite the British interim:

### Relative Popularity of Plan Types In 1764 and 1788

| Type of Plan | Frequency (In Percent) 1764 | 1788 |
|---|---|---|
| COMMON | 64 | 70 |
| ST. AUGUSTINE | 25 | 21 |
| WING | 11 | 9 |

Between 1764 and 1788, there was very little loss in substantial masonry buildings. On the other hand, losses of common-plan houses were heavy. Our tables, dealing primarily with carry-overs, do not point out that many houses were built during the British period. Most of them were inexpensive common-plan houses, much like the ones they replaced. True, there is a handful of blatantly un-Spanish plans (Fig. 27). What Spaniard, for instance, would convert a long range of stables into a dwelling, as did William Watson?[78] In another case only the street façade of Spanish masonry was retained; onto it was built a whole new wooden house, seemingly the one described below. Toward the end of the Revolution, political prisoners sent here from Carolina were on parole and allowed to rent private quarters. One group chose a large wood-built house, belonging to Spencer Man, Esq. very pleasantly scituated near the River, on the North East corner of our Parole Limits . . . this house being two Storys high, and about 75 feet in length contains four large rooms of near 20 feet square on each Floor, with a Piazza the whole length on the South Side, both above and below, so that the four Chambers above, by having the Stairway from one Piazza to the other, are all private, and contains four Lodgers in each. — The Ground belonging to this house being ............feet deep and ditto wide on the back part affords Room for a large Garden, as, also a very roomy Yard of ............ feet front on the Bay. . . . The four Rooms below are disposed of as follows. — the front with a bow window of Three lights next to the water, to be sitting Room for such company, as may be pleased to visit us. The Back Room having a Fireplace, we are to diet in. The other two in the Central part of the house is made use of for a Store room and a Pantry . . .[79]

Notice that the description also fits the "single house" type of Charleston. Is this an example of Charleston influence? But in the main it appears that the British occupation caused no radical change in floor plans.

The pen pictures of the 1760's emphasize several characteristics. Dr. Stork, for instance, said that "two rooms upon a floor" were usual.[80] The 1788 map proves that most common houses did indeed have two rooms, nor was this arrangement at all strange even in the more sophisticated plans. The "chief entrance," said Bartram, was "on the back side of the house or yard"; and Stork adds that "before the entry of most of the houses runs a portico of stone arches."[81] The statements are confirmed in the 1788 map by the large number of porch and loggia spaces, all without exception opening onto the yard, and most of them oriented on the south or east. But from the tax assessor's descriptions it is clear that Stork's "portico of stone arches" could also be wooden posts or masonry pillars.[82]

On north sides, DeBrahm noted, were "double walls 6 or 8 feet asunder, forming a kind of Gallery, which answers for Cellars and Pantries."[83] The 1788 map tends to water down his statement; only a dozen or so such parallel walls are in evidence, generally in houses of the St. Augustine plan.

According to Bartram, street doors were uncommon except in "the grand houses" and taverns. When found, such doors led via a "common passage" (hall) to the yard and kitchens. In confirmation, the 1788 map shows not more than seven or eight such halls, all of them in large buildings.

# WALL MATERIALS
Types of Wall Materials and their Periods of Use
(Numbers refer to list below)

| Wall Materials | \multicolumn{5}{c}{Periods When Used (dating is conservative)} |
|---|---|---|---|---|---|
|  | 1500's | 1600's | 1703-1763 | British | 1783-1821 |
| **Wood** | | | | | |
|   Posts | ═(1)═ | (?) | | | |
|   Boarded frame | ═(2)═ | ═(2)═ | ═(2)═ | ═(3)═ | ═(2)═ |
|   Thatched frame | ═(4)═(5)═ | ═(4)═(5)═ | ═(4)═(5)═ | | ═(5)═ |
|   Shingled frame | | | | ═(6)═ | ═(6)═ |
| **Concrete** | | | | | |
|   Tabby (*tapia*) | ─(7)─ | ──── | ═(8)═ | | ─(9)─(10)─ |
|   Tabby & frame | | | ═(14)═ | | ─(15)─ |
| **Stone** | | | | | |
|   Stone | | (11)(12) | ═(11)═(12)═ | ═(13)═ | ═(11)═(12)═ |
|   Stone & tabby | | | ═(19)═ | | ─(20)─ |
|   Stone & frame | | | ═(16)═ | ═(18)═ | ═(17)═ |
| **Brick** | | | ─(21)─ | ─(22)─ | ─(21)─ |

## Common Names of Wall Materials

### Wood
1. *Savino:* cypress post
2. *Madera, tabla:* wood, board, (timber frame)
3. Timber frame, clapboard, weatherboard
4. *Tablas y paja:* board & straw thatch
5. *Tablas y palma:* board & palm thatch
6. *Tablas y rajones:* board & shingle

### Concrete
1. *Cal:* lime
8. *Ripio:* tabby (probably *ostión*)
9. *Ostión:* oyster-shell tabby
10. *Mampostería:* masonry, meaning *ostión* (rare). See 12.

### Stone (Coquina)
11. *Piedra:* stone, meaning rubble masonry
12. *Mampostería:* rubble masonry
13. Stone, stone-and-lime: rubble masonry

### Combinations
14. *Ripio y tabla:* tabby & frame
15. *Ostión y tabla:* tabby & frame
16. *Piedra y tabla:* stone & frame
17. *Mampostería y madera:* stone & frame
18. Stone & frame
19. *Piedra y ripio:* stone & tabby
20. *Mampostería y ostión:* stone & tabby

### Brick
21. *Ladrillo:* brick, brickmasonry
22. Brickmasonry

(As the divisions in our list show, several synonyms for the same material are to be found. For example wood is called variously *madera, tabla* or *rajón*; tabby is *cal, ripio* or *ostión*; and stone is *piedra* or *mampostería*.)

## 28. WALL CONSTRUCTION

A — Thatch with cabbage palm

B — A post wall. The spaces between posts were filled with sticks and plaster.

C — Florida Indian sentry box (1564). Mud and clay filled the space between the posts.

D — Board Wall. The structure was supported by cypress posts. Joints were probably lapped, fitted or battened.

E — Weatherboard on timber-frame wall.

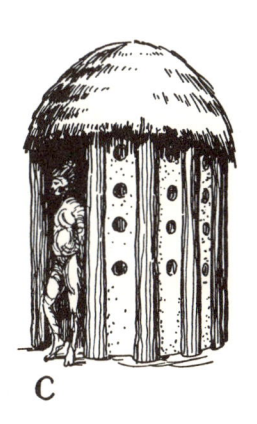

63

## Thatch

Although our records do not specifically mention *walls* of thatch in the 1500's, we can be sure that since they were common in the Indian villages, they were also very much present in the white man's pueblo. Even the poorest fellow could get thatch.

Thatch walls were made by hanging palm fronds upon horizontal poles or slats (Fig. 28A). Though highly flammable, properly made walls were tight and remarkably substantial for several years.

The usual Spanish word for this material is *palma,* denoting thatch made from the fronds of the cabbage palm (Sabal Palmetto). A second common term for it, especially in the 1700's, is *guano.* During the early 1700's another word comes into use: *paja* (straw thatch). This may be a general term for thatch, or it may designate thatch made of a specific material (marsh grass ?) as yet unidentified.

In the 1702 siege, fire destroyed all but a handful of houses and for a decade or more, housing was on an emergency basis. Thatch (*paja*) shelters filled the gap. After about 1720, however, thatch wall construction almost disappeared. By 1763 in all of St. Augustine, only two thatch-wall huts could be found. Yet they were not uncommon outside the city, and a rash of them reappeared when the town swelled with refugees near the end of the British period.[84]

## Wood

Wood was clearly the predominant material during the early days. Pine, oak, cedar, cypress, palm and other woods were available, but there is specific mention of only one for early wall structure. That one is *savino* (bald cypress or pond cypress), "because it does not rot when in the ground." [85] The inference is that post construction was used. In this system, a line of posts (sometimes called palisados or puncheons) was set into the ground to form the house wall (Fig. 28B). Spaces between the posts were filled with sticks and plaster (or clay or mud). The completed wall was whitewashed on both sides. This seems precisely the type construction (*madera y baro y encaladas*) described at Santa Elena during the 1580's, since the Santa Elena houses required sturdy walls to support their flat masonry roofs. Post walls were also known in Florida during prehistoric times (Fig. 28C). Presumably the Indians used clay to seal them. We can assume there was continued use of cypress (*savino*) for wall posts and wherever else a rot-resistant wood was needed.[86]

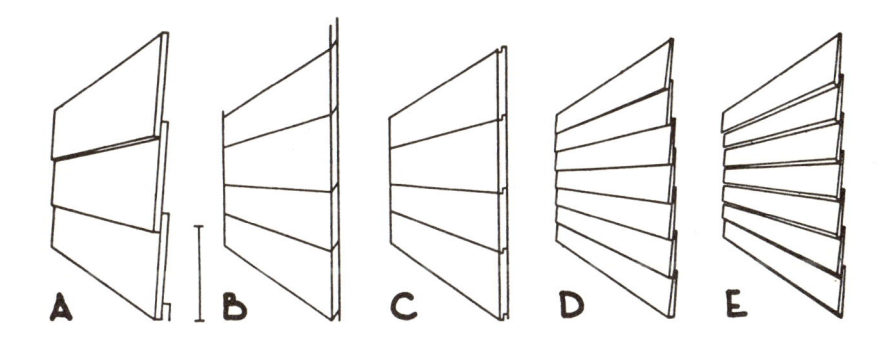

### 29. CLAPBOARDS

A — Edge-lap

B — Beveled edge at 14 St. Francis (Oldest House). This type was also used in New England.

C — Rabetted. Common elsewhere, but no recorded examples in St. Augustine.

D — Feather-edged at 14 St. Francis Street, about 5/8" x 6", with 4¾" to the weather.

E — Feather-edge with molding

Board (*tabla*) walls were on the more important buildings (Fig. 28D). A sketch map (Fig. 4) of the 1590's shows vertical board sheathing on the walls, and this may have been common usage.[87] There are other possibilities, of course. The siding could have been horizontal weatherboarding (Figs. 28E, 29). Or *tabla*, which signifies a sawn (and probably dressed) board in contrast to a rived board (*raja*), may simply mean timber-frame construction instead of post walls.

In any event, board walls became increasingly numerous up to the wholesale destruction of the 1702 siege. During the next 50 years, masonry became the principal material; wooden-walled dwellings were hardly more than 20 percent of the total by 1763. But British builders reversed the trend. In the feverish boom of the early 1780's many timber-frame structures were built, sheathed with feather-edged weatherboards or with clapboards. Probably this siding was dressed; at least the records show clapboards to be distinct from the "rough boards" sometimes used for outbuildings.[88]

Shingled walls seem to have a limited appearance before British times and lasted into the following period. About a dozen of them are recorded on the 1788 map, where the Spanish used the term *rajones* to describe the material. The word implies a large, rough shingle or shake. Most likely it was rived from cypress, as was the English "short shingle" generally used for roofing.

The British records also mention one 16x24-foot "log house" put up by David Marran's seven Negroes as a domicile. However, there is some question whether this was a true log house inasmuch as Marran stated that he bought the timber boards and nails for it. In any event, if it were a log house, it was unique in St. Augustine.[89]

Because red cedar was commonly cut for fence posts by the British,[90] this lasting wood may also have been employed in parts of the house frame. But yellow pine was the wood most generally used by the carpenters. There is no mention of other kinds except cypress, from which shingles were made.

Within a 50-mile radius of the town were 5 sawmills, or tracts surveyed for sawmills. The closest seems to have been a few miles to the southwest on Woodcutter's (Moultrie) Creek. Westward were two: one about 12 miles from town at Saw Mill and Six Mile creeks (where "a command of the Water by Dams and by the Tide" was possible),[91] and the other on the west side of the St. Johns to take advantage of a fine stand of pine. Twenty miles up North River, William Watson had his 200 acres where 20 men worked to supply him with lumber and shingles. Still farther north, on Trout Creek, "Navigable for any Craft necessary for conveying away Lumber," and in "Pine Land . . . very good," was another sawmill.[92] Barges or "flats" usually moved the lumber to market or to port. There was at least one lumber yard at St. Augustine.[93]

## Masonry

The basic materials for St. Augustine masonry were discovered during the 1500's, but do not seem to have been widely used until the 1700's.

*Lime.* Oyster shells, probably from large kitchen middens nearby, were calcined into lime (*cal*) by the early settlers for whitewash and sometimes mortar. In later years tremendous quantities of shell went into the production of lime, or else became the aggregate in tabby masonry. After a century or more of exploitation many con-

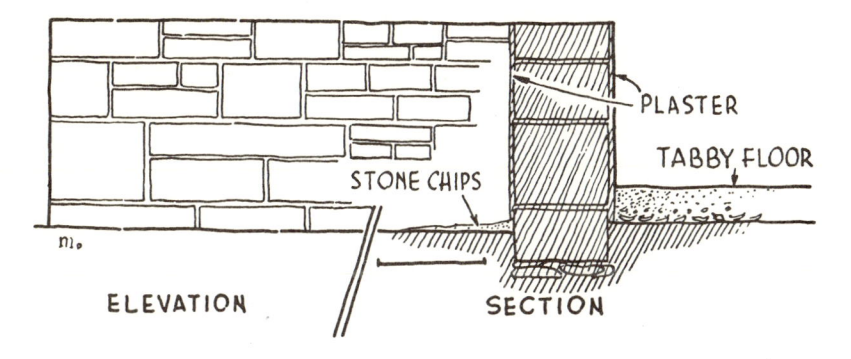

**30. STONE (COQUINA) WALL**
*This is the "coursed-squared-rubble" walling commonly used.*

venient shell mounds were depleted. During the British times one builder complained that his Negroes had to fetch lime from 20 miles away.[94]

*Stone.* Anastasia Island contained major deposits of the shellstone named *coquina* (the Spanish term for shellstone). Oddly enough, most of the records simply call it "stone" (*piedra*). Its discovery was reported no later than 1580, but the first recorded stone construction — a powder magazine of *piedra y cal* (stone and lime) — did not take place until the end of the century. The quarries were not more than three miles away, and most of that was over water.[95]

The building of Castillo de San Marcos (1672-1696) marked the first big stone project and as the work drew to a close, limited amounts of stone became available for the official residences. Citizens could also buy stone in the form of quarry rubble, but exactly how it was used is not certain. During the years after 1703 hewn stone came into such general use that the old quarry played out. The Spanish eventually had to open a new one. Faced with a similar problem, the British found a convenient vein of stone close to the inlet. Afterwards when the sea broke into the pit, this English quarrying was blamed for the erosion that cut away a good chunk of Anastasia Island.[96]

The best houses, and the ones which survived the years, had walls of hewn stone. Standard one-story thickness was one *tercia* (about 11 inches). A two-story wall was at least 1½ *tercias*.[97]

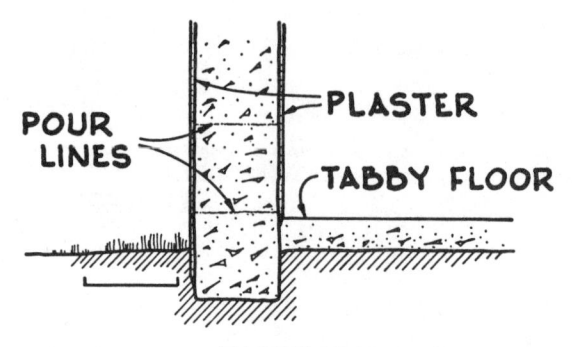

31. TABBY WALL

By present-day standard, house walls had no foundations. The usual preparation was to excavate a trench slightly wider than the wall and about a foot deep. A thin layer of flat stones or oyster shells was tossed in as a sort of spread footing, after which the workmen began wall construction without further ado.

The stone was squared and faced up with a narrow-bitted hatchet. Since the quarry strata varied in thickness, texture and hardness, there was also much variation in the blocks. Consequently most walling was of the type called coursed squared rubble (Fig. 30). The blocks were laid on their natural bed (that is, with their laminae horizontal); side-laid blocks (called "shiners" because of lighter color) were quite rare. Oyster shells or pottery sherds were commonly used in the horizontal joints as levelers or separators. Joints were troweled flush.

*Tabby.* Wall tabby, called *ripio* in 1764 and *piedra de ostión* (oyster-shell stone) in 1788, was lime mortar with oyster shells for aggregate (Figs. 14, 31). "Most of the common Spanish houses," wrote Bartram, "was built of oyster shells and mortar, as well as garden and yard walls."

Structural tabby, like stone, seems rare before 1703. One ruin, found in archeological association with majolica sherds of the 1650-1700 period, might be pre-1700.[98] Perhaps others are awaiting discovery. Strangely enough, tabby construction apparently ended in 1763. In fact, as the table on page 71 indicates, more than 100 tabby houses were lost between 1764 and 1788. Bartam explained that the walls of a common house, having been built room by room over the years as the householder's fortune and need increased, tended to "wind and crack." Numbers of such insubstantial and unoccupied houses were pushed down by the soldiers in order to salvage what lumber they contained for firewood. Often the pushing was easier because many walls were a couple of inches less than the 11 inches (*tercia,* or third of a vara) which seems to have been more or less standard thickness for one-story masonry. The 9-inch wall is probably what Rocque and others called *tabique* (thin wall).[99]

As in modern concrete construction, tabby walls were made by tamping the mortar into wooden forms (Fig. 14). Unlike today's concrete, however, the old lime mortar hardened very slowly. A masonry house might well be under construction for months before you could move in. One means of reinforcing the green mortar and hastening construction was to insert vertical wooden posts into the wall at about 5-foot intervals (Fig. 32). The Spanish term for the technique was *ostión y postes*. The posts not only stiffened the wall, but carried the weight of the roof, thus relieving the new tabby of premature strain.[100]

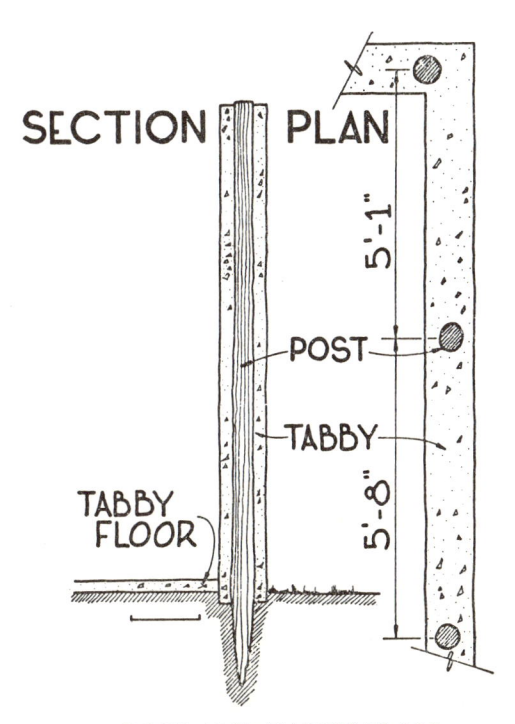

32. POST-AND-TABBY WALL

33. ASHLAR-MARKED PLASTER

*Plaster.* Stone walls were invariably plastered on both sides in order to waterproof the sponge-like shellstone and provide a smooth, clean surface to live with. Work of this period at the fort, which may be accepted as high standard, was smoothly finished with a metal trowel. Efficacy of the finish coat was renewed periodically with coats of whitewash, which built up in surprising number. Fence walls were likewise plastered, since esthetically they were part of the house.

For similar reasons, tabby walls were also covered. The large oyster shell aggregate roughens the surface, forming pockets for water on the outside and dust on the inside, soon converting the textured wall into a moldy, stained and dingy surface which the housewife abhors. Coats of lime plaster on both sides smoothed up the walls and dried out the house.

The colonial plaster undercoat is identical with the mortar used for laying the stones, tan in color with flecks of charcoal, burnt shell chips, and nodules of pure lime. The sand that colors the mix is quite fine. Probably it came from backyard borrow pits. This kind of sand underlies the entire locale. The finish coat is a smooth white application about 1/8 inch thick.

The 18th century fad of marking exterior plaster in imitation of elegant ashlar joints (Fig. 33) may not have reached St. Augustine until the 19th century. Then it was applied to a number of structures, including some old ones which needed replastering.

*Combinations.* Much revealing information on masonry materials comes by comparing data from the maps of 1764 and 1788:

### Wall Materials Used in 1764 and 1788[101]

| No. of Houses | 1764 Material | % | % | 1788 Material | No. of Houses |
|---|---|---|---|---|---|
| 49 | *tabla* (wood) | 14 | 43 | *madera* (wood) | 114 |
|  |  |  | 5 | *madera y rajones* (shakes) | 13 |
| 132 | *ripio* (tabby) | 39 | 5 | *ostión* (tabby) | 13 |
| 106 | *piedra* (stone) | 32 | 36 | *mampostería* (stone) | 94 |
| 24 | *ripio y tabla* | 7 | 2 | *ostión y madera* | 4 |
| 5 | *piedra y tabla* | 1½ | 3 | *mampostería y madera* | 9 |
| 18 | *piedra y ripio* | 6 | 5 | *mampostería y ostión* | 14 |
| 2 | *guano* (palm thatch) | ½ | 1 | *cujes y barro* (wattle and clay) | 2 |
| 336 |  |  |  |  | 263 |

Although the great majority of house walls were a single material, the 1764 map listed three combinations: tabby-and-frame (*ripio y tabla*), stone-and-frame (*piedra y tabla*), and stone-and-tabby (*piedra y ripio*). Tabby-and-frame was the most numerous. The frame part was probably a second story or an addition; but in some instances the explanation of the second material is that Puente has *two* houses in mind, one of each material and both on the same property. In a few cases some of the walls or partitions were built of the other material.[102]

The British of course maintained many of the masonry buildings, remodelled others, and built some new ones. Repairs were necessary in many Spanish-built houses, and some of these were extensive. In one case, a gable wall had to be completely rebuilt. In another, the owner had to "put down" the entire house and rebuild it. But these were exceptional cases. More often the work involved merely additions and improvements.[103]

The Englishmen did not seem to distinguish between types of masonry buildings as carefully as the Spanish did. To most citizens, any masonry structure was a "stone house" or "stone wall house." Occasionally the term "stone and lime" was used, but seemingly not to designate a special kind of masonry.[104]

Stone and wood, during the British time, were used in combination. We are safe in saying that most generally the wood is an addition to the masonry, either beside it or above it. But there is one instance where the dwelling consisted of wooden walls between a pair of stone gable ends.[105] Unfortunately we cannot tell whether this choice of materials was purposeful or circumstantial, or Spanish or English. But it was unusual.

On his 1788 map, Rocque recognized four uses of the material: 1) *tabique de ostión* (literally, thin wall of oyster shell) — exterior walls of tabby about 9 inches thick; 2) *pared* (wall) *de ostión* — exterior tabby wall of standard *tercia* thickness (11 inches); 3) *mampostería* (stonemasonry) *y ostión;* and 4) *divisiones interiores* (partitions) *de ostión*. The latter phrase suggests that the partitions were the walls of an old tabby *casita*, around which a new house had been built.[106]

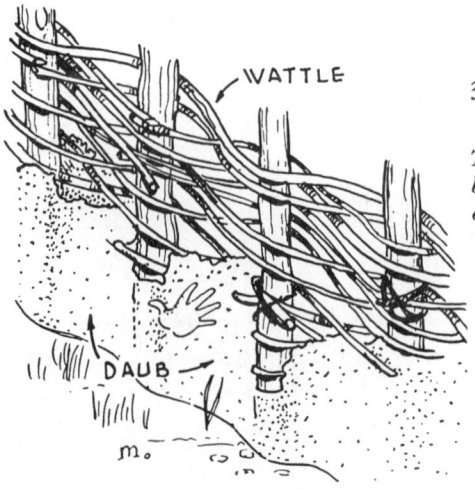

34. WATTLE-AND-DAUB WALL

*The finished wall was smooth, but followed the wavy contour of the wattles.*

The proliferation of names for the various materials between 1764 and 1788 is confusing, but comparison clearly shows these to be equivalent terms:

> stone = *piedra, mampostería*
> tabby = *ripio, ostión*

From them, all the other combinations can be worked out.

Also of interest in the 1788 tally is the presence of two wattle-and-daub (*cujes y barro*) huts (Fig. 34). The respective owners were Juan Yenobar [Genovar?] and Mathias Ponze.[107] Evidently they were men of humble station who drew on primitive experience to build home and hearth. Let us hope their station soon improved. But do not jump to the conclusion that the huts were rough and insubstantial. Similar little houses in the West Indies today show that the construction was strong and durable, especially when the daub is lime mortar.

*Brick.* No examples of colonial brickmasonry seem to have survived. Yet a significant number of 18th century brick fragments have been found, possibly of both Spanish and English origin. They are of unequal quality — some so very poor that they have the look of inferior local materials and manufacture.

Indeed, brick and tile were made here during the 1730's, if not earlier. For in that year, samples were sent to Havana, and there was talk of repairing the brickyard and modernizing the Castillo with brick arches. To get the project under way, an expert brickmaker named Nicolás Gutiérrez from Havana brought 8,000 bricks to build a kiln. Once he saw the yard and the clays, however, Nicolás recommended building the arches out of shellstone.[108]

The few brickbats found in pre-1763 associations have been, with a single exception, inferior and soft and variegated in color from red to ocher. The exception was dark red, hard and well made. It may well have been one of the Havana imports. Average size of the bats was 1⅞"x3¾"x(?). Whole bricks which seem to date from the 1783-1821 period are very red and sized about 2⅛"x3¼"x7". (They conform to bricks of this period in the slave quarters on Fort George Island.) The comparison suggests that the earlier bricks were also about 7" long.[109]

During the British period, brick was used for the first floor and chimneys of the soldiers' barracks. "Good bricks are made here," said the governor. A few specimens of a light red brick about 2¾"x4⅝"x9" are found. They may be relics from British times.[110]

# FACADES
## List of Characteristics

| Item | Before 1700 | 1703-1763 | British | 1783-1821 |
|---|---|---|---|---|
| Height | | | | |
|   1-story | | | | |
|   1½-story | ? | | | |
|   2-story | | | | |
| Openings | | | | |
|   Main entrance via side yard | ? | | | |
|   Street door | | | | |
|   No north openings | ? | | | |
|   Openings all sides | | | | |
|   Doors large, many 2-leaf | ? | | | |
|   6-panel door | | | | |
|   Transoms | | | | |
|   Windows large on street, small on west | | | | |
|   Wooden gratings on all windows, *rejas* on street windows | ? | | ---- | |
|   Inside shutters | | | ---- | |
|   Outside shutters | | | | |
|   Half-lattice on windows | ? | | | |
|   Glazed casements | | | | |
|   Glazed double-hung sash | | | | |
| Cornice | | | | |
|   Parapet, sometimes castellated, on flat roof | ? | | | |
|   Box cornice | | | | |
|   Narrow eave | | | | |
| Features | | | | |
|   Posts, columns or arches (at porches, loggias, or arcades) | ? | | | |
|   Side porch or loggia | ? | | | |
|   Street balcony | ? | | | |
|   Outside stair | | | | |
|   Chimney | | ---- | | |

## 35. STREET ELEVATIONS OF EXISTING HOUSES

### SINGLE-STORY TYPES

A — 57 Treasury  
B — 143 St. George

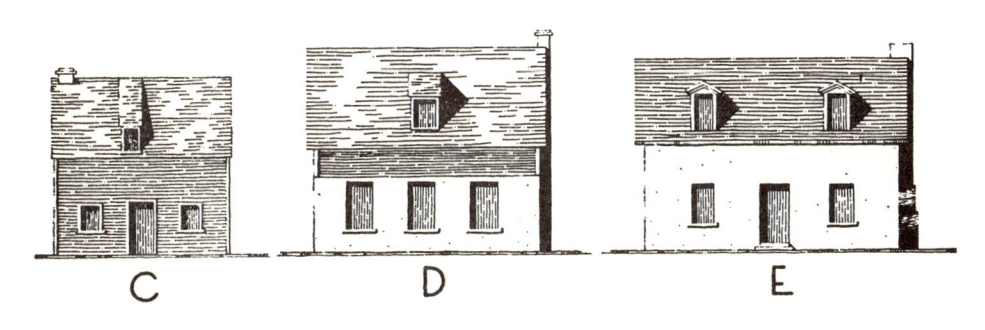

### ONE-AND-A-HALF-STORY TYPES

C — 14 St. George  
E — 250 St. George  
D — 46 Bridge  
F — 54 St. George  
G — 257 Charlotte (reconstruction)

## 35. STREET ELEVATIONS OF EXISTING HOUSES

**TWO-STORY TYPES**

H — 14 St. Francis
I — 224 St. George
J — 42 Spanish
K — 62 Spanish
L — 45 Marine
M — 43 Marine
N — 22 St. Francis

**35. STREET ELEVATIONS OF EXISTING HOUSES**

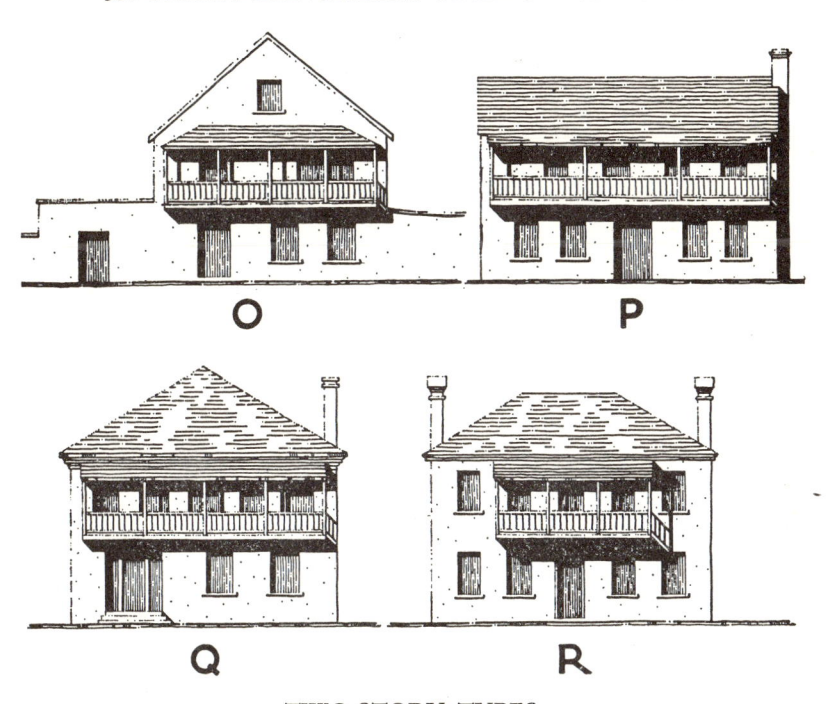

TWO-STORY TYPES

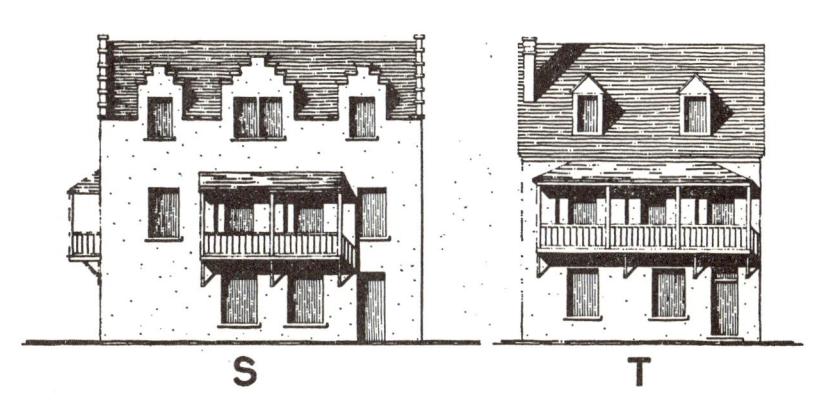

TALL TWO-STORY

O — 32 Aviles
P — 43 St. George
Q — 56 Marine
R — 105 St. George
S — 214 St. George
T — 46 Bay (reconstruction)

## 35. STREET ELEVATIONS OF EXISTING HOUSES

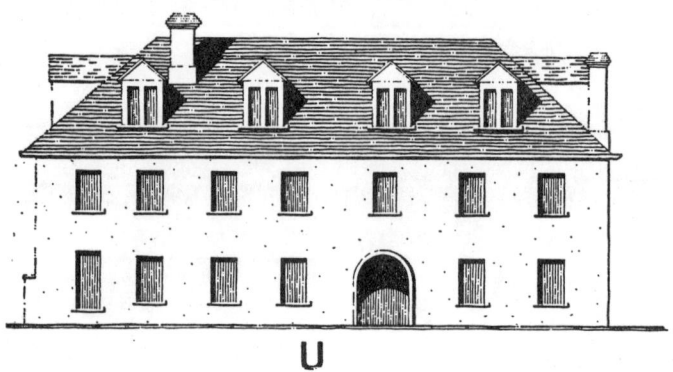

U

V    W

X

**TALL TWO-STORY**

U — 12 Aviles  
V — 20 Charlotte  
W — 20 Aviles  
X — 16 Marine

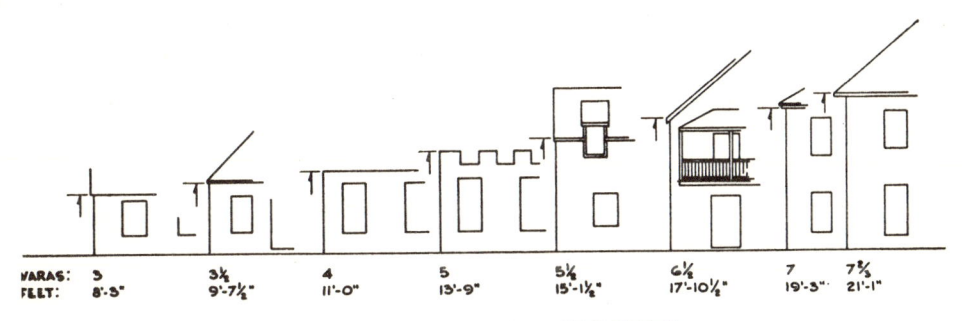

| VARAS: | 3 | 3½ | 4 | 5 | 5½ | 6½ | 7 | 7⅔ |
|---|---|---|---|---|---|---|---|---|
| FEET: | 8'-3" | 9'-7½" | 11'-0" | 13'-9" | 15'-1½" | 17'-10½" | 19'-3" | 21'-1" |

### 36. MASONRY WALL HEIGHTS

Though the people lived on a narrow peninsula and were further constricted by defense walls around the town, almost all their dwellings were separate and detached. There were no row houses.

## Height

For the years before the 18th century, the documents have not yet set forth any data on what the house really looked like, beyond the assumptions we can make from the building materials and, if archeology is involved, from the structural remains. Probably it is true here, as in the history of architecture elsewhere, that the early houses were cramped and with small shuttered wind holes (windows) in the medieval tradition.

What effects the native Indian practices had on Spanish homebuilding is not fully known. The Spaniard was susceptible to native influence — demonstrably more so than the Englishman; but there is no indication that either of them adopted the round house of the Indian. Rather, they clung to the traditional European rectangular dwelling. On the other hand, certainly the Indian taught the white man a great deal about the native woods, the techniques of thatching with local materials, and perhaps even the location of clay deposits.[111]

In the matter of story heights, if there are no dimensions for the early years, we must turn to the masonry buildings of the 1700's (Fig. 36).

The following table is compiled from the 1790 tax list and existing structures.[112]

### Masonry Wall Heights (in *Varas*)[x]

| | | | | | | | |
|---|---|---|---|---|---|---|---|
| HOUSE | | 3 | | 4 | 5 | 5½ | 6½ | 7 |
| WING | | | | 4 | 5 | | 6½ |
| PATIO | | 3 | 3½ | 4 | 5 | | |
| PARTITIONS | | 3 | | 4 | | | |
| KITCHEN | | 3 | | 4 | | | |
| FENCE | 2 | 3 | | 4 | | | |

[x]*Vara* = 33 inches

Four *varas* (11 feet) seems to have been standard wall height for substantial one-story masonry buildings, three *varas* for others. Some one-story buildings had 5-*vara* walls, but these probably included parapets. Occasionally the 5-*vara* wall was listed as "two-story." Very likely it was what we call one-and-a-half, several of which were built during the British period and later. Most two-story survivals from the 18th century carry the 7-*vara* height (about 19 feet). Normally all exterior house walls were the same height, but those on flat-roofed buildings might step down in 1-*vara* steps where roof lines permitted. Similar step-downs might occur over a yard gate and fence when the gate was at one end of the façade and actually part of it.[113]

As to purely British structures: William Watson described a single-story, frame store 10 feet high, and a two-story frame house 18 feet high, both of which he built in 1779. (The store was 18x22 feet, and the house 20x32.) Watson was a carpenter and no doubt his dimensions are accurate. If on this basis the British façades seem lower than the Spanish, however, notice that our English evidence relates only to small buildings, and is painfully scant.[114]

## Doors

In the street front of the houses, doors were uncommon before 1763, said Bartram. Through a gate in the high wall along the street, you came into the yard, perhaps under a porch roof, with the household entry only a few steps away in the loggia or on the porch. All extant historic houses now have a street door (and some have two!). Presumably the change in attitude toward them began with the Britisher's preference for a more direct approach to his domicile, or for business reasons.

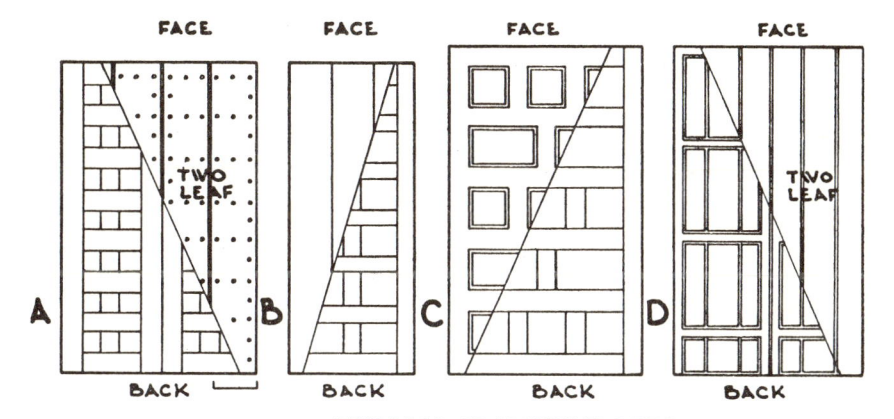

### 37. TYPICAL SPANISH DOORS
*Colonial Spanish doors in St. Augustine were probably like these. The planks in door "D" are tongue-and-groove and beaded both faces.*

Something similar happened to the alleged Spanish practice of building the north wall solid.[115] This was sensible practice for a brasier-and-charcoal-heated household, especially since drafty shutters were the only way to close out the chill winds of winter. English fireplaces and glazed "guillotine" sash made the houses warmer and lighter, and incidentally changed the eyeless appearance of the north wall.

Customarily the Spanish doorway is impressive in size and austere in appearance (Fig. 37). The heaviness of the board-faced door is often obviated by making it in two leaves, only one of which is actually put to use.

Unfortunately, no Spanish doors and very few doorframes have survived. One cause of the disappearance can be laid to insect damage. The doorframe consisted of two long doorposts (jambs) set firmly into the earth or into the masonry, and connected by a lintel at the top (Fig. 38). Such construction was successful in the Caribbean where certain woods resist rot and termites indefinitely. Here it was not. English joinery replaced it with a rectangular frame which, if not actually longer lasting, was a bit easier to replace when the time came. Transoms are not common among the houses of the late 1700's and early 1800's. Those found on houses of earlier date are probably additions.

81

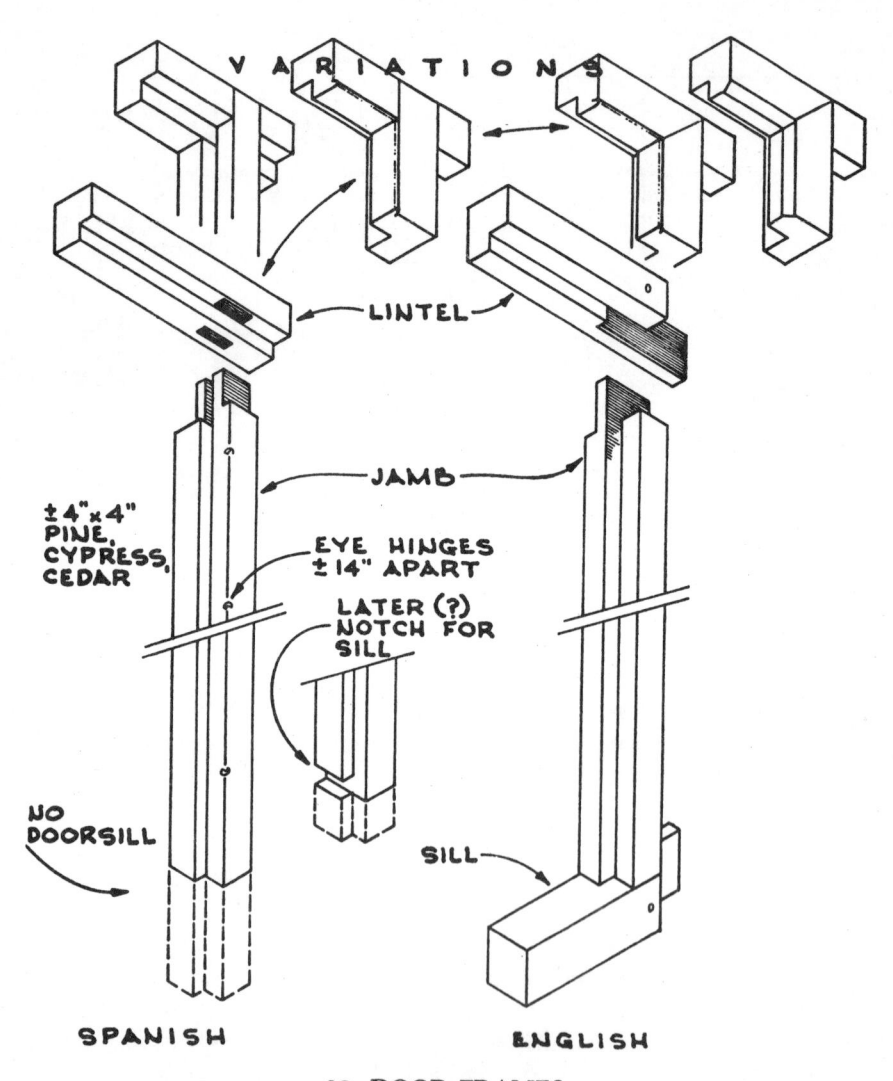

38. DOOR FRAMES

With the new English door frames came new and lighter doors. One English owner of an old house put in a new back door costing "upwards of one Guinea"; another installed "new Doors & Locks throughout the house"; yet another pridefully mentioned the "panneld Doors" in a 1770 frame house.[116] In the British colonies, the

39. SIX PANEL DOOR

6-panel door was in vogue during much of the 18th century (**Fig. 39**). Good examples of it are yet found in St. Augustine, notably in the Fatio House (although this house is later than English period).

In 1787 Roque drew floor plans for a proposed Customs and Counting House (*aduana, tesorería y contaduría*), which joined two old masonry dwellings by a common façade (Fig. 40). The dimensional data are of interest here. The plan shows street doors in 44- and 50-inch widths. The 44-inch doorway appears to be a converted window. The 50-inch one, leading into the customs section, had a foot-high transom above it. Ordinary exterior doors, opening onto the yard or porch, were either 33 or 44 inches. Most were the smaller size, although one, probably a carry-over from earlier times, was 63 inches. Interior doors were pretty well standardized at 33 inches (one *vara*). In other words, the plan gives fair indication that common sizes were 50 inches for street doors and 33 inches for others. Double-leaf doors were much used, even on 33-inch openings. The balcony door (33 inches), the upper third of which had "folding leaves," was probably unusual.[117]

PRIVY

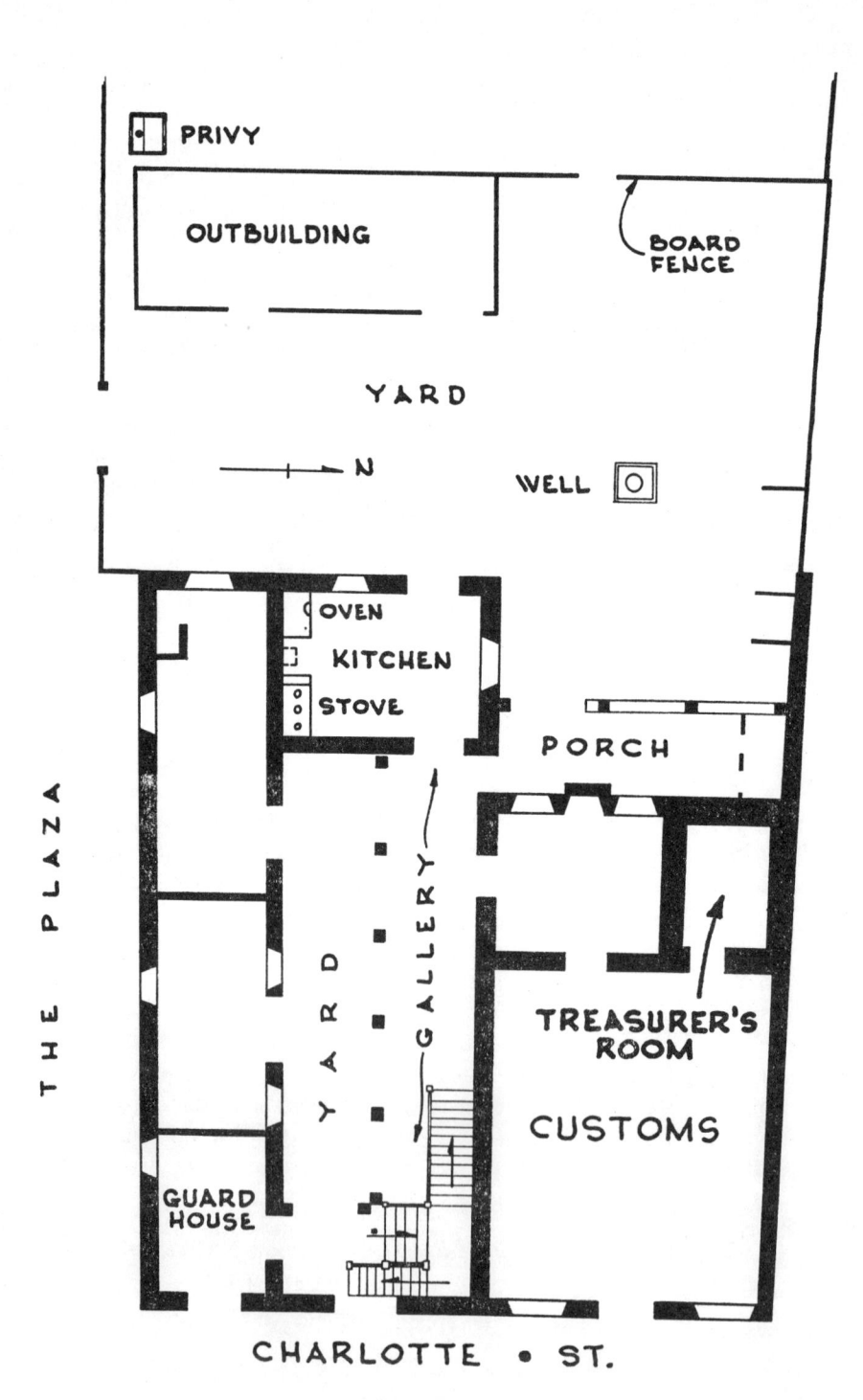

OUTBUILDING

BOARD FENCE

YARD

N

WELL

OVEN
KITCHEN
STOVE

PORCH

THE PLAZA

YARD

GALLERY

TREASURER'S ROOM

CUSTOMS

GUARD HOUSE

CHARLOTTE ST.

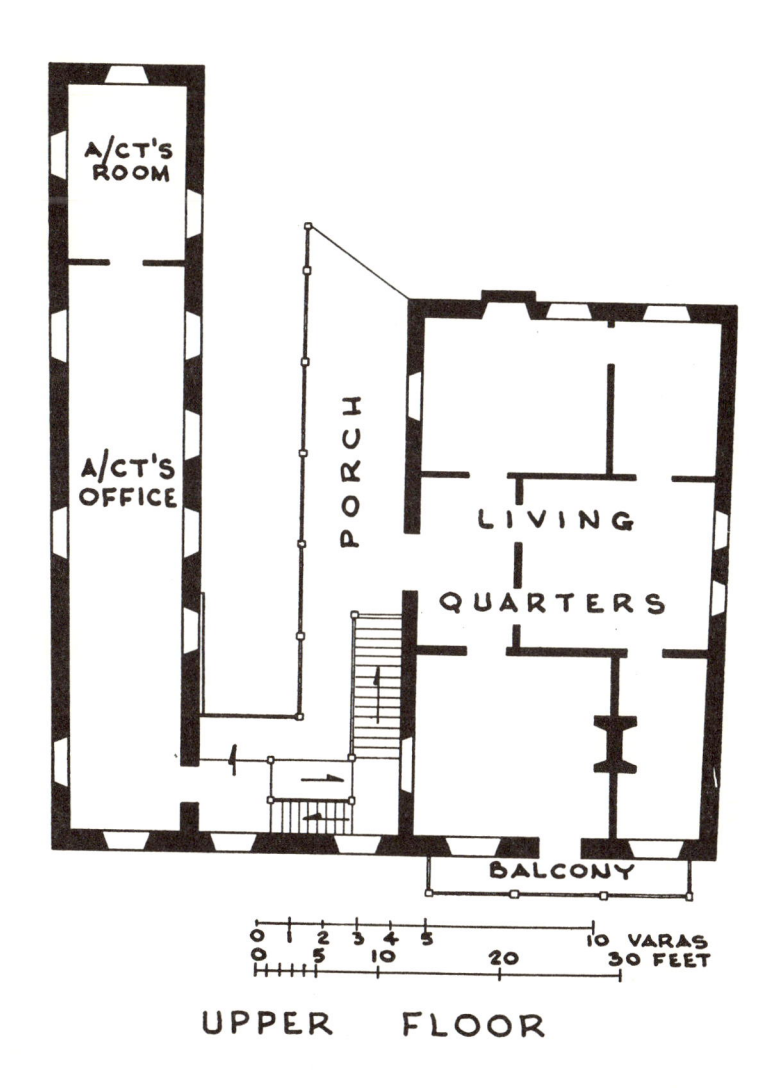

40. 1787 PLAN OF THE ROYAL ACCOUNTANT'S HOUSE

## Windows

Street windows (Fig. 41) were customarily large and high, and so were yard windows if they faced east or south. Windows toward the hot afternoon sun were smaller.

A close grating of wood called a *reja* (pronounced RAY-ha) was built over each street window of the ground floor (Fig. 42). A masonry step under the window carried the weight of the construction and, on occasion, even that of the *señora*. For since the *reja* projected a foot or more into the street, it converted the opening into a screened bay window. This was fine for ventilation, privacy, and for edification of curiosity about what was going on outside.

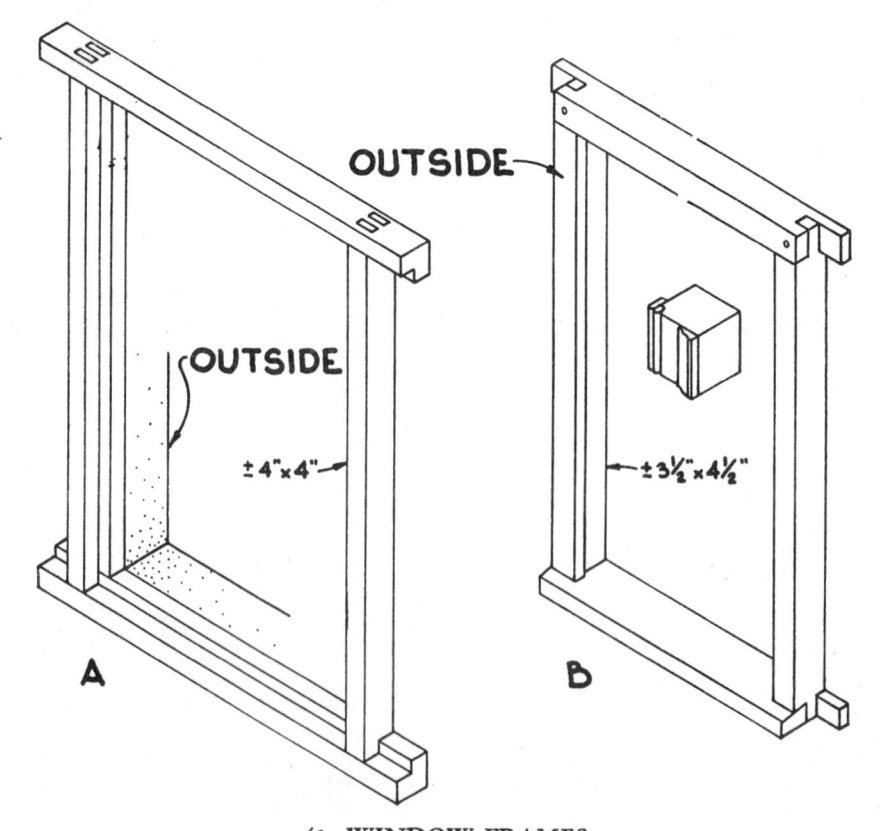

41. WINDOW FRAMES
A — Spanish type for inside shutters (about 1740)
B — Later type for sash and outdoor shutters

42. WOODEN GRATING CALLED A "REJA"

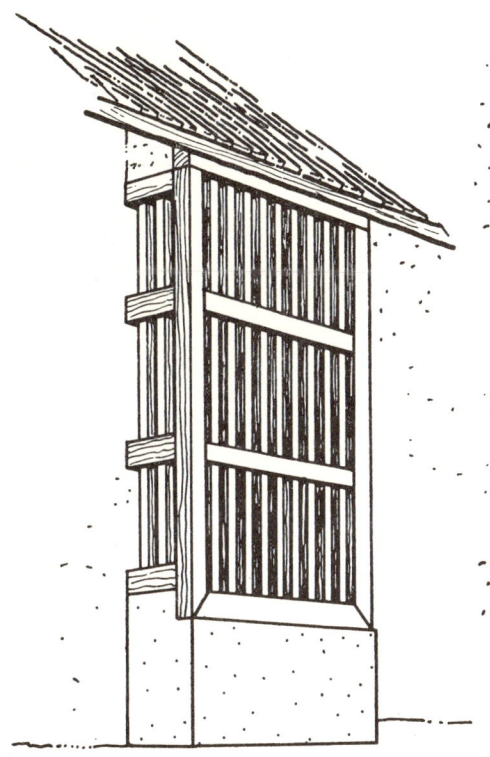

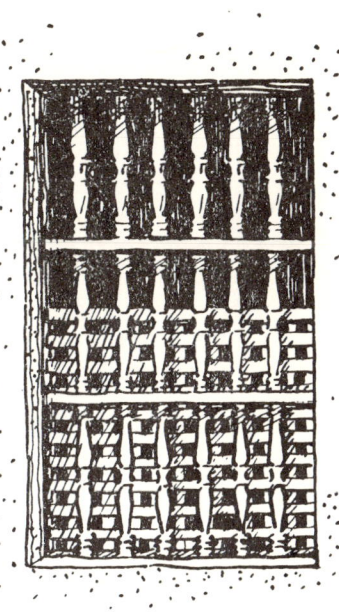

43. A "BANNISTERED AND LATTICED" WINDOW

Though only the street windows had such projection, most other windows were covered by gratings. We need to remember that, in a frontier town and in an age when a householder had to provide his own safeguards, strong gratings were merely good insurance. Bartram described the gratings as "bannisters," which suggests they were lathe-turned spindles.

Another piece of window furniture was the half-lattice, built of 1-inch strips (Fig. 43). It effectively screened the lower half of the opening while permitting unobstructed ventilation above.

All windows were provided with inside shutters (Fig. 44A-B). These were double-leaf shutters, well finished. Many of them had little wickets or doors in one or both leaves. The British period, which brought double-hung window sashes, made the shutter of secondary importance and pushed it outside the house (Fig. 44C). Long sill hooks were perhaps commonly used to keep open shutters

**44. SHUTTERS**

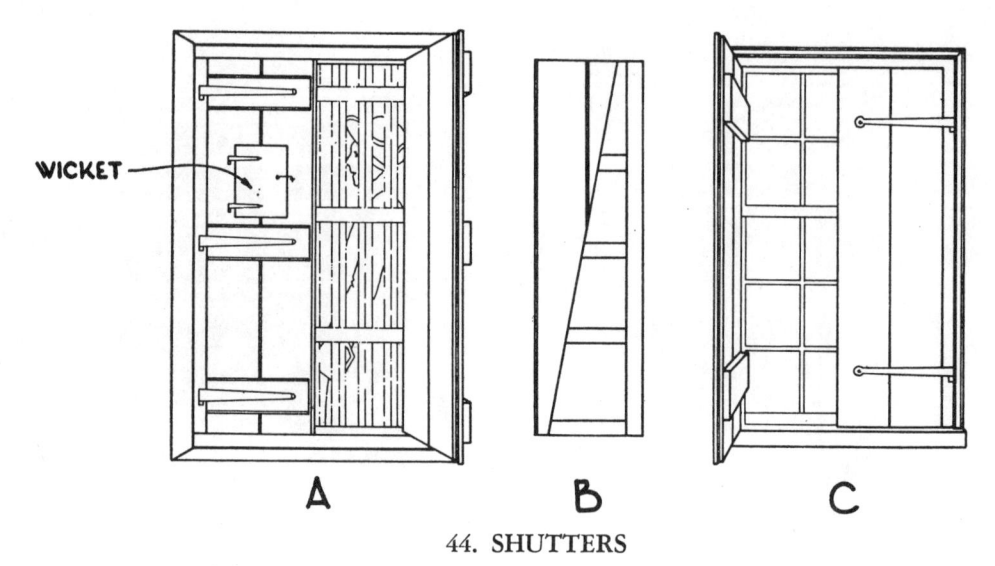

A — Inside shutters. Bartram mentions "strong shutters within side,
B — A probable design
   many of which had a little one in each."
C — Outside shutters

**45. LOAD-BEARING LINTEL**

*One or two wooden lintels were often used over a window instead of a masonry arch.*

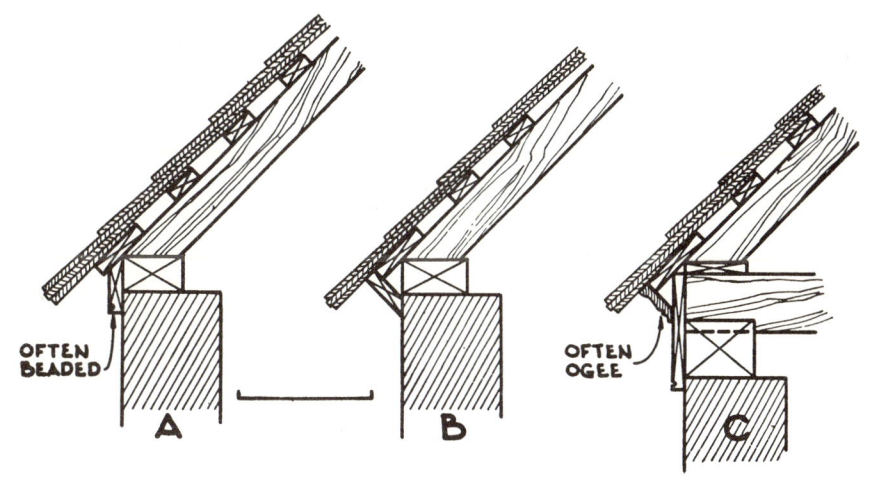

46. TYPICAL EAVES

from banging, but a few T-shaped holdbacks can be seen on masonry buildings in 19th century photographs. Sash was commonly made with six or nine lights, and a typical arrangement might see nine over six on the ground floor and six over six on upper floors.[118]

According to the 1787 Customs House plan, there was considerable variation in window widths. Forty-four-inch openings on the entrance front were the largest; elsewhere in the building were ten 30-inch, seven 33-inch, seven 36-inch, four 39-inch, and two 27-inch windows. Since this was the Customs and Treasury, most windows upstairs and down were protected by four or five iron bars (although in one the bars were wood). Guillotine sash were used, most of them counter-balanced with sash weights. In the old tradition, the structure also had double-leafed inside shutters. Two of them (for 39-inch windows) had four parallel panels.

## Cornices

Thatched roofs, much in the majority at St. Augustine, obviously had no cornices. Wooden shingles, which came gradually into prominence, were very probably in the same tradition, as a 1764 sketch of the Governor's House shows (Fig. 11). Other contemporary evidence is absent, but 19th century photographs of antique structures underline narrow or non-existent eaves, both at gutter line and gable. The fascia board was merely a narrow weatherboard over the plate (Fig. 46).

You would expect the English to bring with them the box cornice so typical of their work elsewhere. Many old flat roofs had to be replaced, and the British carpenters built gables or hips in their stead (Fig. 47).[119] The photograph files show a few molded fascia boards and eave returns which may date from British times, but no examples have been preserved. Cornices which are conspicuous today are usually from the 1840's or later.

Nor has any sample been kept of the "battlements" Bartram observed on flat-roofed houses, except for another 1764 sketch which shows gable parapets on the center section of the town guardhouse, and slender castellations over a narrow cornice of its north porch. The merlons must have been about two feet high. At least that is the approximate difference between the exterior walls and the partitions of the Treasurer's House, allowing for the thickness of the roof, which we know was flat because nine clay spouts were on it. A 4-inch coping with 2½-inch projection on each side was the typical crown for either horizontal or gable parapets.[120]

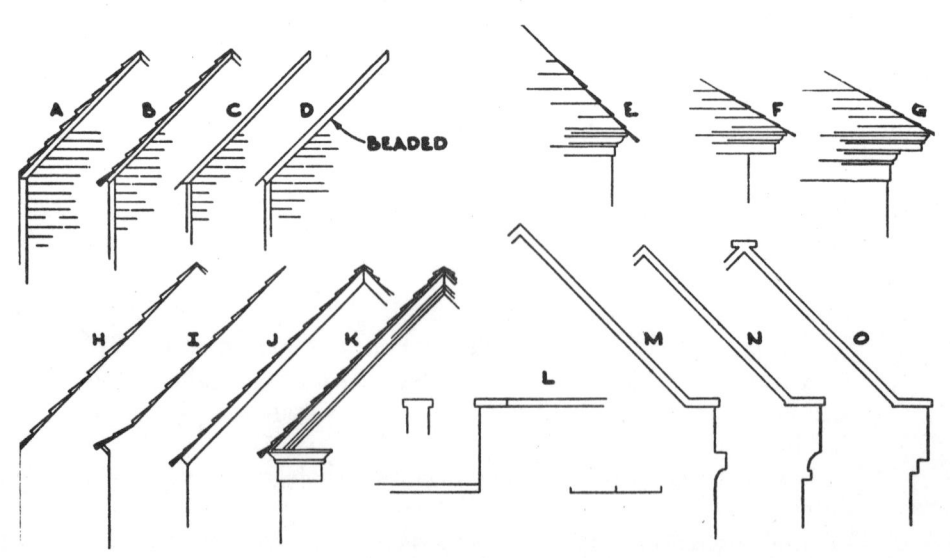

47. GABLES, HIPS AND PARAPETS

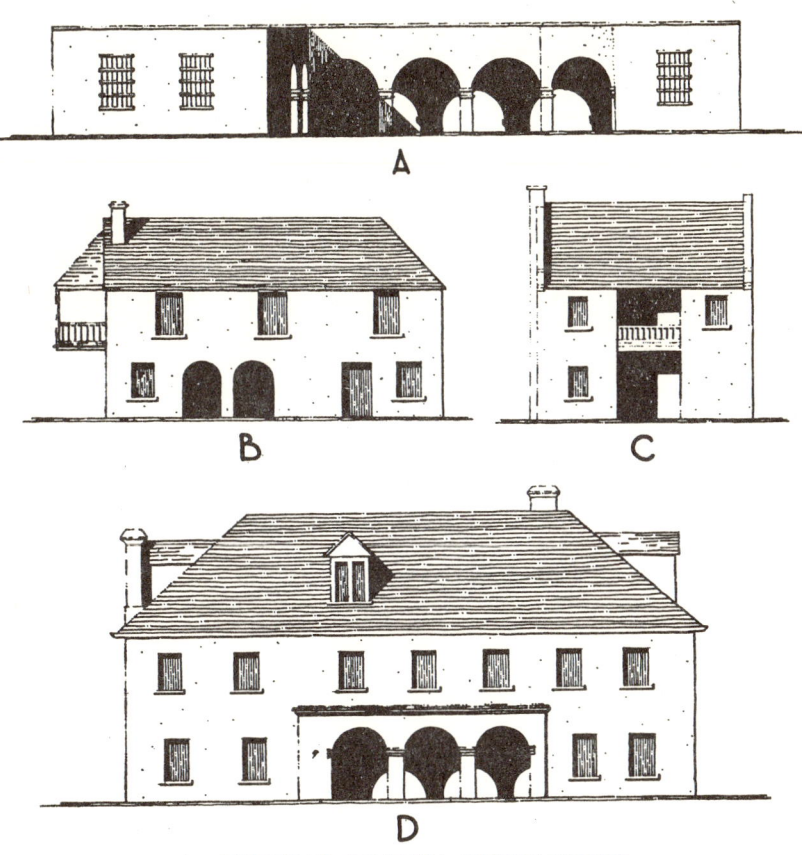

48. TYPICAL LOGGIA ELEVATIONS

## Posts, Columns, Arches, and Porches

"Before the entry of most of the houses," wrote Dr. Stork in the 1760's, "runs a portico of stone arches." [121] Since the good Doctor was writing some of the first promotional literature for St. Augustine since Menéndez' time, we may forgive him for encouraging his readers to believe that virtually all Spanish dwellings were decorated with arched porticos. There were, in fact, often a trio of arches in the loggias (Fig. 48-49). Some of the larger buildings such as the Treasurer's House had arcades. But the common Spanish house seldom had these elegant features. Nor is it probable that stone arches ever outnumbered the wooden posts and masonry pillars, even on the better domiciles.[122]

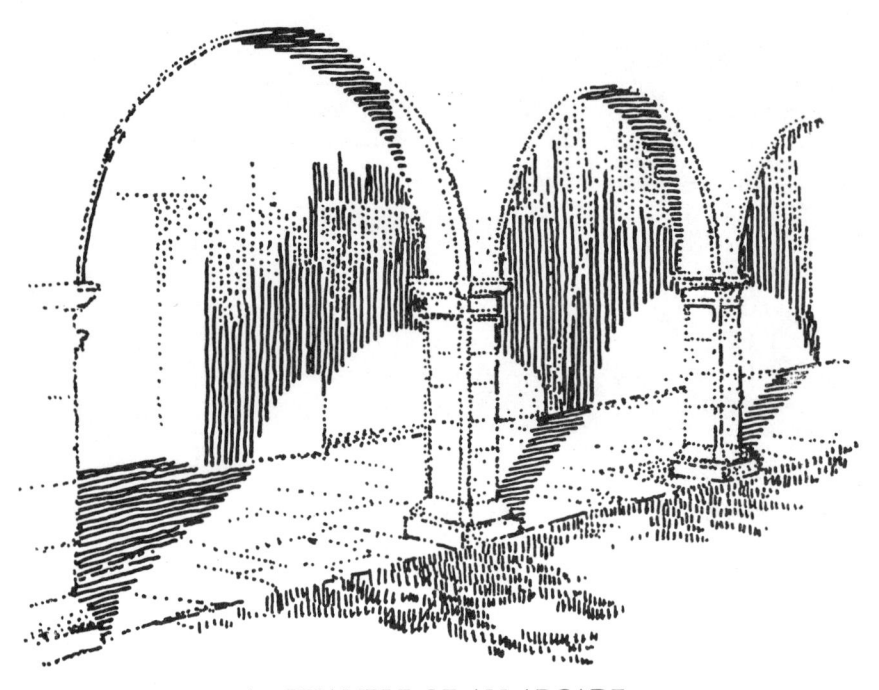

49. EXAMPLE OF AN ARCADE

Nevertheless, the covered gallery — whether porch, piazza or loggia, one-story or two — was a characteristic feature. It was never on the street front, but faced the side or back yard, usually giving shade against the south sun. Bartram told us the width of the typical gallery when he mentioned the 9-foot, tabby-paved walk along the house, because the walk was often the gallery floor (Fig. 55).

The row of arches or pillars supported, in the case of shingle roofs, an extension from the main roof. The posts were sometimes the same height as the house walls. Thus the structure serving in 1790 as dragoon barracks and jail boasted three pillars seven *varas* high. In other instances second floor porch posts were shortened somewhat, to avoid building more roof than the house needed. The change gives a remarkably snug and comfortable look to the building.[123]

DeBrahm, a Swiss engineer with some knowledge of the architectural orders, characterized the supports as "Tuskan Pillars or Pillasters."[124] He had in mind, of course, plain columns and absence of decorative material. Moldings and chamfers were not absent from the work, but the relative coarseness of shellstone kept the moldings few and simple. They are neoclassic in concept. The contours were cut directly into the stone and covered with a thin coat of plaster.

As you would expect, the quality of design and workmanship varies. This fact is obvious in extant examples, where repair or renovation has not "improved" the old work. Design differences are particularly noticeable in arcades, all of which use the *arco de punto* (round arch),[125] springing from a pier that is no higher than one's head (Fig. 49). The piers are rectangular pillars, with base and capital. Some piers are massively broad and carry arches that support a second-story wall. Others are light, with thin, graceful arches. Sometimes the arrises of all elements are rounded off with a convex molding.

Along with many turned wooden posts that are obviously 19th century, old photographs record an occasional set of knobby, spool-like posts similar to certain Spanish lathe work. But this is not conclusive evidence for existence of the type in colonial times.

The records give the British responsibility for building at least one piazza during the 1770's; this one ran the full length of a 40-foot house and had a new room at the end of it.[126] Probably numerous others were also built, because the English, especially the exiles from Charleston, were no strangers to the pleasantness of a piazza. Some houses in later years developed second floor porches which merged with the street balcony and formed a gallery all the way around the building.

## Balconies

The first document to mention balconies seems to be the record of August 25, 1713, which certified that the Governor and his lady did, upon the balconies of the official residence, fling "a large amount" of silver coins to the populace crowded into the street and patio (Fig. 11). The balcony was not often found on the yard sides of the house, since porch construction supported by posts or pillars was more practical there. But on the street side, the *balcón de la calle* (street balcony), according to 19th century photographs, seemed to sprout from almost every two-story house (Fig. 50-51). Even the Britishers built balconies.[127]

93

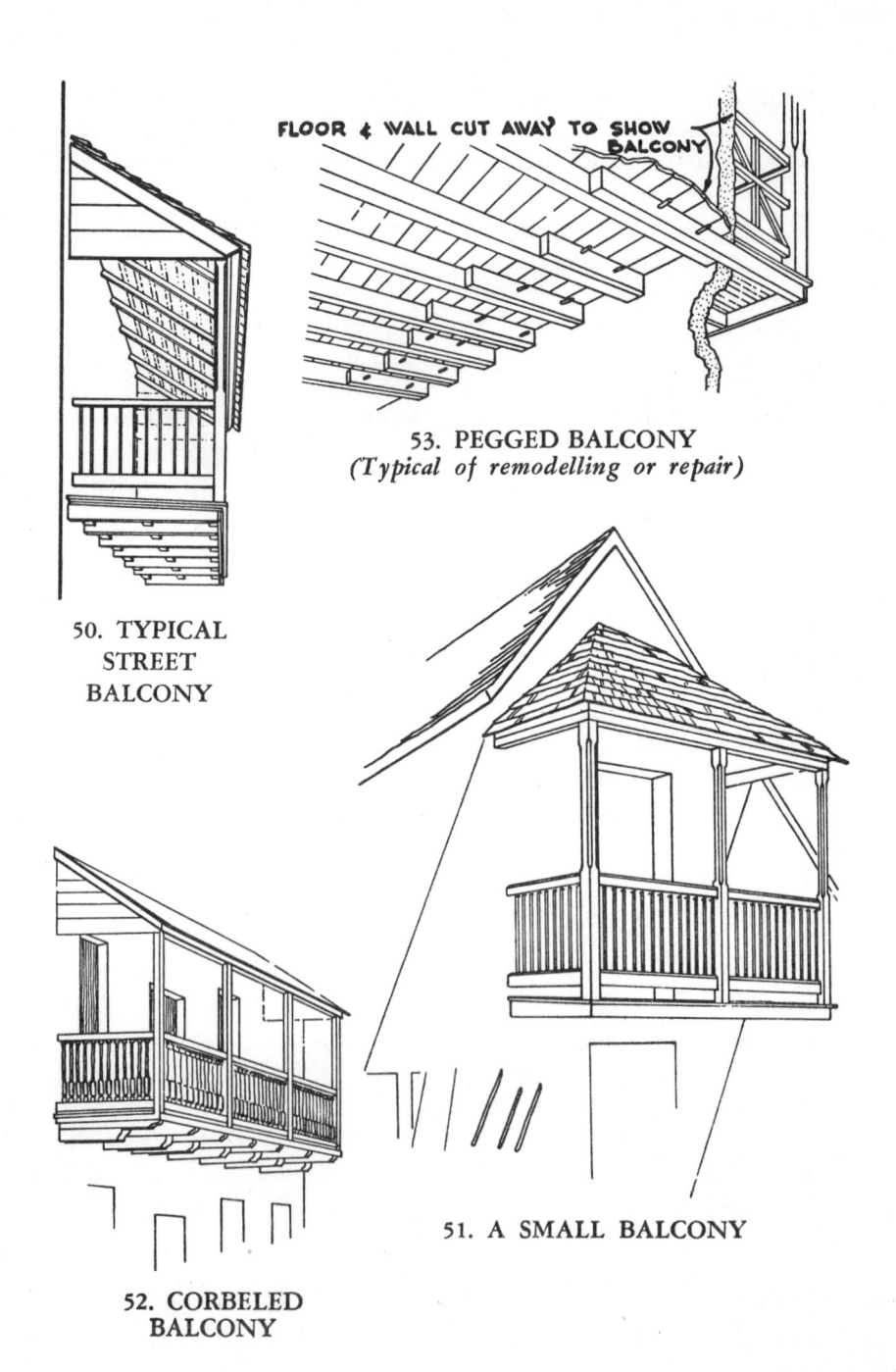

50. TYPICAL STREET BALCONY

53. PEGGED BALCONY
*(Typical of remodelling or repair)*

FLOOR & WALL CUT AWAY TO SHOW BALCONY

52. CORBELED BALCONY

51. A SMALL BALCONY

Constructed upon second-floor joists (*cf.* Fig. 53) that projected through the wall of the house, balconies were about five feet wide. Bartram said they were built with corbeled beams, the upper one extending a foot or more beyond the lower (Fig. 52). The joists were "a convenient distance" apart,[128] which means they might be spaced anywhere from two to three *tercias*. On the average house, the balcony extended across most of the front, so that its roof (it was invariably roofed) protected two or more windows from sun and sudden showers. A center doorway was the usual access.

A 1787 balcony was described thus: 7 2/3 *varas* long by 1 *vara* 6 inches wide, floor to ceiling height 2 2/3 *varas* and 5 inches; roof slope 35°; 4 posts with a balustrade 34 inches high. The floor had 10 joists 2½ x 3½ inches in size and was reinforced by 4 iron brackets.[129]

No examples of Spanish balustrades remain to us. Presumably they were turned spindles, although exposure to the weather might have forced the builders to use a simpler form. Anyway, simplicity came with the years, and brought a plain but finely-proportioned balustrade, well designed from the standpoint of esthetics as well as durability (Fig. 54). The handrail was comfortably rounded on top. The baluster, square in section and slender to the point of elegance, was mortised into the handrail. The foot of the baluster, however, was notched with an inverted V, cut to fit tightly *over* a continuous matching bevel on the bottom rail. The steep bevel on this rail shed water like a roof, and there were no mortises to pocket the moisture and encourage rot.

Other types of balustrades were also used, of course, but the photographs show this kind in wide use during the 19th century.

Balcony posts are as perishable as balusters. The earliest existing ones are light rather than heavy, square in section, with chamfers above the handrail. A lamb's tongue finishes each end of the chamfer.

## Stairways

Bartram's casual mention of the typical courtyard walk "with a staircase at one end to the chambers" is probably best interpreted as a stairway (*escalera*) at one end of the porch pavement (Fig. 55). Where there was a loggia, the stairway could be found off to one side of it, well covered from the weather, but still an "outside" stair. Bartram said the risers were "easy" height, with tabby steps.[130]

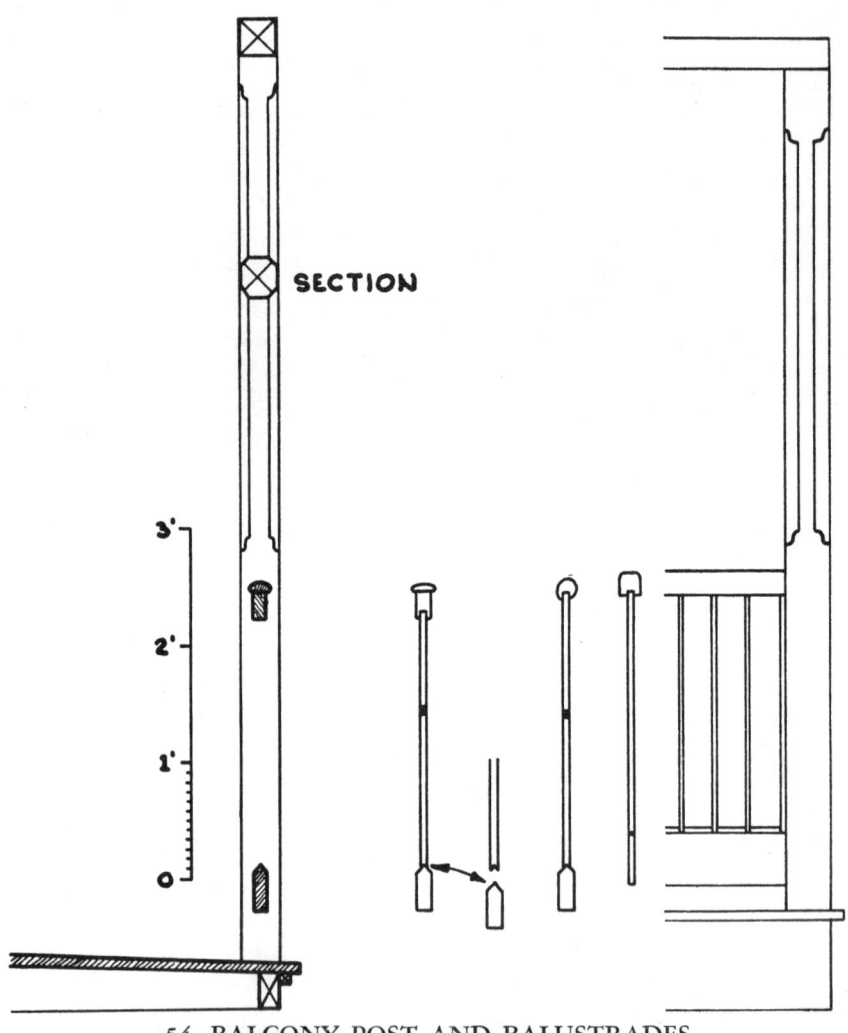

**54. BALCONY POST AND BALUSTRADES**
*The spindles are tapered at the top into mortises (or sometimes a continuous groove) on the underside of the hand rail. The bottom rail is not mortised.*

Although it is likely that some inside stairs existed during the first Spanish period and others were doubtless built by the British, outside stairways continued in popularity. A fine example from the late 1700's is at the Fatio House (Fig. 56). Located at the angle of an L-shaped porch, it is entirely of wood. The risers are comfortable and there is a landing (*entresuelo*) between floors. The balus-

**55. LOGGIA STAIRWAY**
*"A staircase at one end to the chambers; the steps easy, all tabby."* — *Bartram*

ters are turned spindles, graceful and well proportioned. They are lighter than, but not dissimilar to an attractive Puerto Rican spindle of the same period.

Some of the larger houses also had balustraded stairways to the flat roof.[131]

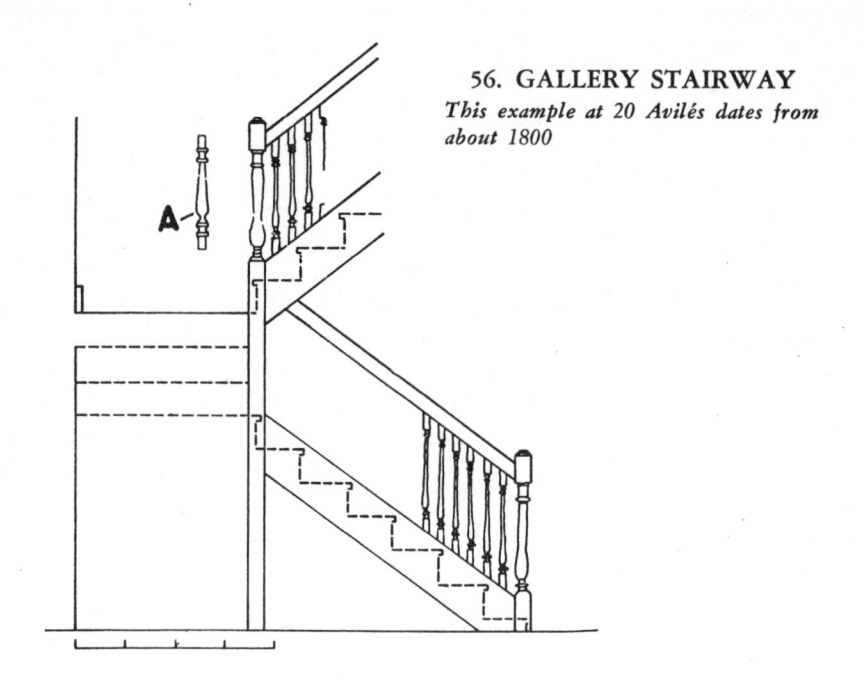

**56. GALLERY STAIRWAY**
*This example at 20 Avilés dates from about 1800*

## Chimneys

The British observers made much to-do over their introduction of chimneys into a chimneyless Spanish town. In point of fact, however, at least two Spanish householders could boast chimneys in both *sala* (living room) and *cocina* (kitchen). One of these establishments was the residence of the Governor. The other was on the northwest corner of Charlotte and Treasury; its *sala* contained *two* fireplaces with glazed tile fronts.[132]

Chimneys were built both of shellstone and brick.[133] When the construction was entirely of stone, before many years it was necessary to repair the fire box with brick, due to the gradual calcining of the stone by the heat. Old photographs prove it was common practice to plaster the chimney stacks, whether of brick or stone. On sponge-like shellstone, plaster was a practical necessity for keeping water out of the house. A soaked stack meant soiled walls.

House chimneys are not massive (Fig. 57). Conventional flat moldings are sometimes absent. Stone chimneys are apt to have a beveled molding.

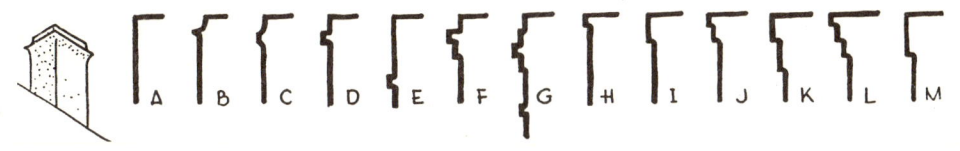

### 57. CHIMNEY MOLDINGS

Even on pre-1760 houses, chimney additions were evidently placed where the householder wanted them, rather than against a gable wall (which might have been easiest and most economical). Hence there were outside stacks, inside, and flush stacks. On existing houses, each type occurs with approximately equal frequency.

Occasionally there is a second-floor fireplace which is not part of the usual ground-to-roof masonry. In such cases the entire weight of the chimney may be supported by the floor joists.

# ROOFS

## Types of Roofing and their Periods of Use
(Numbers refer to names listed below)

| ROOF MATERIALS | PERIODS WHEN USED |||| 
|---|---|---|---|---|
| | Before 1700 | 1703-1763 | British | 1783-1821 |
| Palm thatch | (1) (2) | (1) (2) | | (1) (2) |
| Straw thatch | (3) | (3) | | |
| Shake or shingle | (8) | (8) | (9) (10) | (8) (11) |
| Clapboard | | (6) | (7) | |
| Tabby slab | (4) | (5) | | (4) |
| Tile | | | (14) | (13) |
| Cypress bark | (?) | (?) | | (12) |

## Common Names of Roof Materials

*Thatch*
1. *Palma:* palm thatch
2. *Guano:* palm thatch
3. *Paja:* straw thatch

*Masonry*
4. *Azotea de cal:* tabby flat roof
5. *Azotea:* tabby or tile flat roof

*Wood*
6. *Tabla* or *tablazón:* clapboard
7. Clapboard
8. *Tejamaní:* shingle or shake
9. Shingle: shingle or shake
10. Short shingle: shingle
11. *Rajón:* shake
12. *Cáscara de ciprés:* cypress bark

*Tile*
13. *Teja:* barrel tile
14. Tile: barrel tile

99

# 58. BUILDING A SEMINOLE CHICKEE

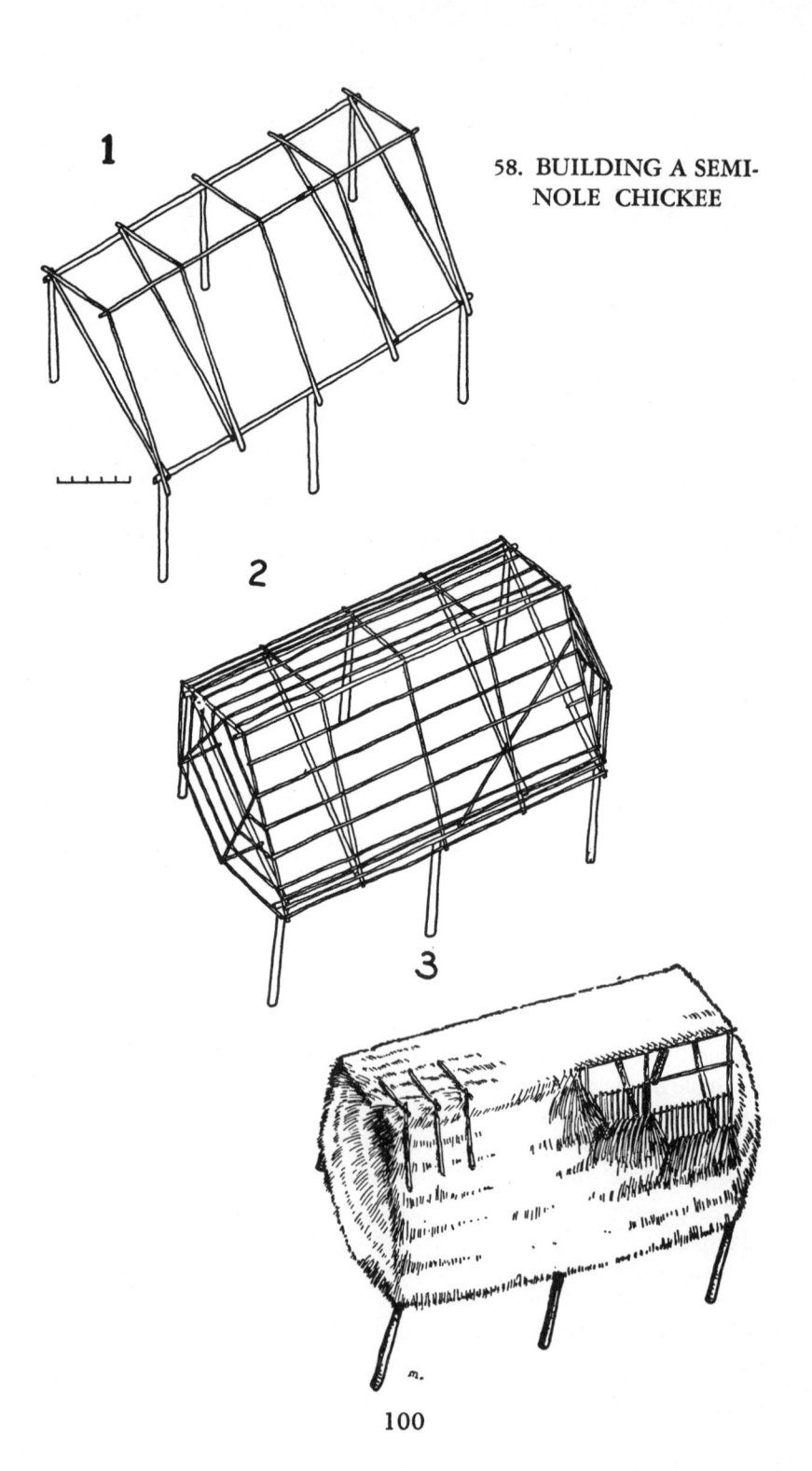

100

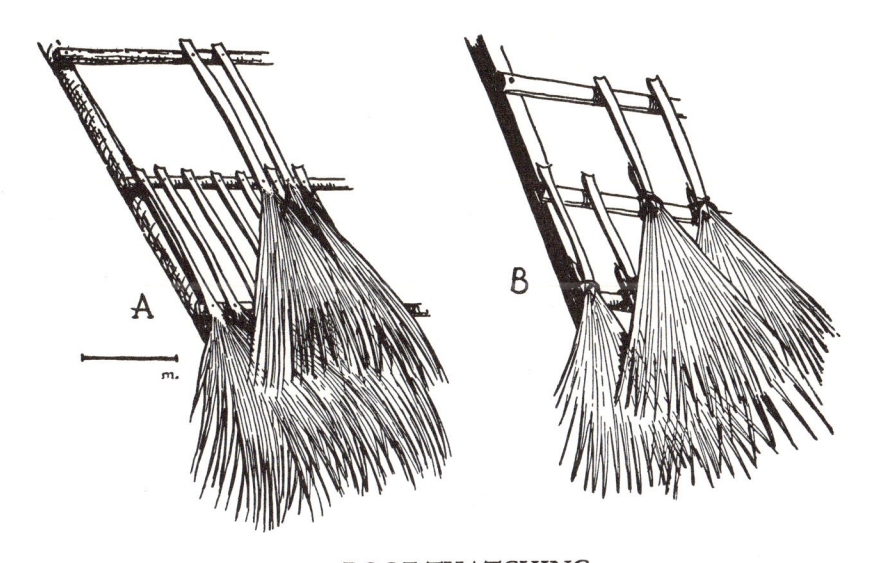

### 59. ROOF THATCHING

Two methods of using fronds from the cabbage palm:

A — Seminole Indian  B — Bahaman

A thatch roof on tabby walls, often with a smoke hole open to the sky, was the "common Spanish house" remarked by Bartram.[134] Palm thatch was the usual roofing material in this part of Florida long before the white man arrived. Nor is it surprising to find it widely used on into the 1800's. The hardy sabal or cabbage palm (so called because of the cabbage-like bud) was plentiful and grew profusely. In fact, palm thatch is still today on the *chickee* of the Seminole Indian (Fig. 58), and to a lesser extent on the beach shelters of other denizens. In the latter case, however, the usual practice was to tack on the scrawny fans from this scrub palmetto— poor substitutes for the heavy, lush frond of the palm tree.

No doubt the thatcher of the 1500's performed his task much like today's workman on the Indian reservation or in the Bahamas, Mexico, and wherever else this variety of palm is used (Fig. 59). Cypress poles, still handy in Florida, may have been used for the laths. The modern Seminole nails the frond to the lath, whereas the oldtimer probably used a fiber cord or a trenail. The frond has a fairly straight stem, long enough for tying to at least two laths. When closely laid and neatly trimmed, the palm thatch roof is tight, attractive and unexpectedly sturdy. Its disadvantages, of course, are flammability, impermanence, and hospitality to vermin. The fire hazard caused it to be prohibited by British law in 1783, but the prohibition was nullified by recession of Florida to Spain.[135]

I have pointed out three Spanish words used to denote thatch. *Palma* and *guano* signify palm thatch. The third term, *paja* which commonly means "straw," denotes a local material as yet unidentified. As late as 1759 it was used for two thirds of the roofs in St. Augustine, so it was plentiful and easy to get. Marsh grass is nothing if not plentiful, and we know it was cut as forage for stock. Possibly this was *paja*. However, its use seems to have stopped abruptly with the Spanish departure in 1764.

The table below shows the relative popularity of the several roof materials in 1759.[136]

| MATERIALS | NO. OF ROOFS |
| --- | --- |
| Thatch (*paja*) | 190 |
| Palm thatch (*guano*) | 64 |
| Shingles or shakes (*tejamaní*) | 26 |
| flat masonry (*azotea*) | 23 |

Thatch was avoided by the British builders until they were forced to it by the housing emergency after 1780. Its use further declined during the later Spanish period.[137]

## Wood

The first identifiable mention of wooden roofs seems to be the affidavits of the carpenters back in 1690 that several government buildings were roofed with shingles, "as is customary in this presidio."[138] From this phrase you would think that most local houses had shingle roofs. But the workmen had in mind only government buildings. For in 1759 no more than 26 shingle roofs could be counted. However, beginning with the British in the 1760's, shingles gained rapidly — they were regarded as very "American" by the English — and by the 1820's had superseded all other types. The wood was cypress; at least, the records I have seen mention no other.[139]

60. SHINGLES

A — Shakes                B — Short Shingles

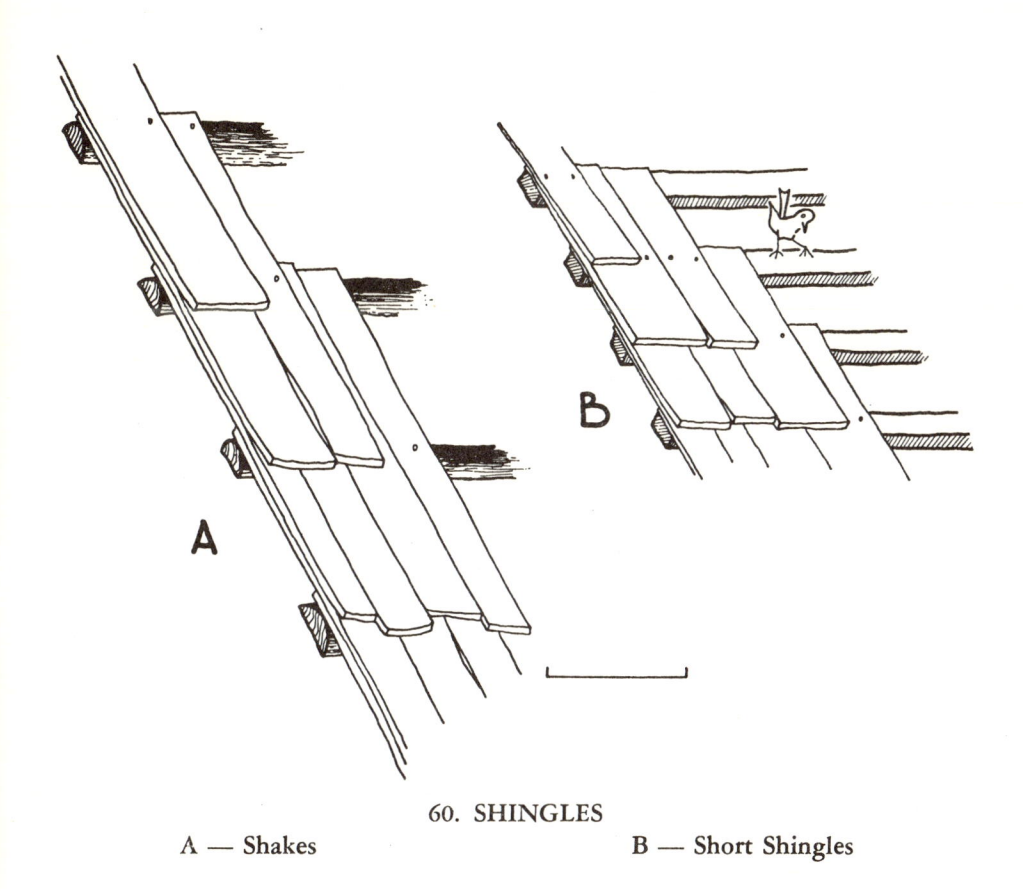

The common Spanish term for shingles is *tejamaní*. In the early period at least, it probably includes shakes (crude shingles) (Fig. 60A). Although *tejamaní* carries over into the later Spanish period, I do not recall having encountered it in the vocabulary of Engineer Rocque. His word for shingle is *rajón*. This derives from *rajar*, meaning "to split." Shingles, of course, were split from blocks of wood. But so were shakes and pickets and laths and some clapboards; and it is sadly evident that Rocque knew them all as *rajones*.

British terminology included *"shingles"* and *"short shingles."*[140] Although most laymen did not recognize a difference and therefore failed to define it, quite likely the short shingles were better finished and made a tighter, neater roof (Fig. 60B).

103

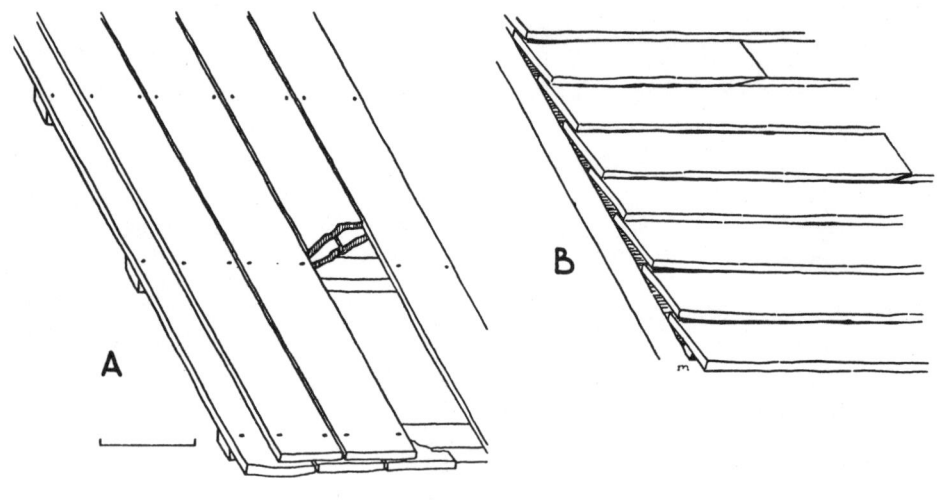

61. CLAPBOARD ROOFS

From earliest times, sawed boards (*tablas*) were used for wall construction at St. Augustine (Fig. 61). During the British period sometimes they also covered pitched roofs. Unquestionably this usage was found in Spanish times too. The English phrase is "clapboard roof." Clapboards (which in British terms were not only weatherboards but also fence boarding) were evidently squared boards, distinctly different from feather-edged siding. Even rough boards could be clumsily overlapped to keep out rain, but a rabbet plane applied to one or both edges of nicely dressed clapboards produced a neat and attractive joint. Clapboard roofs, however, were used only on small structures. Hot sun curled them up and let in the rain.[141]

## Masonry

*Azotea,* meaning flat roof, is a term which carries through both Spanish periods without change. Yet there is no clear-cut evidence in Florida, physical or documentary, which gives us details of its construction. For instance, there is no way for us to define the *açuteas de cal* at Santa Elena during the 1580's beyond saying they were masonry flat roofs. Knowing the locale, we can speculate that the roof was a slab of oyster shell tabby formed over a deck of boards (Fig. 62).[142]

At St. Augustine in 1686, such a roof was used on quarters built around the courtyard of the fort. The 19-foot span between the parapets was bridged by beams *(vigas)* 11 inches high and 16 wide. Random width pine plank 4 fingers (2 ¾″) thick was laid over the beams, and topped by a pour of masonry *(argamasa)*.[143]

In layman's language, sometimes the *azotea* was called a board roof *(techada de tabla)*, probably because the underside of the deck boards would catch a man's eye when he glanced at the ceiling, whereas he might never see the heavy masonry slab above. This seems to have been the case with Father Solana, who in 1759 described the town guardhouse as board-roofed. The 1764 sketch of the structure depicts a castellated flat roof on the north side. Contemporary appraisals give the construction jargon: beams and boards *(vigas* and *tablas)* for the flat roofs *(azoteas)*, plus masonry "fills" *(tortas)*. The latter could be nothing else but tabby slabs.[144]

So far we have found no suggestion in the documents to indicate that *azoteas* were made of anything except planks and tabby. But in 1959 Carver Harris recovered yellow clay tile fragments, brought up by a dredge at the foot of Treasury Street. Much of the rubble from the 1914 fire in the Treasury-Charlotte Street sector had been dumped here. Presumably the broken tile Harris found was from a flat roof — the last of the *azoteas* — known to have been destroyed by the fire. The tile was very close in size to the flat, red tile (¾ x 5 x 10 ¼ inches) used for *azotea* construction in the Caribbean since the 17th century.

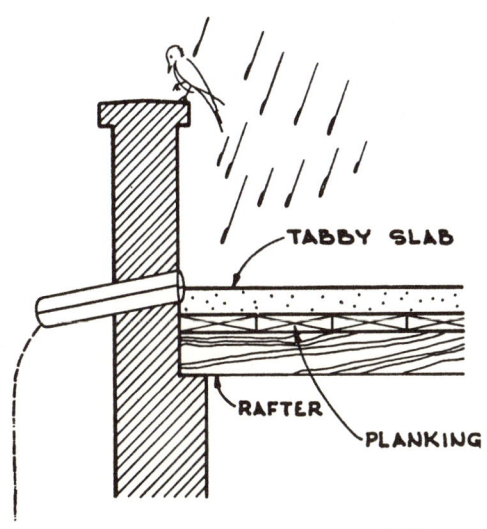

62. TABBY ROOF

105

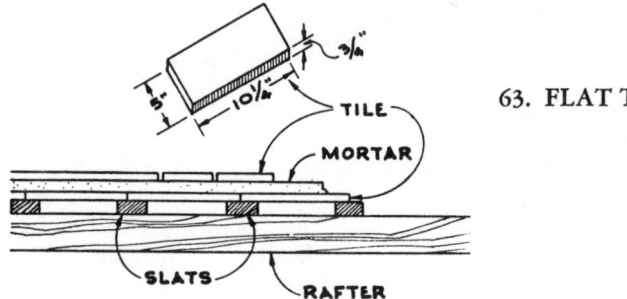

### 63. FLAT TILE ROOF

The Caribbean technique (Fig. 63) is more sophisticated than merely laying a monolithic slab of tabby, and less vulnerable to cracking under stress. Instead of laying a solid deck, the artisan puts down spaced slats, and bridges the slats with rows of tile. Over this solid layer of tile he spreads a thick bed of mortar followed by a second course of tile. Another course or two is sometimes added. Such a roof is from 3 to 6 inches thick.

On the more meticulous work the long slats are replaced by short ones notched right into the beams. A beam or rafter so notched is easy to recognize once you have seen the construction (Fig. 64).

Several such members were among the second floor joists of the Arrivas house. For a long time they had been rafters in a flat-roofed building (the weight of a roof had bowed them permanently, and the top side was lime-burned and moisture-stained). Their building had burned. (The yellow ocher paint on the rafters was scorched and some of the wood was charred.) But the rafters had been salvaged and re-used here as floor joists. (They were laid on their sides to offset the bow.)

These carefully dressed and painted pine rafters were about 17 feet long. Since all ends bore axe marks, this was probably the original length. They were 5 3/16 inches high by 5½ to 6 inches wide. One, rough-sawn and unpainted (and probably unused, for it was also unbowed) was 5 5/8 inches high and 5¼ wide. Another was notched on the underside for 4-inch posts 6 feet apart.

In the West Indies where certain native woods are almost impervious to insects and rot, I have seen century-old roofs of this kind and finding *azotea* tile and rafters in St. Augustine argues for similar construction here. Yet the documents do not mention it, Bartram called the roofs tabby rather than tile, and the archeologists have not found much tile of any kind.

Whether made of tabby or tile, the flat roof was probably on very few of the 17th century houses. The ease with which the town was burned in 1703 confirms the documentary assertions of thatch roofs everywhere. Another argument against widespread existence of the *azotea* in early times is the relatively small number that were built later, even during the post-1703 renascence. Not more than 23 houses (12 percent) boasted *azoteas* by 1759. With proof that only 12 percent of the houses were flat-roofed, Dr. Stork's insistence that "the roofs are commonly flat" must be taken with a grain of salt. Furthermore, the number dwindled to only 11 within the next generation. Obviously it was not easy to keep *azoteas* tight and their beams and boards free from rot.[145]

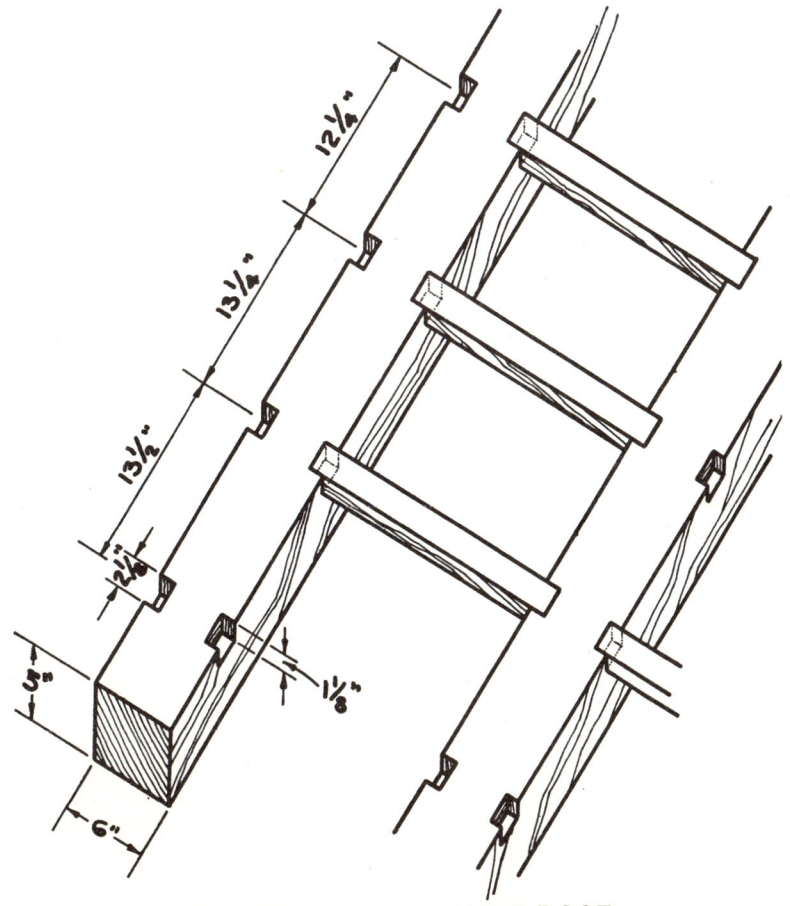

64. JOISTS FOR FLAT TILE ROOF

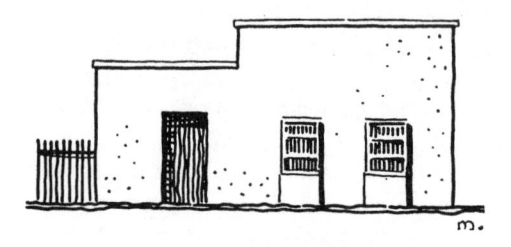

65. FLAT-ROOFED HOUSE

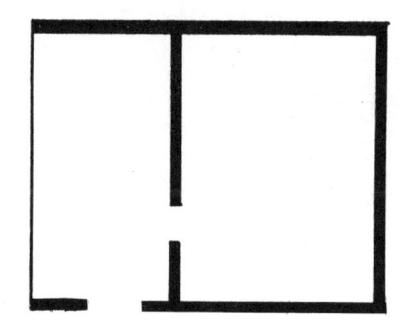

Bartram is reliable in telling us that most flat-roofed houses (Fig. 65) were stone ones. The heavy roofs needed strong walls. Judging by the few known carry-overs, the *azotea* was by no means confined to the more pretentious buildings. *Azoteas* were on six common-plan houses, most of them one- or two-room buildings and only one of them two-story; two St. Augustine-plan dwellings, one of them two-story; and on three of the larger wing-plan structures, including the Treasurer's House.[146]

## Other Materials

Other roof coverings were so little used that to mention them tends to give them more emphasis than they deserve.

There is no evidence that flat roofs made of planks covered with tar and sand, as known in English Georgia, ever came to St. Augustine. Neither pitch nor tar is mentioned as local roofing material. Cypress bark (*cáscara de ciprés*) was found on one lone house in 1788. No other instance is known at St. Augustine, although the Spanish had bark roofs at Apalache during the 1740's and they were also common to Indian house construction as well as to French dwellings in the Mississippi Valley.[147]

Archeology has so far found remarkably few fragments of

roofing tile — only enough to prove tha barrel (semi-circular section) tile was present in the 17th and 18th centuries. One David Yeats, a tiler, did some work on a St. George Street stable (and presumably on other buildings) about 1780. The 1788 map records one house with a tile *(teja)* roof. It was a single-story structure belonging to the crown. Because it was not listed specifically as an *azotea* type, we can infer that the covering was common barrel tile on a sloping roof.

Slate was used for the roof of the new church built during the 1790's, as well as for part of the roof of the customs house.[149]

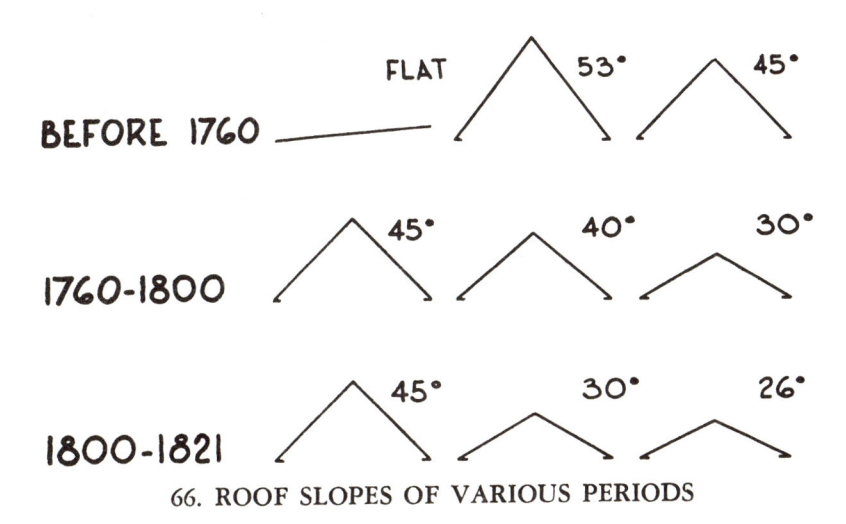

66. ROOF SLOPES OF VARIOUS PERIODS

## Roof Slopes

From the small amount of pictorial evidence illustrating Spanish Florida settlements, pitched roofs (Fig. 66) were not noticeably different from those elsewhere among the southern colonies of North America. To begin with, Indian construction would certainly influence the Spanish builders, especially in the use of native materials unfamiliar to the Iberian newcomers. The 16th century Indian structures around St. Augustine had gable, hip, and beehive roofs. These were thatch, with a pitch of about 45°, except of course for the beehives. Next, the sketch map of St. Augustine in the 1590's depicts boarded gables with thatch slopes pretty close to 45°.[150]

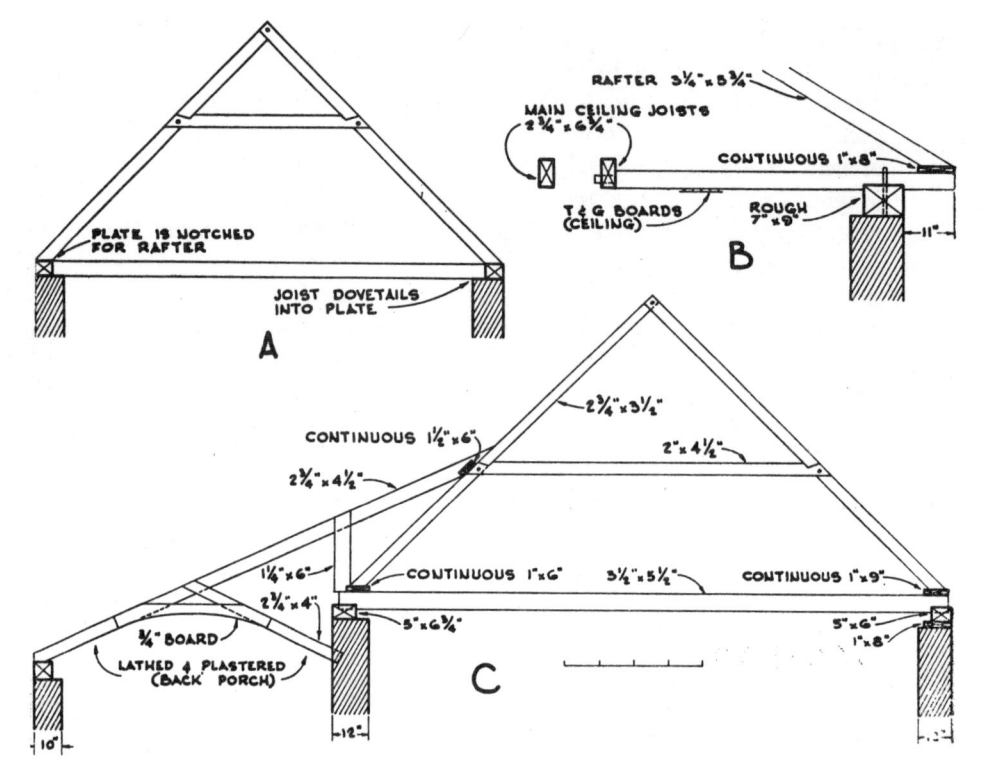

67. ROOF FRAMING

The chances are that the roofs were, if anything, slightly steeper. The early artisans were still influenced by the medieval roof with its breakneck slopes. Not only was a steep roof a good watershed; it provided more headroom in the loft, which in the majority of early houses was the bedroom. Slight evidence of steep slopes at St. Augustine can indeed be found, though in a somewhat roundabout fashion. The Governor's House, pictured in a 1764 sketch, had a gabled shingle roof with 50° pitch or better; and a 53° roof was on another old dwelling. Presumably both roofs had typical pre-1760 lines.[151]

Gables were usually predominant in frontier construction because they were strong, easy to build, and provided a useful loft. As the economy of a community improved and better materials became available, roof designs became more sophisticated (Fig. 67).

Hence the 18th century in the colonies north of Florida saw common roof pitch lowered to 45°, the introduction of additional roof styles, and a growth of dormer windows from tiny vertical skylights into significant features that converted a lightless loft into a pleasant, ventilated room.

It is not surprising, then, to find that the Fatio House along with its many other signs of English joinery has a 45° hip roof with gabled dormers. Nor that the little frame house at 14 St. George Street derives its English-like character from a 47° roof and a long catslide. Though the maps say neither of these houses was built as early as the British period, the carpenters were obviously familiar with the English traditions.

Roof slopes in other places flattened to 30° or less as the 1800's approached. The same thing happened in St. Augustine, but perhaps not until the century was well on its way. The trend toward lower roof lines as the years advanced is well illustrated at the Oldest House. Its early rafters are 47° and 44°; the ones in the last addition are 26°.

Although the coverings have to be replaced periodically, a well-maintained roof can keep its rafters for generations and thus retain its original lines. The following table illustrates a few typical roofs.

## Typical Roofs[152]

| PITCH | TYPE | HOUSE | EST. DATE OF ROOF LINE |
|---|---|---|---|
| 53° | gable | Peña | pre-1760 |
| 50° | gable | Governor's | pre-1760 |
| 50° | gable | Biendicho | pre-1790 |
| 47° | gable-hip | Oldest House | pre-1760 |
| 47° | gable | 14 St. George | pre-1821 |
| 45° | hip | Crown | pre-1788 |
| 45° | gable | Gomila | pre-1821 |
| 45° | hip | Fatio | pre-1821 |
| 42° | hip | Segui | pre-1821 |
| 40° | gable | O'Reilly | pre-1760 |
| 40° | hip | Peña | pre-1788 |
| 38° | hip | 12 Aviles | pre-1821 |
| 35° | gable | Tovar | pre-1821 |
| 30° | gable | Peña kitchen | pre-1788 |
| 30° | hip | 105 St. George | |
| 26° | extension | Oldest House | post-1820 |

Nineteenth century pictures invariably show nothing but shingle roofs (Fig. 68), pitched between 30° and 45° and the majority closer to 45°. Because of the steep pitch, the high gables, and the common practice of extending the house roof over the piazza without a change in slope, when seen in elevation most roofs seem overlarge. From the street, of course, the size of the roof is minimized, especially since the overhang is narrow at gutters and non-existent at gables. Hip roofs, not uncommon, lack the massiveness of the gabled ones, though the slopes may be the same.

Occasionally a "bell cast" roof is seen in the photographs. In this type the main rafters do not overhang the wall of the house. Eaves are formed with little rafters at the lower ends of the main ones, causing the roof line to flare outward like the lip of a bell. The design saved a foot or two on the height of the roof.

A less spectacular variation was to raise the butt of the eave shingle about an inch, whereby the usual "eave droop" was replaced by a perky uplift. This "St. Augustine kick," some say, pushed the rain water away from the walls.

68. SHINGLE TECHNIQUES

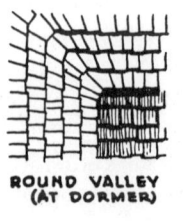

ROUND HIP

MITERED HIP

ROUND VALLEY
(AT DORMER)

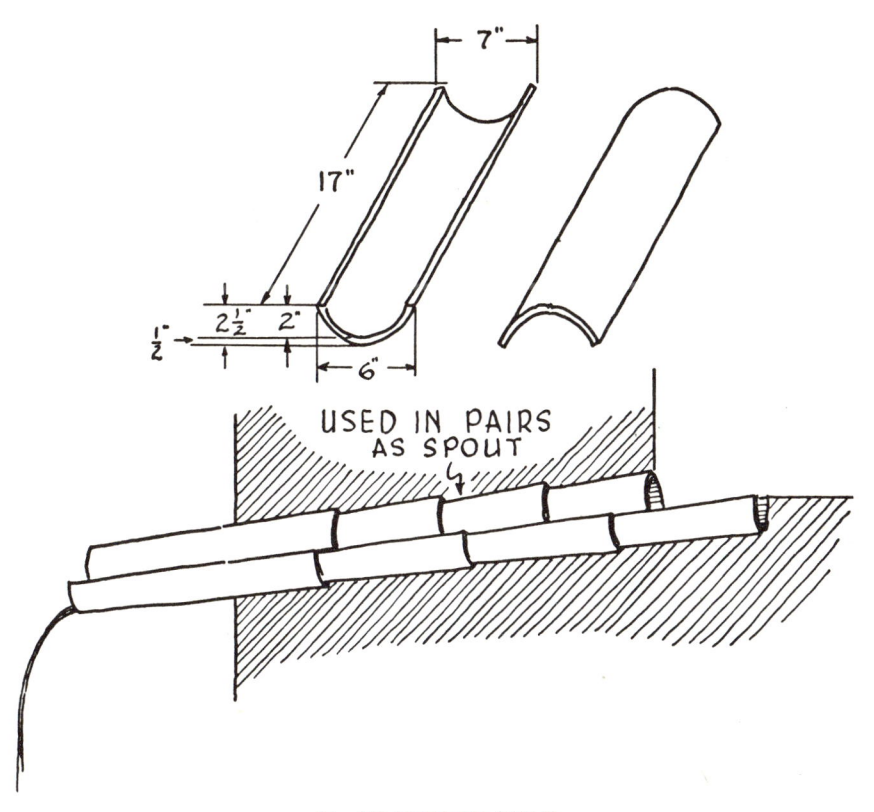

69. "BARREL" TILE

## Spouts and Gutters

The use of spouts through the parapets of flat-roofed buildings was noticed by John Bartram ("pipes, mostly of burnt clay, let through the wall and projecting a foot or more to carry off the water"). Nine of these vitrified spouts (*caños vidriados*) were on the Treasurer's House. Rather than one-piece tubes, however, these were probably pairs of barrel tile, one inverted over the other, as in examples at the fort dating about 1760 (Fig. 69).[153]

It is doubtful that any except the better buildings had gutters. On the Customs House they were fastened to the eaves by iron straps, and led the water into "main pipes" which deposited the flow into the street or the courtyard. We speculate that gutters and pipes were V-shaped troughs of that water-loving wood, cypress.[154]

A

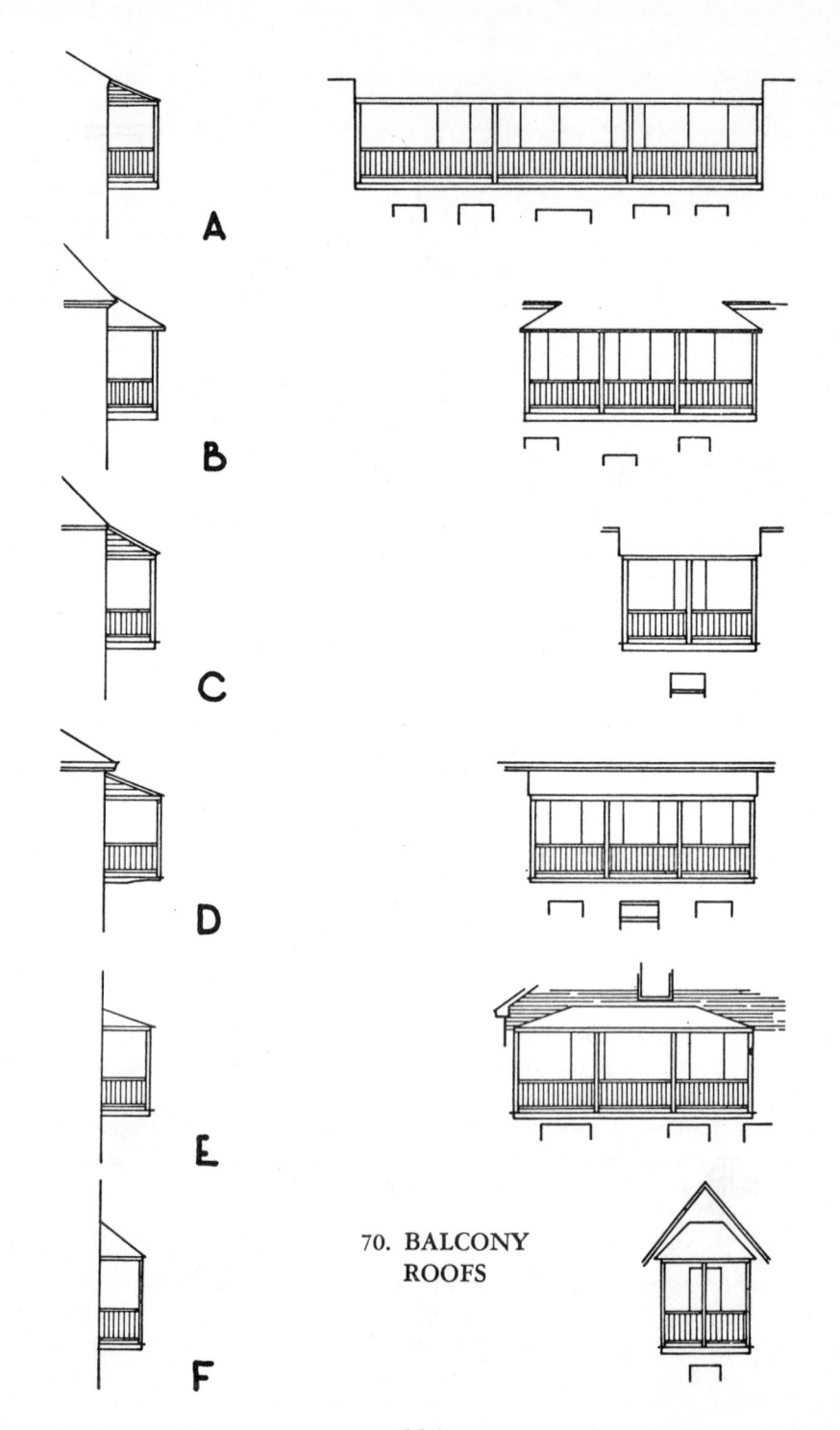

B

C

D

E

70. BALCONY
    ROOFS

F

114

## Balcony Roofs

According to photographic evidence, most balconies were covered with shed-roofed continuations of the house roof, sometimes with a noticeable lowering of the pitch (Fig. 70). The shed ends were sealed with horizontal boards. The eaves had very little overhang and no gutters.

On a gable wall, of course the balcony had its separate roof. At least one high-ceiled, hip-roofed house of the later era begins the balcony roof below the cornice. Not uncommonly the balcony roof itself is hipped.

One known pitch in 1787 (this was probably a carry-over from the first Spanish period) was 35°.[155] It seems, if anything, shallower than we would expect for an early roof. In later years, however, the pitch slumped into the 20's, very likely with some sacrifice of tightness. But who stays on a balcony when it rains?

## Dormers

Because the English did not mention dormers in St. Augustine of the 1760's, we assume there were none. The assumption may be invalid, of course, inasmuch as an observer tends to remark only those features which are strange and unusual to him. Certainly dormers were well known elsewhere in the Colonies; the 18th century had seen them come into their own.

But if the date of their introduction into St. Augustine is late, quite a few examples had developed before 1821 (Fig. 71). One

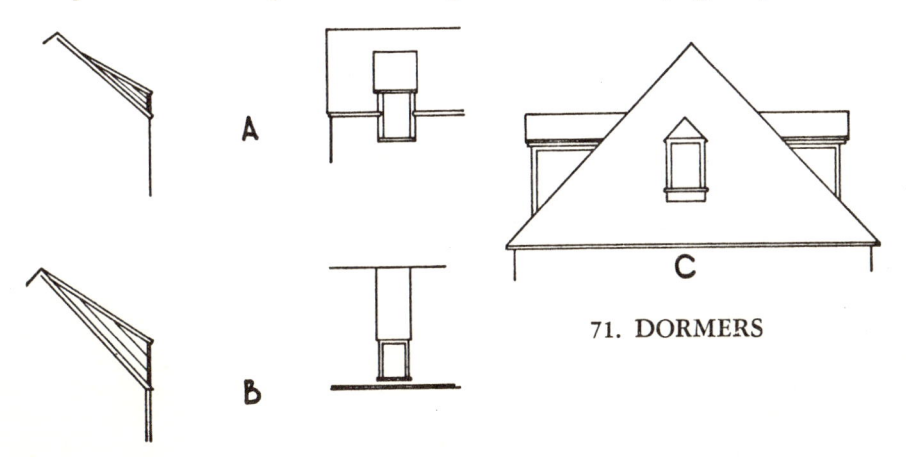

71. DORMERS

115

we can be reasonably sure about is the dormer that is set below the roof plate. This one is an integral part of the house design and not likely to have been knocked through an old roof at the whim of the householder. Several examples of the dormer-in-the-plate type are preserved either *in situ,* or in photographs.

Low dormers of the kind we mention have shed roofs, are found on 1½-story houses, and are small. Gabled dormers are larger, and generally placed upon the two-story house roof.

There is indirect evidence that the 1½-story house existed in Spanish times; a Britisher described the ruined old house he purchased as 16 feet high, which is far too high for one-story and not high enough for two-story. As for British-built 1½-stories, the evidence is positive.[156]

## INTERIORS

### Floors

*Earth.* Beyond question, some habitations boasted no floor but Mother Earth, at least in the early stages of their use. The grey soil of such a floor developed a characteristic dark crust, compact and sometimes quite greasy. Quite possibly the pair of humble dwellings classified in 1790 as *casa terrera* had natural earth floors. The adjective *terrera* signifies humbleness, low-level construction and the like; so the floors were probably at ground level even if they were of another material.[157]

*Wood.* Wooden floors are impermanent and movable. Therefore evidence of them is prone to be lost. With a single exception, I have no data on them until the 1760's. The exception is of questionable value, because it concerns construction in 1745 of a storehouse floor in the fort at Apalache, a long way from St. Augustine. And the work was unusual, perhaps not even in the Spanish tradition, else it would not have been described. This was a floor intended to keep dampness out of the flour barrels. The job was done by a French ship's carpenter serving in the garrison. He put down puncheon joists and planked over them with thick puncheons. This he did, said the commandant, "instead of flooring with round logs which could support the weight of a mountain." The implication is that round logs laid on the ground was the customary way to build a storage floor, but the framed puncheon construction was dryer. Practically speaking, the extra work was a waste of time, because a leaky roof soon afterward turned the flour-house into a pigsty.[158]

However, puncheon floor construction, even if unfamiliar to the Apalache commandant, was so well known in the other colonies that we should not be surprised to find it in St. Augustine and at a very early date.

Likewise, boards sawed for wall construction during the 1500's must also have made flooring (Fig. 72). So even though 1763 is the earliest available record of joist-and-board floors *(vigas y tablas)*, we know that such construction had already been in use a long time. The appraisals of 1763 do furnish other useful information, nevertheless, in stating that wooden floors were found both upstairs and down. Judging by the frequency of each, I would estimate that wood was less used for the ground floor, especially in masonry houses, than for the second floor.[159]

When the British moved in, floors were mended, replaced ("a new floor in the back room"), or enlarged ("her Husband made an Addition . . . floored").[160] Most of the new houses, being timber-frame construction, of course had wooden floors. Under the pressure of massive immigration many small and hastily built structures were

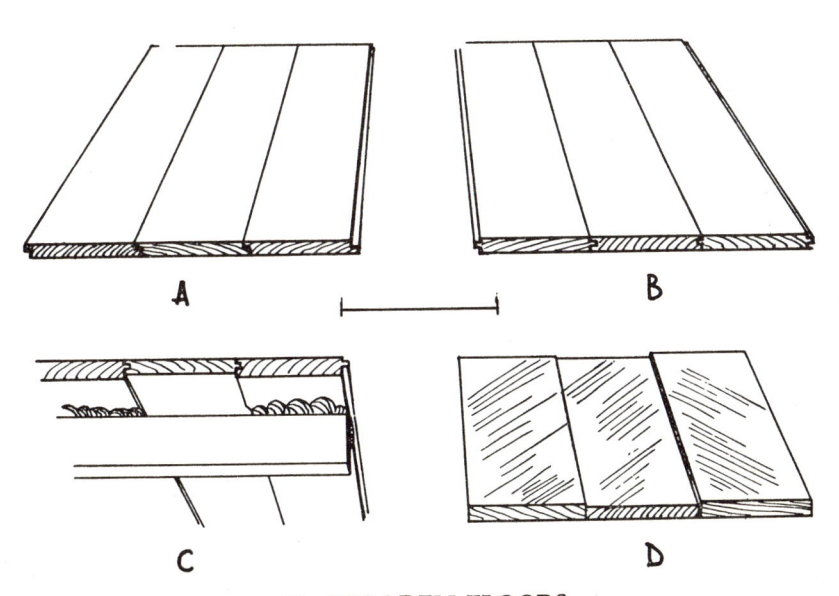

72. WOODEN FLOORS

A — Rabbeted.  B — Tongue-and-groove.  C — Tongue-and groove, showing method of trimming boards to proper thickness at joist. D — "Deal" (undressed boards).

117

put up, and in these circumstances the floors were no better than the houses. In 18th century Savannah, common houses often had floors of rough "deal boards" ("deal" signifying in this case rough-cut lumber about 5/4" X 9" X 12'). See Fig. 72D.) There was ample reason for a similar situation in British St. Augustine. Several sawmills, operated by ambitious and independent businessmen, made lumber more available than ever before. And even more important, the town had plenty of middle-class citizens with the collateral in trade, service, or cash to buy it.[161]

Knowing that the artisans owned the necessary tools is assurance that the better floors were tongue-and-groove tight and smoothly surfaced. But very few of the wide-boarded pine floors are left from the colonial years. Existing examples are random width pine: 1" or 5/4" by 6 3/4", 7 3/4", 8½", 9 3/4", 10½", 11½", plus a 3/8" square tongue. Grooves are 3/8" wide by ½" deep (Fig. 72B-C). Occasionally boards are finished with 2 grooves or 2 tongues instead of alternate tongue and groove. Often the wood is finished 3 sides only. Uneven thickness is compensated at the joist by trimming or filling the boards.

*Masonry.* Tabby floors are permanent in the sense that the archeologist usually finds some of an old floor left. But from the householder's viewpoint, the life of a tabby floor was shorter than he could wish. It is unusual to find *one* tabby floor. What you find is a flock of floors, one on top of the other (Fig. 73). When an old floor became rough and pitted, a new floor was tamped in, right on top of the old one. After a few generations in lively homes, the floor was noticeably close to the ceiling.

The original floor was built on a well-packed base of oyster shell or coquina chippings. Three or more inches of chippings was a usual thing in the military work I have seen. In residential constructions an inch or two of oyster shell, topped by a leveling-off layer of chippings, was common.

Upon this foundation the workmen poured a wet mix of lime and sand and shell. In best-quality tabby, the shell was clean yellow coquina "gravel" from the quarries, most of which would pass a ¼-inch screen. Tabby with this aggregate, when finished, looked like terrazzo. Other aggregates often used included coquina chippings, spalls and oyster shells. The coarser the aggregate, the rougher the floor, although in tamping the mortar (which was an essential part

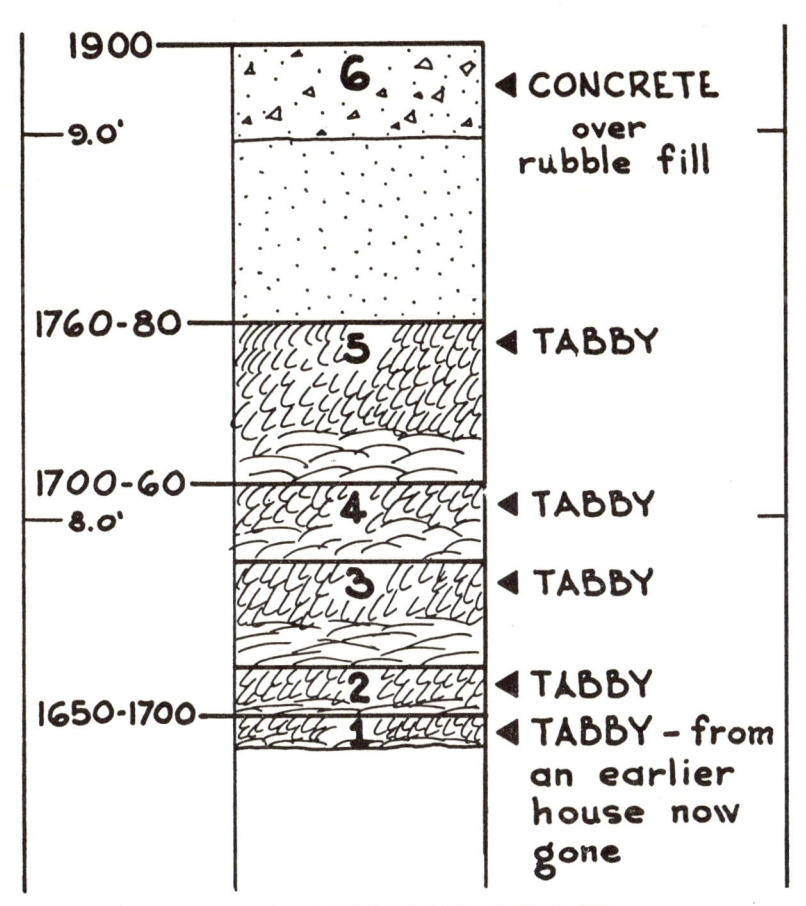

73. MASONRY FLOOR BUILD-UP

of the finishing) the large elements worked down to the bottom and the surface became quite smooth. Two inches was a usual thickness for a layer of tabby, and no doubt screed guides were set up to level off the pour. Contemporary descriptions do not indicate any surface finishing with masons' tools — only a thorough tamping. One observer stated that several applications of linseed oil went on a new floor, each application being tamped well into the slow-hardening mortar.

Where a thick floor was needed, as in military work, two or three 2-inch pours were made, one on top of the other. But for a residence, the single slab was enough until roughened under wear.

Then a few nails might be hammered into it, their heads leveled an inch or two above the surface, and a new tabby tread laid in. The nails heads were your gauges.[162]

John Bartram said that a tabby second floor ("terraced chamber floor") was often to be found in a common tabby-and-thatch house. In such cases we wonder if this were not built the same as a single-story flat-roofed house, with a thatch roof added for dryness. The Spanish phrase (*suelo de azotea*), which might be translated "slab floor," intimates that the floor and roof construction (*torta de azotea*) are similar. [163]

How long tabby has been used in St. Augustine as a floor material is not known. If tabby roofs were built during the 1500's, so were tabby floors. At the fort J. C. Harrington excavated excellent quality tabby floors dating from the 1670's, and in dwellings Hale Smith has unearthed similar floors.

## Partitions, Wall Finishes and Ceilings

The materials for partition walls were almost as varied as for outside walls. The records mention tabby walls (*ostión*), both thin and thick, walls of stone (*mampostería*), board walls (*tablas*), stud walls lathed and plastered (*alfardas, rajones y enlucido*), and in later years even a brick wall.[164]

Although an "old Spanish House" was described in 1786 as having a closet on each of its two floors,[165] closets were not usual conveniences. Instead, chests and wardrobes were used.

Not all houses were finished inside, especially during the hectic last days of the English period. William Watson built a two-story frame house about 1780; it was only "in part lined," he said.[166] Householders then as now wished for interior finishes that were protection against cold and damp, and easy to clean and maintain. Lime plaster was a universal "lining" for a house, whether over stone, tabby, or split lath. All examples of 17th or 18th century work I have seen are smooth — not bumpy — and well finished with a metal trowel. Partition walls were sometimes faced with wood, even in masonry houses. Possibly the wooden facing extended to some of the exterior walls as well. At least in recent times some householders have wainscotted old coquina walls to chair-rail height for the express purpose of sealing out dampness (and the resulting black mold) which crept upward from the foundation. The solution to this problem in colonial days would doubtless have been the same.

74. JOISTS

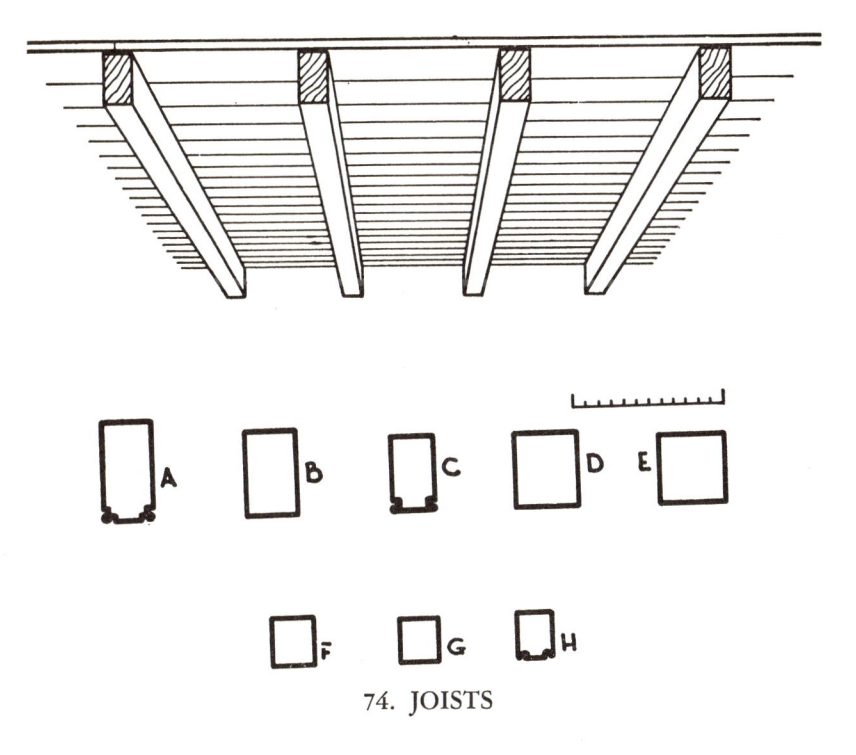

Wall paper seems to have been absent until the British came. Even then, the records yield but a lone example: a 16x43-foot frame house "not lined but papered upon Canvas." Paint was present, but in what quantities and colors the records have not yet fully divulged. Whitewash was by no means limited to outside work; it renovated old plaster and hid any patchwork that was necessary. It seems to have been applied to new work also. British records mention a stone addition "plaistered & white washed on the inside" and a two-story frame house "plaistered & whitewashed which was finished about 1773."[167]

In most cases, plaster walls would have plaster ceilings. However, the 1763 archives list a few flat ceilings (*cielos razos*) made of wood. They were not merely the underside of a flat roof.[168]

The simplest ceiling was the exposed-beam type (Fig. 74). A common bead molding was often planed on the arrises. Some of the existing examples have suffered the indignity of being later lathed and plastered.

# KITCHENS

As with other household features so common as to be taken for granted, kitchens are seldom mentioned in the early records. When mention does occur, the implication of a separate building is strong.[169] There is little doubt that in the better households, if the kitchen were not a separate building, it was at least a separate room. With his customary curiosity Bartram examined one closely:

> I now observed the manner of the kitchens of the better sort [Fig. 75]. The fireplace is raised with stone 2 foot high and 3 broad, and the length of the breadth of the room. And above the floor is open to the slanting roof. There is 1 or 2 openings, a hand's breadth wide and 2 foot long, in the back to let out some smoke. There the back wall is raised 3 foot above the terrace [tabby] roof of the kitchen, from which is carried a slanting roof of terrace, which carrieth of the rain from coming upon the hearth, upon which they have several pots fixed, with holes under each to boil their different soups [Fig. 76]. I dislike this method above any belonging to their houses, as they are all as smoky as an Indian cabin. . . .

However, Bartram intimated, probably with a great deal of truth (although he was not present during the Spanish regime),

**75. A ST. AUGUSTINE KITCHEN**
*(After John Bartram's description)*

122

76. SPANISH STOVE

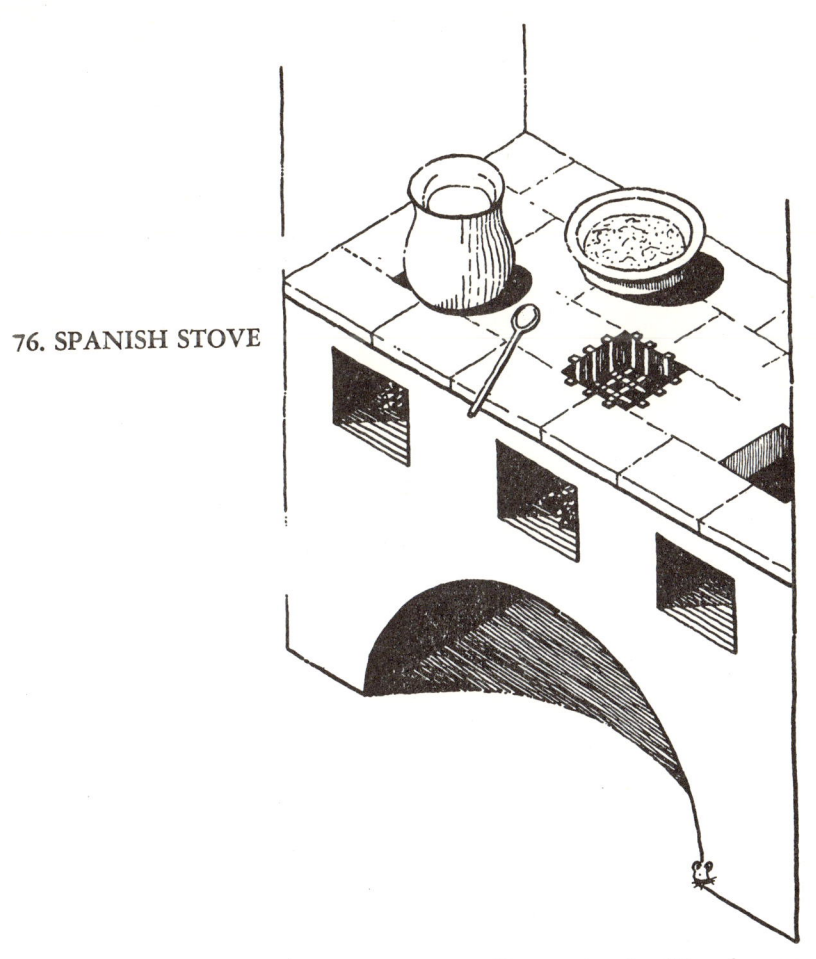

that food preparation played only a small part in the life of most poor householders. They cooked their victuals, "a little of which served them and that very mean," right in the house. Some houses — but by no means all — had smoke holes in the roof. No doubt the mosquitoes were worse in these ventilated ones.[170]

British records confirm the existence of separate kitchens in Spanish households: "a Kitchen detached from the ['Old Spanish'] house"; "a flat roofed Stone out house used by the Spaniards as a kitchen"; "a Stone house and small wooden kitchen." However, in these kitchens English fireplaces soon replaced the charcoal stoves of the Spanish [Fig. 76]. Sometimes other changes were made. The addition of "a very good lodging room" over the kitchen is a recorded — but probably not typical — example.[171]

English-built kitchens also had separate roofs, though in truth some of the houses were hardly bigger than the kitchens ("One framed house 24 feet by 14 . . . and . . . a clap board kitchen"). Englishmen built new kitchens, "rough wooden" kitchens, "large framed" kitchens complete with ovens; and when feasible, they converted other structures to kitchen use.[172]

The 1788 map shows many small outbuildings which can be nothing but kitchens. The later tax appraisals document them specifically: the thatched-wall kitchen of earlier times has disappeared; now they are built of masonry or timber-frame and they had chimneys. Customarily they were 3 or 4 *varas* high, with shingle roofs.[173]

The kitchen of the Customs House (1787) was most likely one of the better ones. It was a 12x15-foot room with 2 doors and 3 windows, tacked onto one of the wings of the building (Fig. 40). An oven and a brick stove (Fig. 76), its "3-burner" top about 28x48 inches, flanked the fireplace.

But with the exception of the fireplace, this kitchen was not vastly different from those "of the better sort" described by Bartram in an earlier era. Instead of the chimney there had been roof vents, but the masonry stove (*fogón*) had been present, and though Bartram failed to mention it, so was the oven (*horno*).[174]

# YARD BUILDINGS
## The Yard

Bartram implies that courtyards were usual ("every court yard had its draw well"). However, the tax appraisals only occasionally mention patio rooms (*cuartos del patio*) or walls (*paredes del patio*), so it is clear that courts or patios in the sense of formally enclosed areas were in the minority. On the other hand, the 1788 map shows that fenced property was the rule, and a man's land might have several fences of one type or another dividing the property for various uses such as houseyard, chickenyard, garden, grove, and so on. The effect, especially in the houseyard, might well be that of a courtyard.[175]

An appealing part of the yard must have been the broad tabby walks Bartram mentioned, and tabby benches along the house walls (Fig. 13). DeBrahm remembered the "arbours of vines, producing

**77. A GRAPE ARBOR**

plenty and very good grapes"; and from more recent times, so do I (Fig. 77). Wonderfully pleasant they were, except for a host of abominable caterpillars which at times dropped upon passersby.[176]

## Wells

Shallow wells furnished the water supply, for the water table is only a few feet down. In the beginning the wells may have been cased with wood (barrels or hollow cypress boles, perhaps), but as the years went by, most of them acquired stone casings (Fig. 78). Ann Hrawbouski, widow of a Tory storekeeper, testified that upon arrival at St. Augustine in 1770, she and her Samuel obtained property with a "Well of excellent Water" cased with "Stone and Lime." I can concur in Ann's testimony; such wells indeed gave clear and potable water in the days before human congestion made them dangerous.[177]

78. WELL CURBS

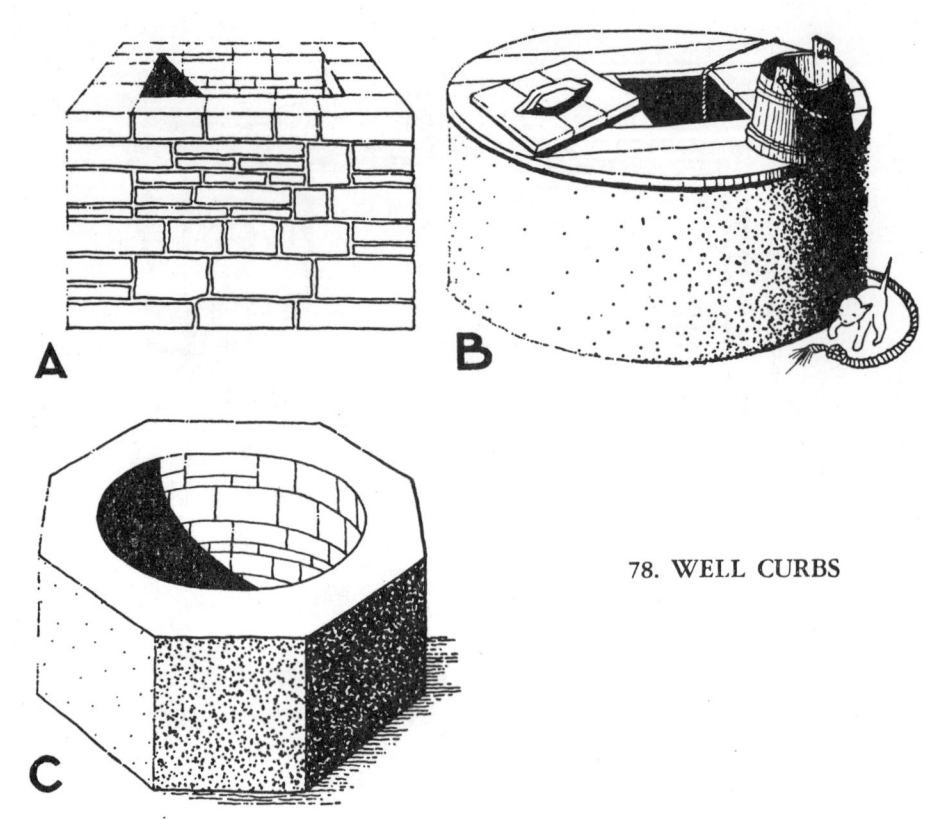

Through the years old ones went out of use and new ones were "sunk." Wells so easily dug (six feet through the light soil was usually enough) were apt to be filled and abandoned if they got in the way of new construction or if they became contaminated. Normally, however, a well could be kept sweet indefinitely by periodic cleanings. This procedure involved removal of debris that had fallen in, and rapid bailing to effect a complete change of water. The bailer stood on the sandy floor of the well and filled and handed up the bailing bucket.

The tax appraisals sometimes indicate a wooden structure at the well; but details of the well houses, if such they were, are unknown. Inasmuch as Bartram called the facility a "draw well," it must have been a rope-and-bucket well.[178] Indeed, many well casings are quite bucket-worn on one or more sides. Obviously the water was lifted by hand without the aid of pulley or windlass.

## Necessaries

Sanitary facilities are poorly recorded, except for occasional and casual mention of the "necessary" (*necesaria*) or "house of office." Thus, while the Governor's House in 1763 had masonry-walled necessaries with separate shingled roofs (each must have stood in solitary grandeur), we remain uninformed as to design and capacity. The void is filled in some measure by a 1787 plan of a privy at the Customs House. Although its finer details have not been preserved, this one-holer measured 39x44 inches, with a seat about a foot wide. The aperture seems to have been a plain circle some 9 inches in diameter.[179]

The refinements mentioned in an 1833 contract for a new necessary on the Governor's House property are probably in the old tradition: "a good double privy . . . of carpenter's work: the holes made oval, and covered with lids on hinges; two for children, lower than the larger ones, and the side privy to be painted blue, with two good coats of paint." The intent of the project was duly carried out, except that instead of wood, a "complete double stone privy" was built. But surely chill masonry was not employed for the interior appointments!

At the other end of the scale from this blue-painted backhouse was a British one built of "rough boards & roofed with the same."[180]

## Stables, Fowl Houses, and Stores

The Governor's House had a stable (*caballeriza*), and doubtless there were others. The British period saw numerous stables, from the hastily-built open shed to an unusual tile-roofed, timber-framed structure. Some were big enough for three, four and six horses. Most were frame buildings, but one was described as having "a stone wall at the back and . . . open in the front." Watson the carpenter converted a large range of stables into a 7-room house, 20x80 feet.[181]

Other outbuildings included the wash house (*lavadero*), the chicken house (*gallinero*), or in the English town the "fowl house" and the pigeon loft. If pigeons were less important as winter food than in medieval times, pigeon pie was nonetheless a welcome change for the table. Some yards also had a "hog house" and various sheds, storehouses and even a strange structure described as "large Stone Cellar in the Yard" with "a small bed Room of Wood adjoining it."[182]

With the British, many shops or stores sprang up, sharing the lot with the residence. Watson built such a one: a "large wooden back Store 30 feet long 18 feet wide & 10 feet high one story high [and short-] Shingled." The store was on the back of a lot occupied by a two-story frame house which was also Watson's creation. Another, also taking up a good part of the house lot, was 12x50 feet. Not all stores were as large as these. Some were only a room in the residence, or an old building converted to the new use.[183]

## Yard Walls and Fences

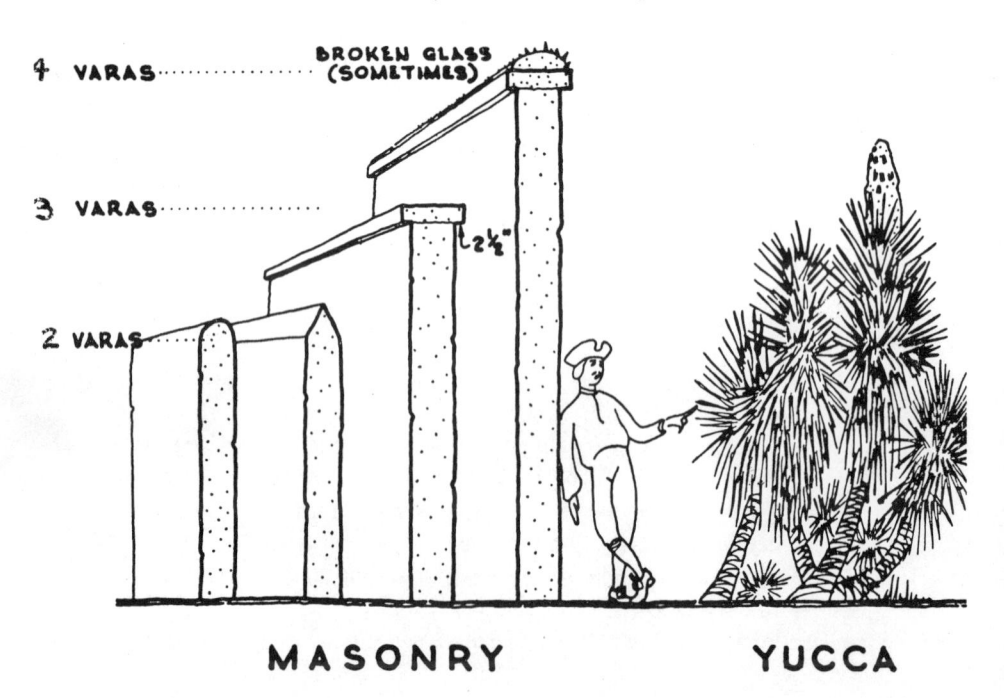

In this frontier community where fruit trees and chickens and kitchen gardens existed side by side, vulnerable not only to human predators but also to raids from the 'coons, cats, deer, foxes and bears close by, fences were a necessity (Fig. 79). Being meant to keep critters out, they were high fences. Recorded heights of masonry walls in 1790, including some "old" walls, were 2 *varas*, 3, 3½, 4 and 5. If as late as 1790 no masonry fence was less than 5½ feet (2 *varas*) high, this was no doubt also the minimum height for almost all fences since early times. It was equivalent to the 6-foot dimension regarded more or less as standard in English practice: Georgia settlers in 1736 enclosed their farm land by "a wooden fence or pales six feet high."[184]

Fences made of pales are still found in the Great Smokies. They were split stakes, stuck in the ground one by another and sharpened at the tops like a miniature palisade.

A stake fence was built around the governor's garden about 1700. There is no reason to believe it was the first of its kind. Certainly it was not the last. A 1763 appraisal of his excellency's garden listed 1,020 fence stakes (*estacas*) and 3 gates, which protected 118 citrus trees along with peach, fig, pomegranate, quince and cherry. Since each *estaca* was appraised at 2 reales (about 25 cents) each, this fence was probably much more substantial than the ordinary rough picket fence of split pales *(rajones)*. A similar fence was built around the barracks in 1788. It was reinforced with stringers, and had double braces angling up from the ground. This was a pine fence, and all below-ground surfaces were tarred.[185]

The data on Rocque's map and key of 1788 are highly informative. The map shows not only that fences were customary on all

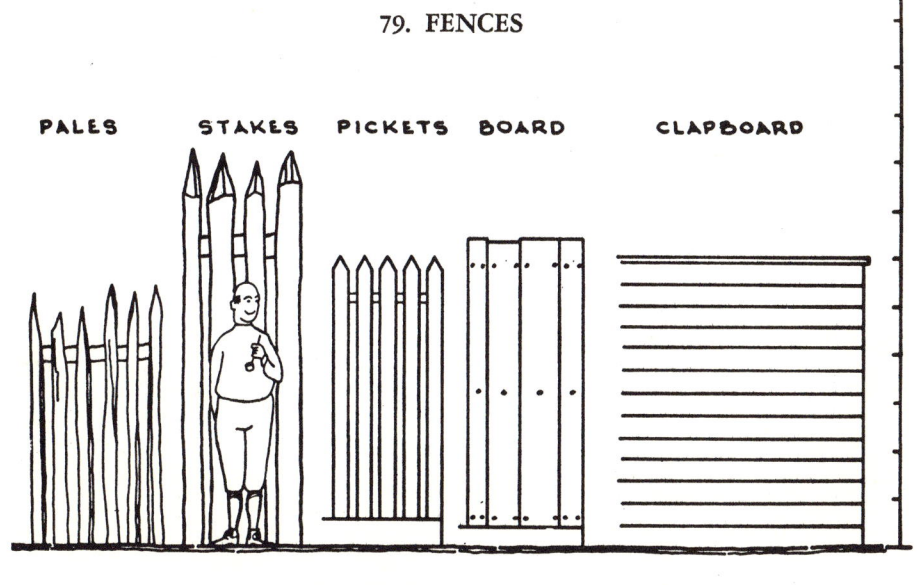

79. FENCES

PALES  STAKES  PICKETS  BOARD  CLAPBOARD

WOOD

properties, but that there might be various subdivisions on a single lot, such as you would expect if the housewife insisted on keeping the chickens from scratching up her green garden. Split pales were in the majority. Some fences were board *(tabla)*, some were yucca *(espinos)*. The yucca or "Spanish bayonet" was known as a formidable barrier since earliest times and cost nothing except the labor to gather and plant them.[186]

Board fences were efficient, but the materials were costly to produce. Presumably "board fence" meant vertical planks nailed close together. This kind of fence was around the Customs House yard in 1787; it was built of 1-inch plank and 6x6-inch posts.[187]

There is good evidence that the Spaniard's vertical board fence was the same thing the Englishman called a "clapboard" fence. For instance, James Scotland in 1777 bought property "well fenced in front with a Stone fence 8 feet high the rest [had] . . . a Clapboard fence." This was clearly a Spanish fence, because it was so old he had to pull it down and build another — "a new Clapboard fence" 6½ feet high. Rebuilding Spanish fences because "the clapboards were mostly rotten" was of necessity a common practice. There were also many instances of fencing unfenced property during these times, and in virtually every case the clapboard fence was the one the proprietor built.[188]

Occasionally a "boarded fence" is mentioned in the records. The distinction between board and clapboard is present, but not clear. When Benjamin Lord closed in his property, it was half with board fence and half with clapboard. Perhaps the clapboard edges were lapped or jointed, thus making a tighter fence than the boards. One man described his fence as having "two or three rails between the Posts & Clapboards nailed upright"; "it was a common Clapboard fence," asserted an eyewitness. But the owner's careful statement that the boards were *upright* suggests that horizontal clapboards on fences were not unusual.[189]

The height of these structures was generally 6 feet, and might go 6½, 7 or 8. An elderly widow said she had a clapboard garden fence "about 4 or 5 feet high." If so, it was uncommon.[190]

The boards were pine. In many cases they were probably "deal" lumber, which measured in the rough 5/4"x9"x12'. Normally the material would be sawed to 6-foot lengths. Hence a well-built fence with a baseboard partly into the ground to keep the chickens from digging out would be exactly 6½ feet high, and no lumber wasted.

The fence boards were probably hung on trenails. Although iron nails are mentioned, they are so few in number and so expensive that they must have been used only to secure the rails to the posts.

The posts, and sometimes the rails, were cedar. A 94-foot fence used 12 or 14 posts, so the maximum spacing was about 8 feet.[191]

The 19th century photographs preserve only two kinds of wooden fences: vertical-board and narrow dressed pickets. Their construction was of course 19th century, but they are not far from the old tradition.

If wooden fences were usual behind the house, masonry walls held their own on the street. A few of the better-off families might even enclose an entire lot with them. Bartram said that most of the garden and yard walls were built of "oyster shells and mortar" (tabby). Many of them were lost during the wholesale destruction of tabby houses in the 1760's, and the only known survivor is on the south line of 214 St. George. Stone walls have fared better. The tax appraisals of the latter 1700's describe a number of stone walls (*mampostería*), and a few examples are still preserved. Evidence indicates that without exception, masonry walls were plastered.[192]

Gateways received special treatment (Fig. 80). Here I do not consider the monumental façade of the Governor's House wall with its huge portal flanked by columns, since this was unique; but 19th century photographs have preserved many examples of the massively simple stone lintel over the gate. The height of the wall is increased 2 or 3 feet in the gateway section. Most examples were flat-arched and wide enough only for single-leaf doors, but occasionally the records mention a big door or gate (*portón*) and we know the gate to the Customs House was a good 6 feet wide with folding leaves.[193]

## Paint

Among the numerous Spanish appraisals I have seen, only one mentions paint. In this case the paint was on a balcony in 1763. Whether the rare mention was due to the virtual absence of oil paint until the 1800's, or whether paint was common enough to be ignored by the appraisers we may never know. I suspect the latter is true, particularly for the 18th century and the better houses. Certainly the British brought their own paints when their time came.[194]

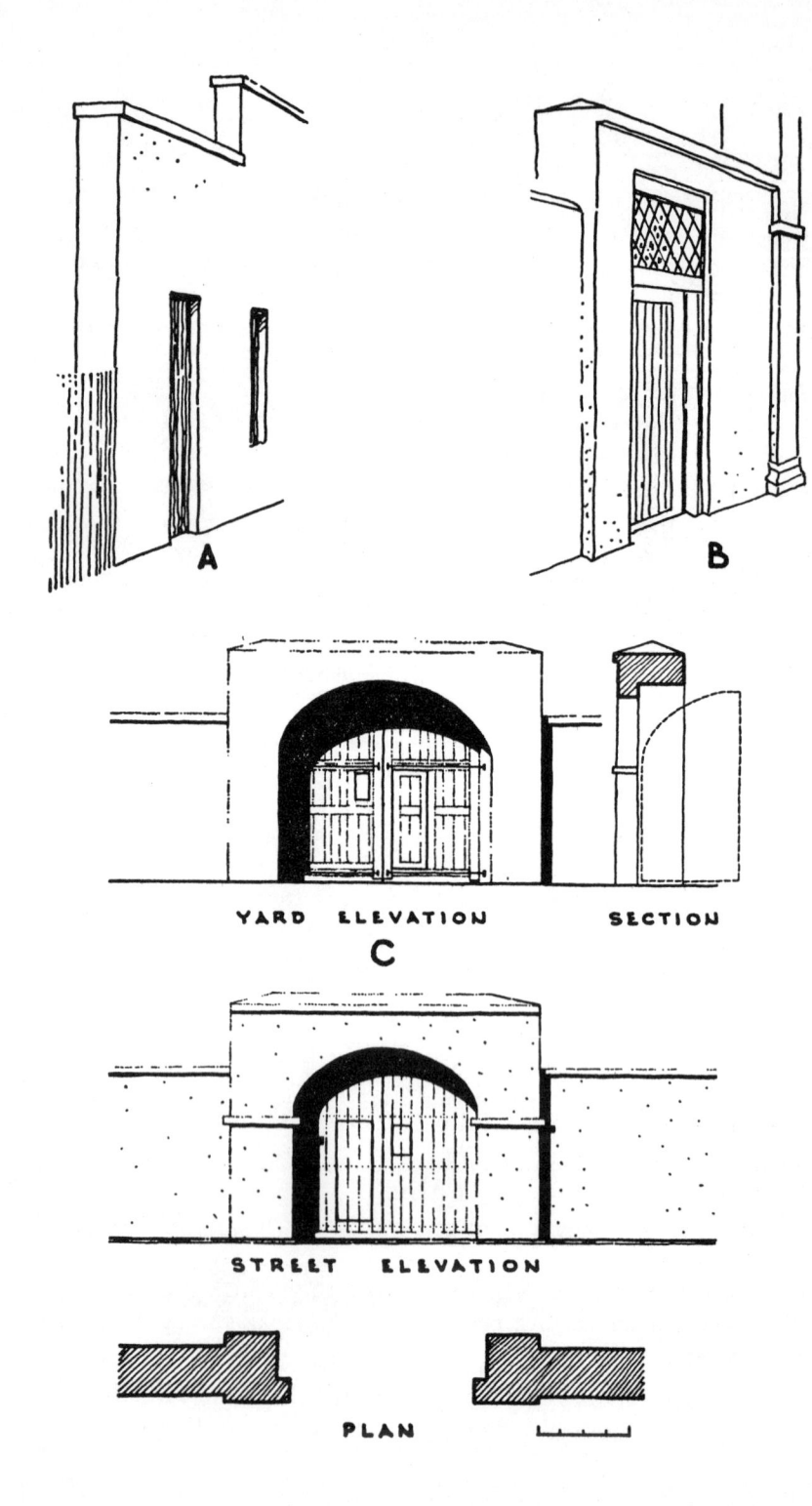

YARD ELEVATION    SECTION
C
STREET ELEVATION
PLAN

80. GATEWAYS

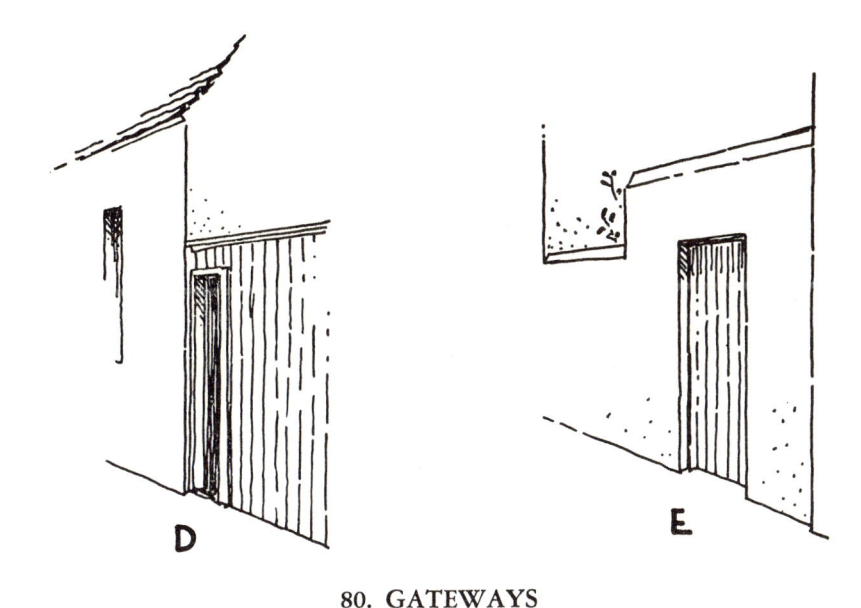

Colors would not be different than those found elsewhere in European countries — white, ochre, red, brown and green possibly predominant. Traces of a characteristic olive green were found on the clapboards of the Oldest House. The color of the "New Red House," an inn completed in 1773, could have been nothing but red. Blue paint was specified for a privy in 1832. Since the colors were probably dry pigments, they could be used in plaster. At the Castillo, crushed red brick was used to color plaster. An attractive ochre-like yellow is known to have been used on some houses now gone.[195]

The most common paint was whitewash. It was ordinary practice on colonial frontiers to whitewash houses inside and out. So it was done at Santa Elena in 1580 and St. Augustine was no exception. There is ample evidence of its use as an all-purpose finish on both wood and masonry.[196]

# SOURCES

THE EVIDENCE relating to the colonial architecture is of three kinds; structural, documentary and graphic. Of structures, there are some 32 existing houses. All post-date 1702 (the year the town was besieged and burned), and 18 of these were erected after 1783. Fourteen can be attributed with reasonable certainty to the 1703-1763 period. Strangely enough, not one can be dated within the British period. Every one of the buildings has, of course, been repaired, remodelled, enlarged, or otherwise modified so that none remains an unadulterated example of period construction.

There are also remnants of buildings long ago demolished, but now uncovered by archeological technique. Obviously this kind of evidence is fragmentary. The digger encounters only floors and foundations. Sometimes there are bits of hardware and roofing materials, and an occasional fallen wall or ceiling. Still, excavated ruins are often the *only* physical evidence of early buildings. The unique value of the data, coupled with the fact that archeology is a technique destructive of the very evidence it uncovers, requires that excavations be conducted with extreme care and meticulous attention to recording.

Historical written records are of many kinds, ranging from general (and sometimes very casual) descriptions of the city to the methodical appraisals of the tax assessor and the detailed inventories found in testamentary papers. In some areas, records are discouragingly voluminous, but frustratingly sparse in others. They will be found in Spanish, English, or Latin. Without attempting to say what and where all these records are, we can give you a general picture:

The major archival source for Spanish material is the *Archivo General de Indias* at Sevilla. Many manuscripts from this and other Spanish archives have been extracted photographically or by transcript and brought to the United States. Notable collections include the Stetson Collection (at the P. K. Yonge Library of Florida History, University of Florida), the Spanish Records of North Carolina (at the North Carolina Department of Archives and History), the Buckingham Smith transcripts (at the New-York Historical Society), and the various groupings in the Manuscripts Division of the Library of Congress, especially the Lowery, Brooks, and Connor collections.

Another collection of major importance in the Library of Congress requires separate mention. This is the governmental archive for the 1783-1821 period, the "East Florida Spanish Papers." A significant part of this archive, dealing with land records, is at the Florida Department of Agriculture, Tallahassee. Other useful records are those of the St. Augustine Cathedral Parish, written in Latin and Spanish and dating from 1594.

Manuscripts in English are mainly those of British archives, such as the Colonial Office Papers and the Audit Office Records (of the Public Record Office, London). The Library of Congress has much from the former, and numerous documents from the latter are published in Siebert's *Loyalists of East Florida*.

Before leaving the subject, a few other comments are in order. For the entire 1565-1763 period, documentary evidence is fugitive and uneven. In the earlier years, crown policy discouraged private ownerships and few property records are known. Thus, descriptions of real estate are encountered more or less by chance in the reports of visiting officials inspecting the presidio, the letters of churchmen painting a word picture of the Florida frontier, or the correspondence, depositions and so on which make up the typical administrative file. Often there is vivid detail, but even at best, this is fragmentary and casual material.

The preparation of property records — at least for the years after 1702 — is certain and their existence somewhere in the archives is probable. Since they are not found in the U. S. collection, a thorough archival search should be made for them. Of the available records, among the more important are the detailed house and land appraisals made by the engineers Juan de Cotilla and Pablo Castelló just before the cession of Florida to Great Britain (1763). Only a few of these appraisals have been located, but systematic search ought to bring more of them to light. Those found were in the land records of the East Florida papers. This archival section, separate from the main archive in the Library of Congress, is found in the Field Note Division of the Florida State Department of Agriculture at Tallahassee.

Extant records from the British period include the colorful descriptions by the notable botanist John Bartram and others, and various claims for property losses suffered by citizens who left Florida when Spanish rule returned. Excellent detail often turns up in the claims. Although conventional property records have not been found, there are useful papers which document the action of many Spanish owners who turned their property over to British agents for disposal.

For the 1783-1821 period the data are voluminous. Of major importance are the periodic official appraisals of property which methodically describe and evaluate each parcel. Likewise valuable are the testamentary papers containing such items as wills and inventories of estates. In addition there are descriptions and reports on the condition of public buildings by the engineers. Such reports are found at the beginning and end of the period and for several of the years in between.

There are numerous maps, but few are useful in architectural study. One anonymous 16th century map graphically depicts early board-and-thatch buildings. There is a colorful print showing the town in 1670, but one suspects the artist was a stay-at-home, drawing through another man's eyes. Nothing else is available until the work of Juan Joseph Elixio de la Puente in 1764. To him fell the task of completing the property descriptions started by Cotilla. Elixio compiled a long list of the real estate, though with less detail than we would like. His list is the key to a schematic map. The map in turn is based upon an accurate engineer's map (perhaps the work of Pablo Castelló), which as yet is lost to us.

Two other maps of the 1760's also seem to have been based upon the missing Castelló map. One is the handsomely drafted but unrealistic Solís map. The other is a fine large-scale map by James Moncrief, crown surveyor for British East Florida.

But far and away the most illuminating source is the "Plano Particular" of Mariano de la Rocque, the government engineer. This remarkable map is an accurate delineation of the town and specifies the materials, size, height, floor plan, ownership and sometimes the roof of each structure. The voluminous detail gives it value not only as a record of 1788 but also as a key to the earlier years. Of almost 300 houses on this map, fully half of them can be identified as survivors from 1763.

There are a few large scale floor plans, such as the 1787 accountant's house. The measured drawings of extant buildings by the Historic American Buildings Survey are useful.

Not many sketches are left from colonial times, but for the traveling artist of later times the buildings of St. Augustine were appealing. And after 1840 came photography. St. Augustine scenes, along with Niagara Falls, were a favorite subject in the stereopticons of the nation's parlors. The photographers, some professional and some amateur, fortunately searched out the city's many aspects and compiled an extensive pictorial record predating the great fires of 1886 and 1914 and the demands of municipal progress. These pictures and other original materials, along with photocopies of most of the various other sources mentioned, have been collected assiduously over many years by the St. Augustine Historical Society, and are available in its library.

**Abbreviations**

    AI=Archivo General de Indias, Seville
    C=Library of Castillo de San Marcos National Monument, St. Augustine
    LC=Library of Congress
    NA=National Archives of the United States
    NC=Spanish Records of North Carolina
        S=Stetson Collection of Spanish Records in the P. K. Yonge Library of Florida History
    SAHS=Library of the St. Augustine Historical Society
        Y=P. K. Yonge Library of Florida History, University of Florida, Gainesville

# BIBLIOGRAPHY

## Primary Sources

### COLLECTIONS

East Florida Spanish Papers. MS. archives of the governors of East Florida, 1783-1821 (and some earlier). LC.
Florida Spanish Land Records. Part of the East Florida Papers. 1783-1821 (and some earlier). Field Note Division, Florida State Department of Agriculture, Tallahassee.
Great Britain. Public Record Office Papers, Colonial Office, Class 5 (Florida). MS. archives. London. LC (transcripts).
Historic American Buildings Survey. Collection of measured drawings and photographs of historic houses. LC.
Lowery, Woodbury L. "Florida MSS." 10v. Transcripts from Spanish and French archival documents, 1512-1680. LC.
St. Augustine Historical Society. Collection of maps, manuscripts, measured drawings, photographs, sketches, views and other historical records, books, and objects.
Spanish Records of the North Carolina State Department of Archives and History, 1566, 1569, 1650-1670, 1783-1802. Photostats from Spanish archives. Raleigh.
Stetson Collection of Spanish Records, 1512-1821 (and some later). Photostats and transcripts from Spanish archives. Y.

### DOCUMENTS

Alacano, Fray Martin de. Memorial. St. Augustine, Aug. 2, 1703 (AI 58-2-14). Y.
Archivo General de Indias: 58-2-8, Cuaderno 2. Residencia of Zúñiga. S.
———. 58-2-4/25. S.
Assessor's Inventory of 1800. Transcript from Assessor's Inventory, no. 320, East Florida Papers (LC). SAHS.
Autos. St. Augustine, Apr. 25, 1712 (AI 58-2-3/56) and June 4, 1717 (AI 58-1-35/60). S.
Castelló, Pablo. Property Appraisals of December 28, 1763: the Governor's House; no. 24, Guardhouse; no. 233, Hospital; no. 22 and 23, Blacksmith Shop. (AI 86-7-11/23). S. Transcribed and translated in Arnade, "Architectural Information," 32 ff.
Córcoles y Martínez, Govr. Francisco de. Letter to Crown. St. Augustine, Jan. 14, 1708. Translation in Boyd, *Here They Once Stood*, 90-91.
———. Letters to Crown. St. Augustine, July 20, 1709 (AI 58-1-30/6); Aug. 13, 1709 (AI 58-1-28/66); Aug. 25, 1713 (AI 58-1-28/109). S.
Cotilla, Juan de. Property appraisals of 1763: houses of Joaquín Blanco, Salvador de Porras, and Antonio de Rodríguez-Juan de Salas, Fla. State Dept. of Agriculture, Field Note Division, City Lots, Bundles 203/19 and 357/6. Transcribed and translated in Arnade, "Architectural Information," 32 ff.
Consejo de Indias. Madrid, Apr. 30, 1703. (AI 58-1-23). NC.
Cruz, Ramón de la. "Inventory . . . of all the Fortresses and Public Edifices . . ." [at St. Augustine, 1821]. Translation from the official Spanish inventory at the cession of Florida. This copy is enclosure of July 10, 1833, letter of Lt. Stephen Tuttle, St. Augustine to Gen. Charles Gratoit, U. S. Engineer Corps, Washington. NA.

## SOURCES

───────. "No. 7. Accountants Office, Treasury & Custom House," in his "Inventory" cited above.

DeBrahm, William G. "History of the Three Provinces, South Carolina, Georgia and East Florida." MS., 1771. Harvard College Library.

"Discrezión de la Planta del Castillo . . ." MS. tracing of plan key, [St. Augustine, 1686]. C.

Elixio de la Puente, Juan Joseph de. MS. key to map entitled "Plano de la Real Fuerza, Baluarte, y Linea de la Plaza de Sn. Agustín de Florida . . ." [St. Augustine] Jan. 22, 1764. Museo Naval, Madrid.

"Estado en que se hallava la Plaza de San Agustín de la Florida." [St. Augustine,] Oct. 29, 1780. East Florida Papers, 176/60. LC.

Franciscans. Letter to the Crown. St. Augustine, Sept. 28, 1713. (AI 58-2-16/2). S.

Hita Salazar, Pablo de. Letter to Crown. St. Augustine, Dec. 15, 1680 (AI 54-5-11/74). S, NC.

───────. Testimony. St. Augustine, 1707 (AI 58-2-8, cuaderno 2), Residencia of Zúñiga. S, NC.

Justís, Govr. Manuel Joseph de. Letters to Govr. of Havana. St. Augustine, March 22 - Aug. 15, 1737. East Florida Papers, v. 37. LC.

León, Capt. Isidoro de. Letter to the Governor of Florida. Apalache, May 21, 1745 (AI 58-2-13/19). Translated by L. L. Wenhold, *Florida Historical Quarterly*, v. 35, no. 3.

Leturiondo, Alonso de. *Memorial a el Rey . . . en que se da noticia de el estado en que se halla el Presidio de San Agustín . . .* n. p. [c. 1701] (AI 58-2-3/14). S.

Méndez de Canzo, Gonzalo. Letters to the Crown, Feb. 23, 1598, and Sept. 22, 1602 (AI 54-5-9). Transcription in Lowery, "Florida MSS.," IV. LC.

Montiano, Govr. Manuel de. Letters to Govr. of Havana. St. Augustine, 1737-1741. East Florida Papers, v. 37. LC.

Nieto de Carvajal, Bernardo. Autos, St. Augustine, Apr. 2 and 4, 1707 (AI 58-2-8). S.

Palazio y Valenzuela, Govr. Lucas de. Letter to Julian de Arriaga. St. Augustine, Jan. 20, 1761 (AI 86-6-6, Santo Domingo 2660). S.

"Plan and View of St. Augustine Castle and Matance's Fort." MS. description of St. Augustine and its defenses, with sketches. N. p. [1743]. C (photostat).

Quesada, Govr. Juan de. Letter to Gardoqui, St. Augustine, Jan. 8, 1793. Enclosure of letter, Gardoqui to the Conde de Alange, Aránjuez, June 16, 1793. (Archivo de Simancas, Guerra, 6916). NC.

Quiroga y Losada, Govr. Diego de. Letters to Crown. St. Augustine, Apr. 1, 1688, (AI 54-5-12/55) and June 8, 1690 (AI 54-5-12/102). S.

Rebolledo, Diego de. Letter to Crown. St. Augustine. Oct. 24, 1655 (AI 58-2-2/2). NC.

Religious and others. Letter to the Crown. St. Augustine, Mar. 4, 1715 (AI 58-2-1/64). S.

Rocque, Mariano de la. "Noticia del estado en que se hallan las Casas de la Ciudad de Sn. Agustín de la Florida." St. Augustine, Oct. 11, 1784. With his map of same date, "Plano de la Ciudad de San Agustín de la Florida." C (MS. tracing).

───────. Reports on the condition of crown property. Dec. 31, 1788 (East Florida Papers, 2023), Dec. 1, 1789 (same, 176-2); Dec. 31, 1789 (same, 2068). LC. SAHS (translations).

Royal Officials of Florida. Letters to the Crown. St. Augustine, July 20, 1689 (AI 54-5-15/68) and Apr. 2, 1707 (AI 58-2-8). S.

St. Augustine Historical Society. "Excerpts from Construction Specifications for church in Ciales, Puerto Rico, c. 1844." SAHS (transcript and translation).

# SOURCES

Solana, Juan. Certifications. St. Augustine, Aug. 25, 1713 (AI 58-1-28/109) and Mar. 4, 1715 (AI 58-2-1/64). S.

Solana, Juan Joseph. Report on the condition of St. Augustine. [St. Augustine, 1759.] Enclosure of Solana's letter to Arriaga. St. Augustine, Apr. 9, 1760 (AI 86-7-21/41). S.

"Ynventarios Tasaciones, y venta en publico Remate de las Casas Y Solares del Rey." St. Augustine, August 19, 1790. Field Note Division, Fla. State Dept. of Agriculture, Tallahassee.

Zúñiga Residencia. St. Augustine, 1707 (AI 58-2-8). S.

Zúñiga y la Cerda, Joseph de. Autos. St. Augustine, Nov. 11 and 14, 1702 (AI 58-2-8). S.

———. Letter to Crown. St. Augustine, Nov. 10, 1702 (AI 58-2-8). S.

## Printed Records

Andrews, Charles M., and Evangeline W. (eds). *Jonathan Dickinson's Journal or, God's Protecting Providence*. Yale University Press, 1945.

Bartram John. *Diary of a Journey Through the Carolinas, Georgia, and Florida from July 1, 1765, to April 10, 1766*. Philadelphia, 1942. Francis Harper (ed.).

Boyd, Mark F. (trans.) "The Siege of St. Augustine . . . in 1702 as Reported to the King of Spain by Don Joseph de Zúñiga y Zerda, Governor of Florida." *Florida Historical Quarterly*, XXVI.

Bry, Theodor de. *America*. Frankfort, 1591.

Connor, Jeanette T. (tr. and ed.). *The Colonial Records of Florida, 1570-1580*. Florida State Historical Society, DeLand, 1925, 1930. 2 v.

Darlington, William. *Memorials of John Bartram and Humphry Marshall* (Lindsay and Blakiston, Phila., 1849).

*East Florida Gazette* (newspaper). St. Augustine, Feb. 28, 1783. Public Record Office, London. SAHS (photostat).

García, Genaro (ed.). *Dos Antiguas Relaciones de la Florida*. Mexico, 1902.

Georgia Historical Society. *Collections of the Georgia Historical Society*. Savannah, 9 v. in 13 parts, 1840-1916.

Hita, Manuel de. Letter to Govr. Enrique White. St. Augustine, April 1, 1807. Translation in *Report of the Solicitor of the Treasury*, 30th Congress, 2 Session, Jan. 30, 1849.

[Kimber, Edward.] "Itinerant Observations in America." *Collections of the Georgia Historical Society*, IV, reprint from *The London Magazine* (1745-1746).

Latrobe, Charles J. *The Rambler in North America, 1832-33*. N. Y. 1835. 2 v.

Moore, Francis. "A Voyage to Georgia." *Collections of the Georgia Historical Society*, I. Savannah, 1840.

*Narrative of A Voyage to the Spanish Main, in the Ship "Two Friends"* . . . Printed for John Miller, London, 1819.

Quesada, Juan de. Letter to the Govr. of Cuba. St. Augustine, May 26, 1792. Translation in *Executive Document no. 21*, 30th Congress, 2nd Session, Jan. 30, 1849.

John Rodman and Elias Wallen. Articles of Agreement, Oct. 12, 1833. *House of Representatives Report*, 25th Congress, 3rd Session.

San Miguel, Fray Andrés de. "Relación de los Trabajos," in Genaro García [ed.], *Dos Antiguas Relaciónes de la Florida*.

Schöpf, Johann D. *Travels in The Confederacy*. Alfred J. Morrison (trans. and ed.). Phila. 1911.

Siebert, Wilbur H. *Loyalists in East Florida, 1774 to 1785*. The Florida State Historical Society, DeLand, 1929. 2 v. Volume 2: *Records of Their Claims and Losses of Property in the Province*.

Spalding, Thomas. Letter in *The Southern Agriculturist* [Magazine], December 1830. Library of Margaret Davis Cate, St. Simons Island, Ga.

———. Letter to N. C. Whiting, New Haven Conn. (Sapeloe, Ga., July

# SOURCES

29, 1844). Transcribed in typescript volume, "Sapeloe Island," pp. 69-73, library of Margaret Davis Cate, St. Simons Island, Ga.
Stork, William. *A description of East-Florida with a Journal Kept by John Bartram of Philadelphia, Botanist to His Majesty for the Floridas . . .* London, 1765.
Wenhold, Lucy L. (trans.). *A 17th Century Letter of Gabriel Díaz Vara Calderón.* Washington, 1936.
———. (trans.) and Albert Manucy. "The Trials of Captain Don Isidoro De León." *Florida Historical Quarterly,* v 35, no. 3. (The translation in this article is from the report of León to the Governor of Florida, Apalache, May 21, 1745 (AI 58-2-13/19). NC.)
Williams, John Lee. *The Territory of Florida.* N. Y., 1837.

### Maps, Plans and Pictures

Boazio. *S. Augustini pars est Floridae* . . . [Map] n. p., [1586]. LC.
"Cortadura y defensas hechas . . . por Don Pablo de Hita y Salazar en el Castillo. . . ." Plan, St. Augustine, 1675 (AI 2-4-1/19, 3). LC 171 (tracing).
Elixio de la Puente, Juan Joseph de. "Plano de la Real Fuerza, Baluarte, y Linea de la Plaza de Sn. Agustín de la Florida . . ." MS. map with detailed key [St. Augustine,] 1764. Museo Naval, Madrid.
———. "Plano del Presidio de Sn. Agustín de la Florida . . ." MS. map with detailed key. Havana, Feb. 16, 1769, LC.
Gordon, Peter. "View of Savannah." MS map. March 29, 1734. De Renne Library, University of Georgia. Reproduced in Nichols, 18.
LeMoyne, Jacques. "Brevis narratio eorum quae in Florida Americae . . ." Narrative with engraved sketches. In Theodor de Bry, *America,* part 2.
"Mapa del Pueblo, Fuerte y Cano de San Agustin de la Florida." MS map, [St. Augustine, c. 1593] (AI 140-7-37). (WL 76, tracing). Also reproduced in Chatelain, *Defenses of Spanish Florida, map. 4.*
Moncrief, James. Map of land ownership, St. Augustine, Florida (no title). [St. Augustine, c. 1765.] Public Record Office, London, Colonial Office, Florida 8. LC (photostat).
Montanus, Arnoldus. *Paganus Hispanorum in Florida.* Engraved view. In Montanus, *De Lieuve en onbekende weereld.* Amsterdam, 1671. LC.
St. Augustine Historical Society. Collection of photographs, sketches and other views of St. Augustine. SAHS.
———. Collection of measured drawings and sketches of historic structures. SAHS.
Rocque, Mariano de la. "Plano inferior y superior de la Casa del Rey destinada para Aduana, Tesorería y Contaduría de esta Plaza." MS. plan, St. Augustine, March 20, 1787. NA.
———. "Plano Particular de la Ciudad de Sn. Agustín de la Florida." MS. map with detailed key, St. Augustine, 1788. The map is in East Florida Papers, LC; the key in Field Note Division, Fla. State Department of Agriculture, Tallahassee.
Solis, John de. "A New & Accurate Plan of the Town of St. Augustine, Engrv'd from the Survey of Don John De Solis, surveyor, who Resided there near Twenty Years . . ." [n. p., c. 1766.] LC.
"View From the Governors Window in St. Augustine E. Florida." Watercolor sketch, [St. Augustine], Nov. 1764 British museum Kings Maps. SAHS (photo)
"View of the Governors house at St. Augustine in E. Florida." Watercolor sketch, [St. Augustine], Nov. 1764. British museum, Kings Maps. CXXII862a. SAHS (photo).
Horton, John S. *View of St. Augustine, East Florida.* Woodcut view, [St. Augustine,] c. 1840. SAHS.

# Secondary Sources

## Unpublished

Arnade, Charles W. "Architectural Information of Early Spanish St. Augustine." Mimeograph, St. Augustine Historical Restoration and Preservation Commission, 1960. SAHS.
Barnette, Stuart. "The Restoration of the Llambias House." St. Augustine, 1954. 2 v. SAHS.
Dunkle, John R. "The Avero Houses — A Location Analysis." Mimeograph, St. Augustine Historical Restoration and Preservation Commission, 1960. SAHS.
———. "Final Geographic Report" [on St. Augustine, Fla., Project of 1960]. Mimeograph, St. Augustine Historical Restoration and Preservation Commission, 1960. SAHS.
Fairbanks, Charles H. "The Excavation of the Hawkins-Davison Houses, Fort Frederica National Monument, St. Simons Island, Georgia." National Park Service, 1952. C.
Historical Records Survey. "Spanish Land Grants in Florida." Mimeograph, State Library Board, Tallahassee, Fla., 1940. 5 v. SAHS.
Manucy, Albert. "The Cathedral of St. Augustine." Mimeograph, National Park Service, 1946. C.
———. "Commerce in Florida from 1763 to 1821, with Especial Reference to St. Augustine." St. Augustine, 1934. C.
———. "Gonzalo Méndez de Canzo." in "Great Men and Great Events in St. Augustine." Mimeograph, National Park Service, 1939. C.
———. "Report on a Field Trip to the Probable Site of Spanish Quarries on Anastasia Island, Near St. Augustine, Florida." National Park Service, 1945. C.
———. "Specifications for a Scale Model of the Town of Frederica in Georgia about 1742." National Park Service, 1960. 2 v. C.
Shiner, J. L. "The Colonial Houses on Broad Street, Frederica, Georgia." National Park Service, 1958. C.
Smith, Hale G. "Final Field Report of the Archaeological Investigations of the Arrivas House." Mimeograph, St. Augustine Historical Restoration and Preservation Commission, 1960. SAHS.
———. "Possible Bricks Manufactured in St. Augustine, Florida, by the Spanish During the First Half of the 18th Century." [Fla. State U., 1960]. 2 p. SAHS.
Stoney, Samuel G. Personal letters to Manucy. Nov. 29, 1960 and May 28, 1961. SAHS.

## Published Articles

Arnade, Charles W. "The Avero Story: An Early Saint Augustine Family with Many Daughters and Many Houses." *Florida Historical Quarterly*, v. 40, pp. 1-34.
Connor, Jeanette T. "Nine Old Wooden Forts of St. Augustine." *Florida Historical Quarterly*, v. 15, nos. 3 and 4.
Florida Historical Society. *The Florida Historical Quarterly*.
Frankfurter, Felix. "History in Brick and Stone and Mortar." *Journal of the American Institute of Architects*. February 1951.
Manucy, Albert. "Tapia or Tabby." *Journal of the Society of Architectural Historians*," v. 11, pp. 32-33. December 1952.
National Geographic Society. *The National Geographic Magazine*. February 1948.
*Revista del Instituto de Cultura Puertorriqueña*. San Juan, P. R., July-September 1960.
Siebert, Wilbur H. "Slavery in East Florida, 1776-1785." *Florida Historical Quarterly*, v. 10, no. 3.

# SOURCES
## Books

Arnade, Charles W. *The Siege of St. Augustine in 1702.* University of Florida Press. 1959.
──────. *Florida On Trial.* University of Miami Press, 1959.
Batsford, Harry, and Charles Fry. *The English Cottage.* London, 1950.
Bolton, Herbert E. *Spain's Title to Georgia.* Berkeley, 1925.
Boyd, Mark F., Hale G. Smith and John W. Griffin. *Here They Once Stood. The Tragic End of the Apalachee Missions.* University of Florida Press, 1951.
Byne, Arthur, and Mildred Stapley. *Spanish Interiors and Furniture.* N. Y., 1928. 2 v.
Chatelain, Verne E. *The Defenses of Spanish Florida, 1565-1763.* Washington, 1941.
Cotter, John L., and J. P. Hudson. *New Discoveries at Jamestown.* National Park Service, 1957.
Curley, Michael J. *Church and State in the Spanish Floridas (1783-1822).* Washington, 1940.
Dodd, Dorothy. *Florida The Land of Romance.* Tallahassee, 1957.
Doggett [Corse], Carita, *Dr. Andrew Turnbull and the New Smyrna Colony of Florida.* The Drew Press,[Jacksonville, Fla.,] 1919.
Forman, Henry C. *The Architecture of the Old South.* Harvard University Press, 1948.
──────. *Virginia Architecture in the Seventeenth Century.* Williamsburg, 1957.
Geiger, Maynard. *The Franciscan Conquest of Florida (1573-1618).* Washington, 1937.
Harrington, J. C., Albert Manucy, and J. M. Goggin. *Archeological Excavations in the Courtyard of Castillo de San Marcos.* St. Augustine, 1956.
Herbella y Pérez, Manuel. *Manual de Construcciones y de fortificación de campaña en Filipinas.* Imprenta del Memorial de Ingenieros, Madrid, 1882.
Jones, Charles C. Jr. *History of Georgia.* Boston, 1883. 2 v.
Jones, S. R. *English Village Homes.* London, 1947.
Kubler, George, and Martín Soria. *Art and Architecture in Spain and Portugal and Their American Dominions.* Baltimore, 1959.
Lowery, Woodbury L. *The Spanish Settlements Within the Present Limits of the United States.* G. P. Putnam's Sons, 1905.
Manucy, Albert. *The Building of Castillo de San Marcos.* Washington, 1942.
──────(ed.). *The History of Castillo de San Marcos and Fort Matanzas from Contemporary Narratives and Letters.* Washington, 1943.
[──────(ed.).] *Seeing St. Augustine* (American Guide Series). St. Augustine, 1937. SAHS.
Mowat, Charles L. *East Florida as a British Province 1763-1784.* Berkley, 1943.
Muller, John. *Treatise Containing the Practical Part of Fortification.* London, 1755.
Nichols, Frederick D. *The Early Architecture of Georgia.* University of N. C. Press, 1957.
Peterson, Charles E. *Colonial Saint Louis: Building a Creole Capital.* St. Louis, 1949.
Smith, Hale G. *The European and the Indian.* Gainesville, Fla., 1956.
Webber, Mabel L. (ed.). "Josiah Smith's Diary. 1780-1781." *The South Carolina Historical and Genealogical Magazine*, v. 33-34.
Weiss y Sánchez, Joaquín. *Arquitectura Cubana Colonial.* Havana, 1936.
West, Erdman, and Lillian Arnold. *The Native Trees of Florida.* University of Florida Press, 1946.

# NOTES

1. Hon. Justice Felix Frankfurter, "History in Brick and Stone and Mortar." *Journal of the American Institute of Architects*, February 1951.
2. San Agustín el Viejo was east of Matanzas Bay. The "new" St. Augustine was replanted at a less exposed site on the west side of the Bay. See [Dr. Caceres,] "Discurso sobre la población de la costa de la Florida . . ." [1574], Depósito Hidrográfico, Colección Navarrete, T. 14E No. 47. This manuscript is transcribed in Woodbury Lowery's "Florida MSS.," II. See also H. E. Bolton, *Spain's Title to Georgia*, 334; and C. W. Arnade, *Florida on Trial*.
3. J. T. Connor [ed. and trans.], *The Colonial Records of Florida*, I, 265.
4. Boazio, "S. Augustini" [map], in *Expeditio Francesci Draki* . . . ; Lt. Thomas Cates' account of the 1586 raid, in Manucy (ed.), *The History of Castillo de San Marcos and Fort Matanzas from Contemporary Narratives and Letters*, 7.
5. Fr. Andrés de San Miguel, "Relación de los Trabajos" in Genaro García (ed.), *Dos Antiguas Relaciones de la Florida*, 205-206. Savino [sic]: Fr. Andrés states that "along the river shores grow many very large *savinas* [sic], from which the Indians make large piraguas [dugouts]." This use would indicate either bald cypress (*Taxodium Distichum* (L.) L. C. Rich.), which grows to a height of 125 feet, or the smaller pond cypress (*Taxodium Ascendens* Brongn.). (See West and Arnold, *The Native Trees of Florida*, 11-12.) *Webster's International Dictionary* (1951) lists sabino as of Spanish origin and signifying bald cypress. Savina (note the *a* ending) may also be translated as savin, meaning red cedar, but under the circumstances this seems an unlikely rendition.
6. "Mapa del Pueblo, Fuerte y Caño de San Augustín," reproduced in V. E. Chatelain, *The Defenses of Spanish Florida*, map 4; Manucy, "Gonzalo Méndez de Canzo," 2.
7. Maynard Geiger, *The Franciscan Conquest of Florida*, 122.
8. Connor, II, 282: "son todas de madera y baro y encaladas por fuera y dentro. Y con sus acuteas de cal . . ." Menéndez Marqués, who wrote the description, said that half the 60 houses at Santa Elena were built this way.
9. For various masonry formulae, see St. Augustine Historical Society, "Excepts from Construction Specifications for Church in Ciales, Puerto Rico, c. 1844." See also M. Herbella, *Manual de Construcciones*.
10. Menéndez Marqués to crown, Dec. 27, 1583, cited in Connor, "Nine Old Wooden Forts," *Florida Historical Quarterly*, IV, 171.
11. Canzo to crown, Feb. 23, 1595, and Sept. 22, 1602, in "Florida MSS.," IV; Manucy, "Gonzalo Méndez de Canzo," 5. Canzo's term began in 1596. After he arrived at St. Augustine he ordered construction of "a house of stone and lime for the security of the powder and munitions" (*una casa de piedra y cal para la guardia de la pólbora y municiones*). The new structure replaced an earlier palm-thatched wooden shelter at the fort.
12. Geiger, 152, 187.
13. Geiger, 187.
14. Manucy, "Gonzalo Méndez de Canzo," 4; see also pp. 2, 6-7.
15. Rebolledo to crown, Oct. 24 1655.
16. Manucy, *The Building of Castillo de San Marcos*.
17. L. L. Wenhold, *A 17th Century Letter of Gabriel Diaz Vara Calderón*. 7.

# NOTES

18. Hita Salazar to crown, Dec. 15, 1680.
19. The magazine housed the armory and lieutenant's quarters. For a detailed report, see J. C. Harrington, A. C. Manucy and J. M. Goggin, "Archeological Excavations in the Courtyard of Castillo de San Marcos, "*Florida Historical Quarterly*, XXXIV, no. 2. See also Manucy (ed.), *The History of Castillo de San Marcos and Fort Matanzas from Contemporary Narratives and Letters*, 19.
20. Quiroga, Apr. 1, 1688, and June 8, 1690.
21. Nieto de Carvajal, Apr. 4, 1707 (AI 58-2-8, fols. 12429-12426). The folio numbers identify the photostat sheets. Also see Residencia de Zúñiga, 1707. Cuaderno 2, fols. 2847, 3430-3429, 3568; E. W. and C. L. Andrews (eds.) *Jonathan Dickinson's Journal*, 84-85.
22. Zúñiga to crown, Nov. 10, 1702. Nombre de Dios, traditionally the site of the first Mass when the settlement was officially established September 8, 1565, was an important Indian mission a short distance north of the fort. See Juan Joseph Elixio de la Puente, "Plano del Presidio de Sn. Agustín de la Florida," 1769.
23. Memorial of Alonso de Leturiondo [c. 1700], chapter XI.
24. C. W. Arnade, *The Siege of St. Augustine in 1702*, 4 ff.
25. Zúñiga autos, Nov. 11 and 14, 1702 (AI 58-2-8, fols. 12935-12932). A musket shot ranged about 250 yards. See Arnade, *The Siege of St. Augustine*, illustrations on pp. 38, 43.
26. M. F. Boyd (trans.), "The Siege of St. Augustine . . . in 1702 as Reported to the King of Spain by Don Joseph de Zúñiga y Zerda, Governor of Florida," *Florida Historical Quarterly*, XXVI, 349.
27. Council of the Indies, Apr. 30, 1703.
28. Nieto de Carvajal, Apr. 2, 1707, fol. 12452.
29. Arnade, "*The Siege of St. Augustine*," 58, citing the memorial of Fray Martín de Alacano, Aug. 2, 1703.
30. Royal Officials of Florida, Apr. 2, 1707, fols. 12476-12439; Córcoles to crown, Aug. 13, 1709.
31. See the 1764 map of Juan Joseph Elixio de la Puente, "Sn. Agustín de la Florida."
32. Córcoles to the crown, July 20, 1709.
33. Boyd *et al*, *Here They Once Stood*, 90; Nieto de Carvajal, Apr. 4, 1707, fols. 12429-12426); residencia of Zúñiga, 1707, cuaderno 2, fol. 3568.
34. Córcoles to the crown, Aug. 13, 1709.
35. Arrivas House, 44 St. George Street.
36. Franciscans to the crown, Sept. 28, 1713 (AI 58-2-16/2). See also Autos, Apr. 25, 1712.
37. Autos, June 14, 1717.
38. Certification by Juan Solana, Aug. 25, 1713.
39. Religious and others to the crown, Mar. 4, 1715.
40. AI 58-2-4/25, fol. 11570.
41. "Plan and View of St. Augustine Castle and Matance's Fort," [1743].
42. Palazio to Arriaga, Jan. 20, 1761; Juan José Eligio de la Puente, key to ms. map, "Sn. Agustín de la Florida," 1764.
43. William Stork, *A Description of East-Florida*, 12.
44. William G. DeBrahm, "History of the Three Provinces," 298.
45. John Bartram, *Diary of a Journey*, 52, 55.
46. Obviously Bartram is not using "terrace" in its presently accepted meaning. (See *post*, his phrase "roof of terrace," etc.) A natural cement known at the time was called "terrass" (John Muller, *Treatise Containing the Practical Part of Fortification*, 111-112), hence Bartram writes "terraced" much as we would write "cement." Presumably the construction he describes is tabby, although

145

# NOTES

not the coarse oyster shell tabby he later mentions. Castillo de San Marcos has a solid tabby roof and floors (see Manucy, "Tapia or Tabby," *Journal of the Society of Architectural Historians,* XI, 32-33). John Lee Williams (*The Territory of Florida,* 118) mentioned tabby floors and roofs still in use at St. Augustine during the 1830's. Today there are a few floors yet in existence, but no tabby roofs are preserved elsewhere than at the fort.

47. This is *tapia* or tabby construction. The technique is described in detail by Thomas Spalding in *The Southern Agriculturalist* of December 1830. Although Spalding's experience was with colonial and plantation tabby in Georgia, the basic technique (lime mortar mixed with shell aggregate and tamped into plank forms) is the same as the Spanish.
48. Elixio map key, 1764. The key has 393 identifications.
49. Bartram to P. Collinson, Aug. 26, 1766, in William Darlington, *Memorials of John Bartram and Humphry Marshall,* 283-284. Another innovation was a law prohibiting the use of roofing thatch in St. Augustine. However, since this regulation was not promulgated until 1783 (by which time British sovereignty was almost ended), the law may have been ineffective. See the *East Florida Gazette,* Feb. 28, 1783.
50. Siebert, *Loyalists in East Florida,* II (Claims), 152-153. Hereafter cited as *Loyalists* 2/.
51. *Loyalists* 2/113-120.
52. *Id.* 2/196.
53. *Id.* 2/87-89.
54. *Id.* 2/87-88.
55. Nichols, *The Early Architecture of Georgia,* 26.
56. *Collections of the Georgia Historical Society,* 1/23.
57. C. C. Jones, *History of Georgia* 1/156-160, quoting a December 21, 1733, deed then in the office of the Georgia Secretary of State.
58. Nichols, 26; S. R. Jones, *English Village Homes,* 88-89.
59. Nichols, 18.
60. Mowat, *East Florida as a British Province,* 30-31; *Loyalists* 2/127, 146-147, 180.
61. *Loyalists* 2/21, 22, 31, 36, 86.
62. *Id.* 2/84, 155-160.
63. *Id.* 1/208, 209; Schöpf, *Travels in the Confederation,* 2/231.
64. *Loyalists* 2/20-23, 30-32, 63-64, 70, 84, 88, 116-120, 126-128, 130-133, 144-145, 147, 152-153, 158-160, 179-180, 182, 189-190, 196.
65. Schöpf 2/229.
66. Mowat, 145-147; Loyalists; Mariano de la Rocque, "Noticia del estado en que se hallan las Casas de la Ciudad de Sn. Agustín de Florida," October 11, 1784.
67. Gov. Juan Quesada, letter of Jan. 8, 1793.
68. Schöpf 2/230-231.
69. Latrobe, *The Rambler in North America,* 35-36.
70. Manuel de Hita to Gov. Enrique White, April 1, 1807.
71. Manucy, "Commerce in East Florida," iii, 24-26, 38.
72. Arnade, "The Avero Story"; Dunkle, "The Avero Houses — A Location Analysis."
73. Manucy, "Commerce," 29-37, 42-45.
74. Rocque, "Descripción de Plano Particular de la Ciudad de Sn. Agustín de la Florida," 1788.
75. [Manucy, (ed.),] *Seeing St. Augustine,* 28-29.
76. Mariano de la Rocque, "Plano Particular de la Ciudad de Sn. Agustín de la Florida." The key is entitled "Description del Plano Particular de la Ciudad de San Agustín de la Florida Oriental = Año de 1788." Hereafter the plan and pertinent items in the key will be cited thus: 1788/1 (*etc.*).
77. Juan Joseph Elixio de la Puente, map "San Agustín de la Florida," with key. Hereafter cited thus: 1764/1 (*etc.*).
78. *Loyalists* 2/158-159.
79. Mabel L. Webber (ed.), Josiah Smith's Diary, 1780-1781." *The South Carolina Historical and Genealogical Magazine,* XXXIII, pp. 11-12.

See also 1764/178; 1788/97; "Ynventarios Tasaciones" (St. Augustine's Tax List of 1790), nos. 45, 21 and 88. Hereafter cited as 1790/22, etc.
80. William Stork, *A Description of East-Florida*, 12.
81. John Bartram, *Diary of a Journey Through the Carolinas, Georgia, and Florida from July 1 1765, to April 10, 1776*, p. 52; Stork, 12.
82. 1790/21, 45 and 88.
83. William G. DeBrahm, "History of the Three Provinces." 298.
84. Córcoles to the crown, July 20 and Aug. 13, 1709; autos, Apr. 25, 1712; Schöpf, 2/231.
85. Andrés de San Miguel, "Relación de los Trabajos," 205-206.
86. Connor, *The Colonial Records of Florida*, II, 282; Theodor de Bry, *America*, II, plate 30. The artist was Jacques LeMoyne, a member of the French Florida colony of 1564.
87. "Mapa del Pueblo, Fuerte y Caño de San Agustín," in Chatelain, *The Defenses of Spanish Florida*, map 4.
88. *Loyalists* 2/31, 64, 120.
89. *Id.* 2/70.
90. *Id.* 2/31, 184, 189.
91. *Id.* 2/204.
92. *Id.* 2/194.
93. *Id.* 2/36, 94, 129, 157, 192.
94. *Id.* 2/31.
95. Montiano to Güemes, No. 145, April 7, 1739 (East Florida Papers, v. 37, pp. 168 ff.; Loyalists 2/31. See also Manucy, "Report on a Field Trip to the Probable Site of Spanish Quarries on Anastasia Island"; and *ante*, nn. 13, 15.
96. Quiroga, April 1, 1688, and June 8, 1690.
97. 1790/36, 38, 69, 89, 188, 249. An exception to these standards was the former house of the royal treasurer, with a wall 1 *vara* thick on Treasury Street, and ½ *vara* on St. George. See 1790/174 and 249.
98. Hale G. Smith, "Final Field Report of the Archaeological Investigations of the Arrivas House," 11.
99. Bartram, 52:, 1790/36, 38, 69, 89, 188, 249.
100. 1788/129.
101. The data are compiled from the 1764 and 1788 maps.
102. Cf. 1788/113, 115, 124 and others showing these practices.
103. *Loyalists* 2/20, 31.
104. *Id.* 2/20, 84, 113, 117, 120, 128, 130, 132, 152, 189.
105. *Id.* 2/189.
106. *Id.* 2/189. Also see especially 1788/45, 46, 106, 110, etc.; 1788/101, 123; 1788/208, 250, etc.; and 1788/124.
107. 1788/20, 72.
108. Justís to the Governor of Cuba, March 22, 1737, and two letters of August 12, 1737.
109. Hale G. Smith, "Possible Bricks Manufactured in St. Augustine, Florida"; personal observations at Arrivas House excavations.
110. British Public Record Office Papers, Colonial Office 5/556, no. 14, p. 593; personal observations at Arrivas House excavations.
111. Cf. H. G. Smith, *The European and the Indian*.
112. Based on measured drawings of 20 existing houses, and 1790/21, 32, 36, 38, 45, 66, 69, 89, 112, 124, 174, 188, 227, 229, 249.
113. 1788/91, 92, 98, 100, 115, 139, 172, 245; 1790/21, 38, 66, 69, 112, 174, 188; *Loyalists* 2/147, 189.
114. *Loyalists* 2/31, 158; cf. 119.
115. DeBrahm, 298.
116. *Loyalists* 2/20, 120, 126.
117. "Plano inferior y superior de la Casa del Rey destinada para Aduana Tesorería y Contaduría de esta Plaza . . . 1787," (hereafter cited as Rocque, 1787); Ramón de la Cruz, [description of the] "Accountants Office, Treasury & Custom House." 1821, (hereafter cited as Cruz, 1821).
118. Bartram, 52; *Loyalists* 2/20, 31, 46, 120, 126, 189.
119. *Loyalists* 2/20-23.
120. "View From the Governors Window in St. Augustine E. Florida. Novr: 1764"; 1790/98.

# NOTES

121. Stork, 12.
122. These and the related conclusions are based upon study of the 1788 plan and key, the various property appraisals and existing buildings.
123. Bartram, 52; 1790/229.
124. DeBrahm, 298.
125. 1790/45.
126. *Loyalists* 2/189.
127. Certification by Juan Solana, August 25, 1713 (AI 58-1-28/109); 1790/36, 38; *Loyalists* 2/118.
128. Bartram, 52.
129. Rocque, 1787; Cruz, 1821.
130. Bartram, 52.
131. Juan de Cotilla, 1763 appraisal of Antonio de Rodríguez-Juan de Salas property (357/6 folio 1), in Arnade, "Architectural Information."
132. Pablo Castelló, 1763 appraisal of the governor's house (AI 86-7-11/23); Juan de Cotilla, 1763 appraisal of Rodríguez Salas property (357/6, folio 1); both in Arnade, "Architectural Information."
133. *Loyalists* 2/20, 126, 179, 189.
134. Bartram, 52.
135. *East Florida Gazette,* Feb. 28, 1783.
136. Juan Joseph Solana, April 22, 1759.
137. 1788 key.
138. Quiroga, April 1, 1688, and June 8, 1690.
139. Edward Kimber, "Itinerant Observations in America," *Collections of the Georgia Historical Society,* IV; *Loyalists* 2/64, 157.
140. *Loyalists* 2/158.
141. Id. 2/23, 31, 36, 64, 152; cf. Peterson, *Colonial St. Louis.*
142. Connor, *Colonial Records,* II, 282.
143. "Descrezión de la Planta del Castillo . . ." The Spanish expression is "tablones de varia de pino de quatro dedos de grueso." Four *dedos* = 2¾ inches.
144. Castelló appraisals of 1763, especially the governor's house, guardhouse, and the hospital. Although Solana's 1759 report states that the hospital was also plank-roofed, the 1763 appraisal indicates otherwise; the roofs were all shingled.
145. Juan Joseph Solana, 1759; Stork, 12; 1788 key.
146. 1788/5, 42, 92-95, 99, 107, 127, 141, 185.
147. *Collections of the Georgia Historical Society,* I, 134, 140, 146; 1788/48; Isidoro de León to the governor of Florida, May 21, 1745 (AI 58-2-13/19), in Wenhold, *op. cit.;* Peterson, *Colonial St. Louis.*
148. *Loyalists* 2/20; 1788/226.
149. Manucy, "The Cathedral of St. Augustine"; Cruz, 1821.
150. Jacques LeMoyne de Morgues, plate 30 in Theodor de Bry, *America;* "Mapa del Pueblo, Fuerte y Caño de San Agustín" (AI 140-7-37).
151. "View of the Governors house . . .", cited above.
152. Cruz, 1821; "View of the Governors house"; 1788/88, 92, 93; measurements of existing houses.
153. Bartram, 52; 1790/89.
154. Cruz, 1821.
155. *Ibid.*
156. *Loyalists* 2/30-32, 147, 189-190.
157. 1790/2, 3.
158. Isidoro de León to the Governor of Florida, May 21, 1745.
159. Castelló appraisal of governor's house, hospital and blacksmith shop; Cotilla's appraisal of the Salvador de Porras house.
160. *Loyalists* 2/31, 118, 196.
161. Id. 2/94, 157, 164, 192, 194, 204; Collections of the *Georgia Historical Society,* I, 23.
162. See Manucy, "Tapia or Tabby," *Journal of the Society of Architectural Historians,* XI, 32-33, for additional detail.
163. Bartram, 52. In two-story houses, the bedrooms (chambers) were customarily on the second floor. See also the Cotilla appraisals of the Rodríguez-Salas and Blanco houses; Castelló appraisal of the governor's house.
164. Cotilla and Castelló appraisals; 1788/17, 24, 65; 1790/38; Cruz, 1821.

## NOTES

165. *Loyalists* 2/84.
166. *Id.* 2/158; *cf.* 63-64.
167. *Id.* 2/118, 180, 196.
168. Cotilla appraisal of the Rodríguez-Salas property. Ceiling carpentry *(cielos-rasos)* was appraised separately from roof carpentry *(techos azotea)*, and was of almost equal value.
169. Cotilla and Castelló appraisals.
170. Bartram, 52, 55.
171. *Loyalists* 2/84, 117-118, 126, 132-133, 189, 196.
172. *Id.* 2/64, 118, 189, 196.
173. Autos, June 14, 1717; 1788/42; 1790/36, 89.
174. Cruz, 1821; Bartram, 55; Cotilla appraisal of the Porras house; Castelló appraisal of the governor's house.
175. Bartram, 52; 1790/45.
176. Bartram, 52; DeBrahm, 298.
177. Loyalists 2/21, 130.
178. Castelló appraisal of the hospital, guardhouse, and governor's house; Cotilla's appraisal of the Porras house; Bartram, 52.
179. Castelló appraisal of the governor's house; Rocque, 1787; Cruz, 1821. About the same time a 4-compartment, shingle-roofed latrine was built at the barracks. It had receptacles that could be removed for cleaning. See Rocque's report on the condition of crown property in 1788.
180. John Rodman and Elias Wallen, Articles of Agreement, October 12, 1833; *House of Representatives Report,* 25th Congress, 3rd Session, p. 223; *Loyalists* 2/31.
181. Castelló appraisal; *Loyalists* 2/21, 126, 157-159, 189.
182. Castelló appraisal of the governor's house; Cotilla appraisal of the Porras house; *Loyalists,* 2/31, 118, 126, 128, 180, 196.
183. *Loyalists,* 2/189, 196.
184. 1790/38, 45, 89, 124, 129; *Collections of the Georgia Historical Society,* I, 82-83.
185. Nieto de Carvajal, April 4, 1707, folios 12429-12426; Castelló appraisal of the governor's house; Rocque's report on the condition of crown property in 1788.
186. 1788 key, concluding note.
187. Cruz, 1821.
188. *Loyalists,* 2/31, 36, 118, 189.
189. *Id.*, 2/21, 23, 84, 189, 196.
190. *Id.*, 2/31, 36, 84, 118, 189; *cf.* 32.
191. *Id.*, 2/31, 36, 84, 189.
192. Bartram, 52; 1788/18; 1790/38, 45, 202-203.
193. Cotilla appraisal of Rodríguez-Salas house; Cruz, 1821.
194. Cotilla appraisal of Rodríguez-Salas house; *Loyalists,* 2/114, 196.
195. *Loyalists,* 2/114, 118; Rodman and Wallen, cited above.
196. Peterson, cited above, 23; *Loyalists,* 2/118; Connor, *Colonial Records,* II, 282.

## NOTES ON PICTURES

**Abbreviations:**
- 1764 = Elixio map and key of this date
- 1788 = Rocque map and key of this date
- 1790 = Ynventario Tasaciones (Tax List)
- SAHS = St. Augustine Historical Society

No.
1. After SAHS photo.
2. 1788/88, 92-95; SAHS photos.
4. Line facsimile of "Mapa del Pueblo."
5. After photo, *National Geographic Magazine* (Feb. 1948), 224.
6. After Manucy, *The Building of Castillo de San Marcos,* 6, 9.
7. After 1675 and 1680 Hita Salazar plans. Harrington *et al,* 104 ff.
9. After H. G. Smith, "Archaeological Investigations of the Arrivas House."
10. After "View from the Governor's Window."
11. After "View of the Governor's House."

# NOTES ON PICTURES

12. After SAHS photo.
13. After Barnette's reconstruction at 31 St. Francis.
14. Description in Spalding's letter to Whiting, July 29, 1844.
16-17 After SAHS photos.
18. After SAHS photo.
19. Line facsimile of 1788 block by T. R. Johnson, in SAHS.
21. A: 1764/64, 1788/45 (masonry-tabby), 1790/101.
    B: 1764/61, 1788/49 (masonry, thatch roof).
    C: 1764/170, 1788/88 (2-story masonry), 1790/19 (outside chimney later).
    D: 1788/9 (wood, thatch roof), 1790/49.
    E: 1764/238, 1788/189 (wood), 1790/232.
    F: 1764/66, 1788/44 (2-story masonry), 1790/102.
    G: 1764/168, 1788/86 (2-story, masonry-wood), 1790/16-17.
    H: 1788/14 (wood).
    I: 1764/340, 1788/249 (tabby), 1790/192.
    J: 1764/103, 1788/70 (masonry), 1790/70.
    K: 14 St. George (1½-story timber-frame).
    L: 62 Spanish (2-story stone).
22. A1-2, B1: conjectural; B2, E1: SAHS photos; C, C1: 14 St. George; C2: 250 St. George; D, D1: 224 St. George; D2: 20 St. Francis; E, E2: 62 Spanish.
23. 31 St. Francis, based in part on Barnette's "Restoration of the Llambias House," II, plates 85-88.
24. A: 1764/162, 1788/115 (tabby), 1790/69; B: 1764/147, 1788/100 (2-story masonry, 1790/66; C: 1764/81, 1788/5 (masonry, part 2-story, flat roof), 1790/45; D: 1788/90 (masonry-wood); E: 42 Spanish (stone); F: 1764/205, 1788/127 (masonry), 1790/27; G: 12 Avilés (2½-story masonry).
25. A: 1764/205, 1788/127, 101 Charlotte; B: 54 St. George; C: 14 St. Francis; D: 42 Spanish.
26. A: 1764/274, 1788/193 (masonry), 1790 / 177; B: 20 Avilés; C: 1764/193, 1788/141 (masonry), 1790/89, 143 St. George.
27. Left: 20 Avilés; right: 16 Marine.
28. A: After photo, courtesy R. H. Stewart, National Geographic Society; B: after Peterson, *Colonial St. Louis*, pl. 3-7; C: after LeMoyne, pl. 30; D: conjectural, after "Mapa del Pueblo"; E: personal observation.
29. A: After SAHS photo of Marine St.; B: 14 St. Francis; George Watson, personal statement; C: Watson, personal statement; D: 14 St. Francis; E: 40 Bridge St. (recent).
30-31 Personal observation.
32. H. G. Smith, "Archaeological Investigation of the Arrivas House," (House 1) p. 11; personal observation; south lot boundary wall, 214 St. George.
33. Personal observation.
34. Smith's excavations at San Francisco near Tallahassee recovered clay daub imprinted with wattles (see Boyd *et al, Here They Once Stood*, pl. 7-8). Plaster-daub huts are extant in the West Indies. Corner posts and other members, including plates, are framed with barked logs. All joints are mortised. Sometimes the uprights are anchored in a base wall of masonry, of rectangular section and about 3 feet high. The plaster is lime mortar mixed with clay, and painted with whitewash.
35. B: conjectural restoration after 1790/89; F, K, N, O, P, R: conjectural restoration of ground floor openings; X: restored after SAHS c. 1886 photo.
36. 1790.
37. A-C: after Byne and Stapley, *Spanish Interiors and Furniture*, II, pl. 217; D: San Juan, P. R. (SAHS photo no. 1841).
38. Personal observations, especially at 14 St. Francis, 44 St. George, Castillo de San Marcos.
39. 20 Avilés.
40. After Rocque, 1787.

## NOTES ON PICTURES

41. A: personal observation at Castillo de San Marcos; B: same at 62 Spanish and elsewhere.
42. After Weiss, *Arquitectura Cubana Colonial*, pl. 150.
43. After San Juan, P. R. (SAHS photo no. 1811); Bartram.
44. Frederik C. Gjessing, personal statements re Puerto Rican colonial practice; Byne and Stapley; Bartram; B: conjectural, after SAHS photo no. 1841; C: SAHS photos.
45. Personal observation at 42 Spanish and elsewhere.
46. A-C: William F. Sánchez, personal statements re local practice, 14 St. Francis and elsewhere; C: after SAHS photos.
47. A: 14 St. George; B-C, H-J, N: after SAHS photos; D: 46 Bridge; E, O: after SAHS photos of 65 St. George; F: 105 St. George; G: 62 Spanish, L: 32 Avilés wall; after SAHS photos of Avilés at Green; M: 42 Spanish.
48. A: 143 St. George; B: 14 St. Francis; C: 42 Spanish; D: 12 Avilés.
49. 101 Charlotte.
50-51 After SAHS photos.
52. Conjectural, after Bartram, using Puerto Rican elements (SAHS photos nos. 1814, 1829, 1831).
53. 31 St. Francis.
54. 20 Avilés, 44 St. George, SAHS photos.
55. Barnette's reconstruction at 31 St. Francis; Bartram.
56. 20 Avilés; A: *Revista del Instituto de Cultura Puertorriqueña*, no. 8, p. 37.
57. A, C, F, H-M: after SAHS photos; B: 14 St. Francis, 43 Marine; D: 14 St. George, 54 St. George; E, G: 31 St. Francis.
58. After Bob Halgrim photos of Seminole construction (1960).
59. A: after Halgrim photos; B: after J. C. Harris photos of construction in Bahama Islands, B.W.I.
60. Personal observation.
61. A: after SAHS photo, shack just south of fort; B: conjectural.
62. Conjectural.
63. Personal observation.
64. 44 St. George; San Juan, P. R., observations by W. F. Sánchez, F. C. Gjessing, and writer.
65. 1764/269, 1788/220 (tabby), 1790/239; after SAHS photo (southwest corner of Avilés and Green).
66. See table in text.
67. A: 31 St. Francis, after Barnette; B: 62 Spanish; C: 42 Spanish.
68. After SAHS photos.
69. Ravelin, Castillo de San Marcos.
70. A: after SAHS photos of 43 St. George; B, C, F: after SAHS photos of Charlotte St. houses; D: 105 St. George; E: 20 St. Francis.
71. A: 54 St. George; B: 46 Bridge; C: 20 Avilés.
72. A, D: conjectural; B, C: 14 St. Francis, 44 St. George, 214 St. George.
73. After Smith, "Archaeological Investigations of the Arrivas House."
74. A-B, D-F: 44 St. George; C: 42 Spanish; H: balcony joist, 20 Charlotte.
75. Conjectural, after Bartram; and personal observation.
76. After Bartram; personal observation.
77. Personal observation.
78. A: personal observation, typical; B: 31 St. Francis; C: 42 Spanish.
79. Masonry: 1790, 20 Charlotte, 32 Avilés wall, personal observation. Yucca: 1788. Wood: 1788; Rocque Dec. 31, 1788, report; *Loyalists* 2/21; SAHS photos; personal observation.
80. After SAHS photos; A: southwest corner Avilés and Green; B: northwest corner St. George and Cathedral; D: Marine; E: 44 St. George; C: 46 Bay (gate is conjectural reconstruction).

# GLOSSARY

*Key to references* (see Bibliography for complete citation of titles):
Arana:   L. R. Arana, personal communication.
Gjessing:   F. W. Gjessing, personal communication.
Peterson:   C. E. Peterson, *Colonial St. Louis.*
Smith:   H. G. Smith, "Bricks."
1580:   Connor, *Colonial Records,* 2/282.
1583:   Connor, *Fla. Hist. Quarterly,* 4/171.
1595:   García, 205-206.
1598:   Canzo to crown, Feb. 23 (Lowery, IV).
1686:   Discrezión de la planta del Castillo.
1688:   Petición de Ana Ruiz.
1709:   Córcoles to crown, Aug. 13.
1713:   Juan Solana certification, Aug. 25.
1715:   Religious and others to crown, Mar. 4.
1737:   Justis to Güemes, Mar. 22.
1745:   Wenhold in *Fla. Hist. Quarterly,* 35/248-249.
1756:   *Cartografía de Ultramar,* V. 2/68.
1759:   Solano to crown, Apr. 22.
1760:   Palacios to Arriaga, Jan. 20.
1763A:   Cotilla, property appraisals.
1763B:   Castelló, property appraisals.
1764:   Puente, property map and key.
1765A:   Bartram, 52, 55.
1765B:   Stork, 12.
1765C:   Darlington, *Memorials,* 283-284.
1765D:   DeBrahm, 298.
1776:   British Public Record Office, CO 5/556.
1780:   Siebert, *Loyalists, II.*
1784:   Rocque, "Noticia del Estado," Oct. 11.
1788:   Rocque, property map and key.
1790:   Quesada, "Ynventarios Tasaciones."
1821:   Cruz, "Description of Public Buildings," No. 7.
1844:   Spalding letter, July 29.
1849:   U. S., Executive Document 21, Jan. 30.

**alacena, alasena.**
Pantry, storeroom. (1763A: Blanco.)
**albañilería,**
   **alvañilería.**
Masonry. (1763A: Blanco, Salas.) See *mampostería.*
**alfarda.**
Stud, light wooden beam. *Tabiques de a., rajones, y enlucido* (1788-65): partitions framed in wood, split laths, and plastered.
**alto.**
Story, floor, height.—*De a.:* 2-story.—*Casa de mampostería de un a. en una de las divisiones* (1788/6): masonry house with a 2-story section.—*Casa de mampostería con a. de madera* (1788/103): masonry house with wooden second story.—*Casa de madera de dos altos* (1788/109): 3-story frame house.—*Una pared con 14 varas de largo y 3½ de a.* (1790/45): a wall 14 varas long and 3½ high.—*Dos paredes de un a. con 12 varas de largo y 4 de a.* (1790/45): on one floor, two walls 12 varas long and 4 high. See *cuerpo, piso.* Fig. 36.
**aposento.**
Room, bedroom. (1763A: Blanco.)
**arcade.**
A series of arches supported on piers or pillars; an arched, roofed, or covered passageway.—"A row of pillars or arches generally supports a roof continuing from the common roof" (1765A). See *corrido de arcos.* Figs. 48, 49.

# GLOSSARY

**arco.**
Arch.—*Dos arcos de medio puntos con tres pilares de cantería* (1790/45): two round arches with three squared-stone pillars. Figs. 48, 49.

**argamasa.**
Mortar. (1686). See *ormigón*.

**argamasar.**
To make mortar; to cement with mortar.

**armadura.**
Framing; shell of a building; framework; trestle.—*Armaduras y suelos en mal estado* (1788/5): framing and floors in bad condition.

**armario.**
Wardrobe.—*Armarios de madera pintada* (1763A: Rodríguez - Salas): painted wooden wardrobes.

**arris.**
The sharp edge formed by the meeting of two surfaces.

**asentar.**
To place, fix, seat, adjust, sink, settle.—*Donde van asentadas las vigas para los quarteles* (1686): where the roof beams for the quarters are seated.

**ashlar**
Masonry of squared stones in regular courses, bonded uniformly and set with fine joints. (Not usually applicable to St. Augustine work.) See rubble.

**atajadiso,**
    **atajadizo.**
Partition.—*A. de tablas* (1763A: Porras): board partition. See *tabique*.

**azotea,**
    **acutea,**
        **sotea.**
Flat roof, generally a tabby slab supported by solid board sheathing. Also a flat roof made of two or more layers of brick-like tile supported upon spaced wooden slats. Mortar is laid between each layer of tile. Each tile is about ¾ x 5 x 10¼".—*Açuteas de cal* (1580): flat roofs of tabby.—23 of 303 houses were *piedras y sotea* (1759): squared stone masonry and flat roofs.—*Edificio hecho de sotea* (1759): flat-roofed building.—*Vigas y tablas de la a. del cuerpo de guardia* (1763B: governor's house): beams and boards of the flat roof at the guardhouse.— "Flat roofs are terraced [*i.e.*, made of tabby] on the top," with stone battlements (1765A).—"Roofs are commonly flat" (1765B).—*Techos de azoteas* (1788/5): flat roofs, possibly of azotea tiles. See *teja*; also *caño*. Figs. 62-65.

**azulejos.**
Glazed tile.—*Chimeneas con frentes de a.* (1763A: Rodríguez-Salas): fire places faced with glazed tile.

**balcón.**
Balcony; a balustraded platform extending from the wall of a building.
—Coins were thrown to the crowd from the balconies of the Governor's House (1713). — *B. de 12 varas* (1763A: Porras): a balcony 12 *varas* long.—*B. a la calle de 18 varas con techado de texamaní y cielo razo* (1763A: Rodríguez-Salas): street balcony 18 *varas* long with shingle roof and flat ceiling [this balcony was painted and had three glazed windows and a door].—*12½ varas de b.* (1763B: Governor's House): balcony 12½ *varas* long.—*B. en dicho alto* (1763B: Blanco): upper balcony.—"All or most [houses are] with pleasant covered balconies" (1765A).—"Commonly [houses are] with large windows and balconies" (1765B).—"Built a large framed wooden house 3 rooms on a floor and a balcony in front, 2 stories high" (1780/118).—*Un b. de la calle* (1790/36) and *un b. a la calle* (1790/38): a street balcony. Figs. 50-54, 70.

**baluster.**
One of a set of posts or uprights supporting a handrail and, with the handrail, forming a balustrade. Figs. 54-56.

**barraca.**
Hut; in Spain, a hut with floor excavated below ground level (Arana).
—*De las 133 casas de madera, 111 son barracas de ninguna consideración* (1788 *nota*): of 133 wooden houses, 111 are worthless huts. (The reference is doubtless to English-built shacks of the 1780's.)

**barro, baro.**
Clay, mud, daub.—*De madera y baro* (1580): puncheon and clay or post and pan.—*Cujes y b.* (1788/72): wattle and daub. Cf. *embarrado, palisado*.

153

# GLOSSARY

**batten.**
A strip of wood used for nailing across two or more other pieces (as the halves of shutters) to hold them together, or for covering the joint or crack between two boards. Figs. 28D, 44.

**bead.**
A narrow half-round molding.

**bidriera.**
See *vidriera*.

**board.**
*Tabla:* a piece of sawed lumber usually not more than 2½" thick and from 6 to 12" wide. See batten, deal, plank, *tabla*. Figs. 4, 28-29.

**bomba.**
Large water jar. (1763A: Rodríguez-Salas.)

**brick.**
*Ladrillo:* a structural unit of burned clayey material, in the form of a rectangular block. Samples of brick and tile made at St. Augustine were sent to Havana in 1737. Soon afterward 8,000 brick were received from Havana to build a kiln at St. Augustine, but the records do not indicate a thriving manufactory (1737). Because "good bricks are made here," brick was later proposed for the barracks construction (1776), and used for the first floor walls and for chimneys (1848). Brick was also used for a partition in the Customs House prior to 1787 (1821). No colonial brickmasonry seems to have survived, but a significant number of 18th century fragments and a few whole bricks have been found. They are of unequal quality and there are some very poor ones which may well be of local manufacture. In the table below, which is based on Smith ("Bricks"), Gjessing, and personal observations by Karl Masters and the writer, asterisks mark specimens found in St. Augustine:

| SIZE (inches) | DATE | IDENTIFICATION | ORIGIN |
|---|---|---|---|
| *1 7/8 x 3 3/4 x ? | pre-1750 | local kiln spoil? | Arrivas House, A, B, D, E |
| *1 7/8 x 3 3/4 x ? | Pre-1750 | Havana? | Arrivas House, G |
| 2 x 3 5/8 x 7 1/4 | c. 1800 | — | Fort George slave quarters |
| *2 1/8 x 3 1/4 x 7 | c. 1800? | Spanish ? red | Arrivas House, H |
| *2 1/4 x 3 1/2 x 7 1/2 | c. 1800? | Spanish ? red | Arrivas House, H |
| 2 x 4 1/2 x 11 1/2 | — | Spanish | Puerto Rico |
| 2 x 5 1/2 x 11 1/4 | 1500's | Spanish | Puerto Rico, El Morro |
| 2 1/4 x 4 x 11 | — | Spanish | (Britannica) |
| *2 3/4 x 4 5/8 x 9 | c. 1780 | English ? orange | Arrivas House I |
| *2 7/8 x 4 3/4 x 9 1/2 | c. 1780 | English ? orange | Arrivas House, I |
| 3 x 4 x 9 | c. 1750 | Old Virginia | (Britannica) |
| 2 1/4 x 3 3/4 x 8 | modern | U. S. | (Britannica) |

**cal.**
Lime; lime mortar, plaster; tabby. In Florida lime was calcined from shells, usually oyster shells from Indian middens.—*Azoteas de c.* (1580): flat roof of tabby.—*C. muerta:* slaked lime.—*C. viva:* quicklime.—*C. y canto* (1764/1): mortar and squared stone (masonry at Castillo de San Marcos).—"Lime brought 20 miles" (1780/31).

**campana.**
Mantel of fireplace. (763A: Rodríguez-Salas.)

**canal.**
Gutter. (1763A: Rodríguez-Salas.)

**cantería.**
Art of cutting stone; building made of squared stone; unit of squared stone.—*Casa de c.* (1788/5): *casa de piedra* (1764/81): squared stone masonry.—*Pilares de c.* (1790/45):

# GLOSSARY

square stone pillars.—*C. de rafa* (1763A: Rodríguez-Salas): buttressed masonry (?).—"The best houses are generally built of hewn shell stone" (1765A).

**canto.**
Quarry stone: block (1764/1.) See *cal*.

**caño.**
Spout, pipe, gutter, ditch, conduit; specifically a clay tile spout.—Nine *caños vidriados de las azoteas* (1790/89): 9 vitrified spouts from the flat roofs. See *azotea*. Figs. 62, 69.

**carpintería.**
Carpentry.—*C. de 5 puertas, 2 ventanas, piso de dentro y techo* (1790/21): carpentry of 5 doors, 2 windows, interior floor, and roof.

**casa.**
House.

**cáscara de ciprés.**
Bark of the cypress tree (probably bald or pond cypress).—*Cobija de c. d. c.* (1788/48): roof of cypress bark.—Bark roofs were not uncommon elsewhere in primitive societies (Peterson, 21). C. warehouses mentioned at Apalache (1745) were probably storehouses sheathed or roofed with bark; "from May on is the time for stripping the bark." However, the latter references may relate to the gathering of bark for trade or medicine.

**casita.**
Small house. (1790/104.)

**castellation.**
Battlement. See merlon.

**caballeriza, cavalleriza.**
Stable. (1773B: Governor's House.)

**cerca.**
Fence, wall, hedge.—*C. principal de la calle* (1688): principal wall on the street.—*La c. que linda de la parte de Alonso García falta de rajones* (1688): the fence along the García property line needs pales; *c. del corral* (1763B: Governor's House): yard fence.—*1020 estacas de la c. de dicha huerta* (1763B: Governor's House): 1020 stakes in the fence of the said garden.—*Todas las cercas de las casas y solares, la mayor parte son de rajones de madera, algunas de tablas, y otras de espinos* (1788 *nota*): most of all the fences of the houses and lots are wooden pales, some are board and others yucca.—"Most garden and yard walls were built of tabby" (1765A).—Many clapboard fences, common in British colonies, were built in St. Augustine (1780/20ff.).—*Una c. de mampostería con 13 varas de largo y 2 de alto* (1790/38): a masonry fence 13 *varas* long and 2 high. See *muro, ostión,* pale, *pared, rajón, tabique.* Fig. 79.

**chamfer.**
A diagonal cutting off of an arris; the flat surface created by slicing off the square edge of a corner of wood or stone. Fig. 54.

**chimenea.**
Chimney.—*c. campanario y picota* (1763B): bell tower and finial (?).—*C. en la cozina con su campana y cañon de 12 varas* (1763A: Rodríguez): chimney in the kitchen with mantle and flue 12 *varas* high.—*2 chimeneas en la sala con frentes de azulejos* (1763A: Rodríguez): 2 chimneys in the drawing room with glazed tile fronts.—"There were no chimneys, but English officers are having them built" (1765A).—"The English drive the chimney through the tops of the house roofs" (1765 C).—"No house had any chimney for a Fire-place" (1765D).—"A new stone chimney" (1780/126, 189).—Brick chimneys (1780/179).—*Dos chimeneas de tercia de grueso* (1790/112): 2 chimneys 11" thick; *casa de madera con una c.* (1790/148). Fig. 57.

**chiquero.**
Pigpen. (1688.)

**cielo.**
Ceiling; roof.—*C. raso* [of a balcony] (1763A: Rodríguez-Salas): flat [i.e., plastered] ceiling; compare with *maderas de los techos azoteas* (ibidem).

**cimientos.**
Foundations.—*Casa de madera, c. de piedra* (1790/77): wooden house, stone foundations.

**clapboard.**
In England originally a size of board, especially of split oak, used for making staves and wainscoting. In the American colonies it came to mean a narrow board, often thicker at one edge than the other, used for weatherboarding frame buildings, for roofing and fences. Usually clapboards were laid horizontally and overlapped.

# GLOSSARY

—"One framed house covered with feather edge boards, and a clap board kitchen" (1780/64). — "A small wooden house with a c. roof" (1780/36).—"A small boarded house with a c. roof" (1780/152).—"A necessary of rough boards and roofed with the same" (1780/31).—"C. fence 4 or 5 feet high" (1780/118), "6 feet high" (1780/36, 189), "6½ feet high" (1780/189).—"A partition c. fence" (1780/64). — "Clapboards were mostly rotten [so had to refence] with pine boards" (1780/31). —"A common c. fence . . . [with] clapboards nailed upright" (1780/23). See *tabla, rajón*, weatherboard. Fig. 28E, 29, 61, 79.

**cobertizo.**
Hut, shed.—*Cobertizos de mampostería, cobertizos de madera* (1784): masonry huts; wooden shacks.

**cobija.**
Cover, roof.—*C. de palma* (1788/10): palm thatch roof.—*C. de rajones* 1788/1): shingle roof.—*C. de teja* (1788/226): tile roof. See *azotea, techo.*

**cocina, cosina.**
Kitchen.—*Un pretil en el patio de rajones que corría desde la puerta de la calle hasta la c.* (1688): In the patio a fence of pales which ran from the street gate to the kitchen.—*Casa de mampostería con la cosina de madera* (1788/42): masonry house with a wooden kitchen.—*Dos diviciones de la c. con 10 varas de largo y 4 de alto y una tercia de grueso* (1790/89): 2 partitions in the kitchen, 10 varas long, 4 high and 11" thick.—23 *varas de mampostería de largo de las paredes de la c. y 3 de alto* (1790/36): masonry of the kitchen walls 23 varas long and 3 high.—*Una chimenea en dicha c.* (1790/36): a chimney in the said kitchen. See kitchen.

**cajón.**
Drawer of a piece of furniture. (1763A: Rodríguez-Salas.)

**colgadizo.**
Shed; shed roof; gallery.—The guardhouse had *un c. de tabla* (1759): a gallery built of boards.—*C. ó corredor* (1788/153): gallery or corridor.

**comedor.**
Dining room. (1759.)

**court.**
Inclosure, yard; a clear space wholly or partly enclosed by a wall or the like, or by buildings.

**courtyard.**
A court; or space enclosed by walls.

**coquina.**
Spanish for shellstone: a conglomerate composed of fragments of marine shells. Fig. 6.

**coquina chippings.**
The detritus that results from cutting coquina into blocks. The spalls were used as aggregate in some types of masonry, or as fillers and spacers. The finer chippings, being quite "sharp," compacted efficiently and were sometimes used as pavement, as a foundation for and an aggregate in tabby floor or pavement, and as "dry" patching for pavement.

**coquina shell or 'gravel.'**
The unconsolidated mixture of sand and shell found between the strata of coquina. It was sometimes used in making tabby.

**corbie-steps.**
(From Old French *corb* = raven.) A series of step-like projections on the sloping sides of a gable; crow-steps. Fig. 35S.

**corral.**
Yard, especially that part of the yard devoted to garden (1688).

**corrido de arcos.**
Row of arches (1759). See arcade.

**costado.**
Wing of a building; side—*Los dos costados 30 varas y 5 de alto* (1790/66): the two sides 30 *varas* long and 5 high.

**cuartel.**
Quarter, district; quarters, barracks, dwelling.—*C. de dragones* (1790/229): dragoon barracks.

**cuarto.**
Room, chamber, hall.—*Un c. del patio* (1790/45): a room on the patio.—*Cuartos altos* (1763A: Rodríguez-Salas): upper rooms.

**cubierta, cubierto.**
Covered, roofed; roof, shed, cover.—The 1759 document lists:
 23 *piedras y sotea*: 23 stone walls and flat roof
 64 *tablas y guano*: 64 board walls and palm thatch roof
 26 *techadas de taxamaní ú tablazón de la misma*: 26 roofed with shingles or planks

# GLOSSARY

*190 cubiertas de paja:* 190 covered with thatch.

The phraseology of the listing suggests that both roof and walls of the 190 houses were thatched.—*Casa terrera de mampostería cuvierta de taxamaní* (1790/): masonry hut roofed with shingles.

**cuerpo.**
Body; entire part of a building up to the cornice or entablature; floor (story) of a building; mass.—*Casa de tabique de hostión el primer c., y el segundo de madera* (1788/189): house with a first floor of thin-walled tabby and second floor of wood. See *alto, piso.*

**cuje.**
Withe; horizontal pole.—*Casa, la mitad de cuje, y embarrado, con algunos pilares de mampostería, y la otra mitad de madera, cobija de rajones* (1788/20): house, half wattled and roughly plastered, with some masonry pillars; and the other half wood; roof of shakes.—*Casa de cujes y barro* (1788/72): house of wattle and daub. Fig. 34.

**culata.**
Rear part; rooms at the rear (1763A: Rodríguez-Salas).

**deal.**
(England and American colonies.) A board of fir or pine cut to any of several specified sizes. *Standard deals* from which the others were sawed were usually 3" x 9" x 12'. *Whole deals* were 1 ¼" thick; *split deals*, ⅝"; and *five-cut stuff*, ½" or less. Pieces less than 6' long were called *deal ends.* Fig. 72D.

**dedo.**
A finger; a small part; 1/48 of a vara castellana (32.9").—*Tablones de varia y pino de quatro dedos de grueso* (1686): random width pine planks 4 fingers (2 ¾") thick.

**despensa.**
Pantry. See *espencita.*

**división.**
Partition; section; division.—*Casa de un alto en una de las divisiones* (1788/6): house with an upper story in one of the sections—*Casa de mampostería y divisiones interiores de madera* (1788/17): masonry house with wooden partitions.—*Algunas divisiones de madera* (1788/112): some wooden partitions.—*Varias divisiones, las mas de ellas sin techos* (1788/149): various sections [of a house], most of them without roofs. — *Dos divisiones de pared* (1788/149): 2 sections of wall.

**door.**
See *puerta.* Figs. 37-39.

**embarrado.**
Plastered roughly, often with clay or mud. (1788/20; Gjessing.)

**encalado.**
(*Encalar:* to whitewash; to lime.) Whitewashed. — *Casas encaladas* (1580): whitewashed houses.

**enlucido.**
Plaster; plastered. (1788/65.)

**entablada.**
Sheathed or covered with boards or planks. — *Las vigas entablado con tablones de varia y pino* (1686): the beams covered with random width pine planks. Fig. 28D-E, 29.

**entablar.**
To cover with boards; to board up; to plank.

**entresuelo.**
Stair landing; mezzanine.—*E. principal* (1763A: Porras): main landing—*Primer e. (ibidem):* first landing.

**escalera.**
Stairs, stairways; ladder.—*Una e. de mampostería* (1790/38): a masonry stairway. — Stairs to the flat roof (1763A: Rodríguez-Salas.) See *varanda.* Figs. 55-56.

**espalda.**
Back. See *frente.*

**espencita.**
A small pantry — *Una e. de piedra* (1790/45): a stone pantry. See *despensa.*

**espino.**
Thorn: yucca, or Spanish bayonet.—*Cercas de espinos* (1788 nota): yucca hedge. See yucca. Fig. 79.

**estaca.**
Stake; pale; picket. — *1020 estacas de la cerca de dicha huerta* (1763B: Governor's House): 1020 stakes in the fence of the said garden. See *cerca.* Fig. 79.

**esquina.**
Corner, angle. — *Casa de mampostería, las paredes maestras y esquinas, los tabiques de alfardas, rajones y enlucido, de alto* (1788/65): 2-story house, the main wall and corners of masonry, the partitions framed in wood, split-lathed and plastered.

# GLOSSARY

**expensa.**
See *despensa*.
**fábrica.**
Structure. (1790/250.)
**fence.**
A wall or barrier.—"A clapboard f. 4 or 5 feet high" (1780/118).—"A clapboard f. 6 feet high" costing 900 clapboard @ 9 s. per 100, 28 posts, and 54 nails @ 1 s. each (1780/35-36).—Property in 1777 had an 8' stone fence in front, the rest clapboard and new clapboard fence 6½' high was later erected (1780/189). —"Clapboards were mostly rotten [and Robertson had to re-fence] with pine boards and cedar posts.... One side was 27', the other 67' long and it was 8' high. He paid 16 per 100' of pine boards. There were 12 or 14 cedar posts which cost 7 shillings each. Besides this there was the expense of nails and it was put up by a negro who was at work upon it between 3 and 4 days and to whom he paid 2 dollars per day" (1780/31). —"He fenced in the lot with post, rails and clapboards. It might take 100 posts with 2 or 3 rails between the posts, and clapboards nailed upright ... he bought the posts and rails" (1780/21). — "New boarded fence cedar posts 7 feet high (1780/84).—"Fenced lot, half with boarded fence, half with clapboard fence" (1780/196). "Put up a boarded fence all around the lot with cedar posts and rails" (1780/189). See *cerca, muro, pared*. Fig. 79.
**fogón.**
Hearth. — *F. de cantería* (1763A: Blanco): hearth of cut stone.
**freestone.**
Any stone which can be freely worked or quarried, as coquina. — St. Augustine houses were "built of freestone" (1765B).
**frente.**
Front, façade. — *Casa 17 varas de pared por el f. y espalda 20* (1790/1): house walls 17 *varas* on the front and 20 on the back.—*Casa que llaman la Tesorería antigua linda por el f. la calle que sale a la Puerta de Tierra ... mampostería del frente y espalda con 42 varas de largo* (1790/89): house that is called the Old Treasury on the front borders the street to the Land Gate ... masonry on the front and back [is] 42 *varas* long.

**gable.**
The triangular wall enclosed by the sloping ends of a ridged roof. Fig. 47.
**gallery.**
Covered walk or promenade, piazza or portico; veranda; balcony; raised platform or passageway along the outside or inside the wall of a building. Figs. 48-49.
**gallinero.**
Chicken house; coop. (1763A: Blanco.) — *Falta una puerta de g.* (1688): a door of the chicken house is gone.
**gate.**
See *puerta, portada, portal*. Fig. 80.
**guano.**
Palm thatch; palm leaves used for thatching; any palm tree. — 65 of 303 houses were *tablas y g.*: board and thatch; Guadalupe church was stone with g. roof (1759).—*Casa de g.*: (1764/388; 1790/135): palm thatch house.—*G. y madera* (1790/120): thatched wooden house—*Maderas y g.* (1790/21): boards (?) and thatch. See *paja, palma*, thatch. Figs. 58-59.
**guarniciones.**
Decorations. (1763A: Rodríguez-Salas.)
**habitación.**
House, dwelling, habitation. (1763A: Blanco.)
**hip roof.**
A roof with sloping ends and sides. Fig. 47.
**hormigón.**
See *ormigón*.
**horno.**
Oven, kiln. (1790/60.)—"Built an oven" (1780/21).—*H. de cal*: limekiln—*H. de ladrillo*: brick kiln.—*Hornillo*: small oven. (1763A: Blanco; 1763B: Governor's House.) See kitchen, oven.
**hostión.**
See *ostión*.
**huerta.**
Garden; grove, orchard. (1763A: Governor's House; 1764/18.)
**kitchen.**
Room where cooking is done; *cocina*. —*Un pretil en el patio que corría desde la puerta de la calle hasta la cocina* (1688): a fence in the patio from the street gate to the kitchen. This suggests a detached kitchen.— "Detached stone kitchen 16' x 20'" (1780/120).—"A kitchen detached

158

# GLOSSARY

from the [old Spanish] house" (1780/84). — "Small stone house, used as a kitchen." Later an upper bedroom was added (1780/132).— "A flat-roofed [stone?] outhouse, used by the Spaniards as a kitchen" (1780/117-118). — Converted "other building" to kitchen and store (1780/196). — "Clapboard kitchen" (1780/64).—"Converted a wall to a kitchen" (1780/189). — "Repaired kitchen" (1780/189). — "Built a large framed kitchen with an oven and a chimney" (1780/118). — "New stone chimney to kitchen" (1780/126). See Bartram (1765A) for the classic description of Spanish kitchens. See *cocina*. Figs. 40, 75-76.

**labadero, lavadero.**
Wash house; laundry. (1763A: Blanco.)

**ladrillo.**
Brick; perhaps also the tile used in construction of flat roofs (Fig. 63). See brick, *teja*.

**lamb's tongue.**
Termination of a chamfer in an ogee, or S-shaped cut.

**lindar.**
To abut, to border, to be contiguous. —*Casa linda al frente la Calle Real* (1790/229): the front of the house is on Royal Street.

**lined.**
Covered on the inside, as the interior plaster of a house.—"A wooden framed house in part lined" (1780/158).—"A frame house not lined but papered upon canvas" (1780/180).

**loggia.**
A gallery or arcade open to the air on at least one side; especially one contained within the body of a building and serving as an open-air room. Figs. 24D-G, 27, 48.

**madera.**
Wood; any type of wooden house construction, but after 1700 probably timber frame boarded or clapboarded.—*M.* (1595): puncheon walls of bald cypress.—*M.* (1709): probably puncheon construction, since Córcoles seems to denote frame construction with the word *tabla*.—78 of 342 houses were wood (1764).— *Tablas* (1764/43, 98) = *madera* (1788/28, 79): timber frame.—

*Casa de m.* (1788/1): timber frame house.—*M.* de *alto* (1788/4: 2:story timber frame.—*M. y rajones, cobija de palma* (1788/9): timber frame and shingle [walls], palm thatch roof.—*Casa de maderas, dos chimeneas, cimientos de piedra* (1790/77): Frame house, 2 chimneys, stone foundations. See fence, *raja, rajón, tabla*. Figs. 28, 29.

**madre.**
Main beam, key member, principal support of a structure.—*Una m. de las principales* (1688): a main support of the second floors.

**mampostería.**
Masonry; stonework generally, but not exclusively (1788). The following usages show that *m*. is not always a synonym for coquina masonry.— "All houses are built of masonry" (1765D).—*M. y cantería* (1788/5): tabby (?) and squared stone rubblework.—*M. y maderas* (1790/75): masonry and timber-frame.—*Madera y alguna parte de m. y hostión, de alto* (1788/123): timber frame and part masonry and oyster shell tabby, 2-story. — *M.* (1788/49, 69, 65, 112) = *ripio* (1764/61, 102, 105, 160): tabby (?). — *M.* (1788/6, 141, 127) = *piedra* (1764/82, 193, 205): squared rubble work (?). See especially discussion under *piedra*. See also *albañilería, cantería,* tabby, *ripio, ostión*. Figs. 30-33.

**merlon.**
The solid part of a battlement or parapet, between two openings.

**molding.**
Any of various ornamental contours given to cornices, jambs, *etc.*; a shaped strip of wood used for ornament.

**morada.**
Residence, habitation.—*La casa de mi m.* (1688): the house where I live.

**muleta.**
Post, prop, support. (1688; 1763B: Governor's House.)

**muro.**
Wall.—*Muros de división* (1763B: *Cuerpo de Guardia*): partition walls. —*Casa con su terreno cercado de m. de piedra* (1790/202-203): house with its lot enclosed by a stone wall. See *cerca, pared, tabique*, wall. Figs. 28-34, 36, 79-80.

159

# GLOSSARY

**necesaria.**
Necessary, house of office, latrine, privy. (1763B: Governor's House.)
**ogee.**
A molding having an S-shaped curve in profile; any S-shaped curve or line.
**oratorio.**
Oratory; a small chapel, especially one for private devotion. (1759).
**ormigón, hormigón.**
Masonry, especially concrete—*Torta de o.* (1756): tabby slab. See *argamasa*, tabby.
**orno.**
See *horno*.
**ostión.**
Large oyster shell; masonry using oyster shell aggregate, tabby, *ripio*. (1790/192.)—*Piedra de o.* (1760): tabby.—*Tabique de hostión* (1788/45): thin wall (about 9") of tabby. —*Casa de tabique de o. y postes, con alto de madera* (1788/129): tabby-and-post thin-walled house, with timber-frame second story. See *mampostería, poste, ripio*, tabby, terrace. Figs. 31-32.
**oven.**
See *horno*, kitchen.
**paint.**
Pigment mixed with oil or water and applied to a surface as a protective or beautifying coating.—P. used on balcony (1763A: Rodríguez-Salas).— "The New Red house" [an inn c. 1770] (1780/114).—"Repaired old Spanish house and painted it" (1780/196). — Antique color evidence on existing historic houses: yellow, red, green, white. See whitewash.
**paja.**
Straw, thatch made of material other than palm, as reeds or marsh grass (?). — "Scanty shelters of straw" (1709).—*Cubiertas de p.* (1759): straw thatch roofs. See thatch.
**pajizo.**
Thatched with straw. (1760).
**pale.**
A narrow board used in fencing; pointed stake or picket. ("Stakes stuck in one by another like pales. Defoe's *Captain Singleton*, vii). See *Cerca, estaca, rajón*. Fig. 79.
**palisado construction.**
Wall construction formed by setting posts upright in the earth. The tops were spiked or mortised into the plate. Spaces between the posts were about equal to their diameter, and were channeled and filled with rubble work or wattle and plaster. The wall was plastered on both sides. (Peterson, 36-37.) This is similar to the puncheon construction described by Forman, or traditional English post-and-pan. Examples were excavated at Frederica, Ga., an English settlement of the 1730's. See *barro, poste*. Fig. 28B-C.
**palma.**
Palm tree; palm thatch, specifically thatch made from the fronds of the cabbage palm (sabal palmetto); guano. — "Palmetto thatched roof, which was very tight" [on common tabby house] (1763A).—*Cobija de rajones y p.* (1788/23: roof of shingles and palm thatch. See *guano, paja*, thatch. Figs. 58-59.
**parapet.**
The portion of wall above the roof-gutter. Fig. 47.
**pared.**
Wall.—*Paredes de cerca* (1763B): fence walls or surrounding walls.— *P. corrida* (1790/45): continuous wall (this one was 32½ *varas* long by 4 high.—*P. de división* (1763B): partition.—*Paredes maestras* (1763A; 1788/65): main walls. — *Pared de patio* (1790/117): patio wall. See *cerca, muro, tabique*, wall. Figs. 28-34, 36, 79-80.
**pasadizo.**
Corridor. (1763A: Blanco.)
**pasamano.**
Handrail, especially of a balustrade. (1763A: Blanco.) Fig. 54.
**patio.**
A court, as of a house, especially an inner court open to the sky; courtyard; yard.—*Una pared del p. con 14 varas de largo y 3½ de alto* (1790/45): a patio wall 14 *varas* long and 3½ high.—*Un cuarto del p.* (1790/45): a room on the patio.
**piazza.**
Porch; gallery. — "Entrances shaded by Piazzas supported by Tuskan Pillars or Pillasters against the South Sun" (1765D).—"Put up a piazza the whole length [of the house] and a room at the end of it" (1780/189). Fig. 24A-C.

# GLOSSARY

**piedra.**
Stone, specifically coquina. The term commonly used to designate coursed squared rubble wall construction of coquina, which was invariably plastered on both sides.—Discovery c. 1580: "an abundance of stone near the sea" (1583). — First recorded use: between 1596-1598 (1598).— 124 of 342 houses were stone (1764). — *Cimientos de p.* (1790/77): stone foundations.—*Chimenea de p.* (1790/38: stone chimney.— *P. de ostión:* See *ostión.* — "Two dwelling houses built with stone and lime and a well built with the aforesaid materials" (1780/130).—Stone was brought 3 miles by Negroes (1780/31). This tabulation demonstrates the confusion in the names of the building materials:

| NUMBER OF APPARENT CARRY-THROUGH BUILDINGS | DATE | |
|---|---|---|
| | 1764 | 1788 |
| 52 | piedra | mampostería |
| 4 | piedra | mampostería y ostión |
| 1 | piedra | mampostería y cantería |
| 6 | piedra | mampostería y madera |
| 1 | piedra | ostión |
| 2 | piedra | ostión y madera |
| 7 | piedra y ripio | mampostería |

Clearly the *piedra* of 1764 is identical with the *mampostería* of 1788, with some exceptions. Renovation and remodelling with new materials no doubt accounts for many apparent discrepancies. See *cantería, coquina, mampostería, ostión.* Figs. 6, 30, 33.

**pilar.**
Pillar, post, column, support, pedestal. (1688).—14 masonry pillars (1763B guardhouse).—"Tuskan Pillars" (1765D).—"Row of pillars or arches generally supports a roof continuing from the common roof" (1765A). — *Pilares de cantería* (1790/45): cut stone pillars.— *Pilares de mampostería* [in a wattle and plaster house] (1788/20): masonry pillars.—*Tres pilares de mampostería con 7 varas de alto* (1790/229): 3 masonry pillars 7 *varas* high. See *poste.* Figs. 48-49.

**pilastra.**
Pilaster; a rectangular column with base and capital, inserted in a wall and projecting about ¼ of its breadth.

**piso.**
Floor, story, loft, apartment, ground level; flooring, pavement, tread, footing. See *alto, cuerpo, suelo.*

**plank.**
A heavy, thick board; typically, a sawed board 11″ to 18″ wide and 3″ to 6″ thick.

**portada.**
Gate; large door. (1763B: Governor's House.) Figs. 11, 80.

**portal.**
Porch, portico, piazza; entrance, entry; gate.—The Guardhouse had two *portales* (1759): porticos. Figs. 10, 80.

**portico, portigo.**
A porch; structure consisting of a roof supported by columns, usually attached to a building as a porch, but sometimes detached as an ambulatory.—*Portigos* (1763B: Governor's House): shelters at the garden gates. —"Portico of stone arches before the entry of most houses (1765B). Figs. 48-49.

**portón.**
Large door. (1763A: Rodríguez-Salas.)

**poste.**
Post, pillar.—*Ostión y postes* (1788/129): post-and-tabby construction. Posts were embedded vertically in the masonry wall about 5′ apart during the pouring process. They reinforced the masonry (which has low tensile

161

# GLOSSARY

strength) and probably helped the slow-setting masonry to support wooden members such as rafter plates.— 6 *posteles* (1790/188): 6 posts. See *palisado, pilar, ostión.* Figs. 32, 77.

**poyo.**
Masonry bench. (1763B: Guardhouse.) Fig. 13.

**pozo.**
Well.—*P. revestido* (1763B: Governor's House): well lined with masonry. — *Posso de piedra* (1763B: Guardhouse): same. Fig. 78.

**pretil.**
Rail; breast-high fence.—*Un p. que corría desde la puerta de la calle hasta la cocina* (1688): a fence which ran from the street gate to the kitchen.

**principal.**
Second floor. (1688).

**puerta.**
Door; gate.—*Carpintería de puertas y ventanas* (1790/45): carpentry of the doors and windows. See *portada, portal.* Figs. 37-39, 80.

**puncheon.**
A short upright timber in timber frame construction; a slab of timber or a piece of split log with the face roughly dressed, used for flooring, etc. ("Floors of rived puncheons, hewn smooth on one surface." Roosevelt, *Winning of the West,* i. 7.) See *palisado.*

**quartel.**
See *cuartel.*

**quarto.**
See *cuarto.*

**rafe.**
Eaves. Fig. 46.

**raja.**
Split; cleft or rived board. 1788/121.)

**rajón.**
Split wood; shake, shingle, *tejamaní,* used for covering walls and roofs; split lath; cleft clapboard (?).—*Rajones medianos labrados* (1688): split pales, partly smoothed.—*Cercas de rajones de madera* (1788 nota): fences of split wooden pales.—*Casa de rajones* (1788 / 10): shingle house. — *Casa de madera y rajones* (1788/9): timber - frame (clapboard?) and shingle house.—*Casa de rajones, cobija idem* (1788/39): shingled house and roof.—*Casa de madera, cobija de rajones* (1788/1):

timber-frame (clapboard ?) house, shingle roof.—*Tabiques de alfardas, rajones y enlucido* (1788/65): partitions of wooden studs, split lath and plaster. See *madera, tejamaní,* weatherboard. Figs. 29, 60-61.

**reja.**
Grating; especially the projecting frame of wood on street windows.— *Rexas de la cerca del patio* (1763A: Rodríguez - Salas): gratings in the patio fence.—"Large windows next the street, all bannistered and projecting a foot or more from the house wall." Windows facing the yard had flush gratings. (1765A.)—East windows projected -6" to 18" into the street. (1765D.) Fig. 42.

**remate.**
Capital of a column or pilaster. (1763B: Governor's House.)

**retablado.**
Shelf. (1763B: Governor's House.)

**ripio.**
Term used in 1764 to designate masonry other than squared stonework, principally tabby; *ostión.*—*Casa de piedra y r.* (1764/118) = *casa de mampostería de alto, con algunas divisiones interiores de hostión* (1788/124): 2-story squared stone house, with some tabby partitions.—*Casa de ripio y tablas* (1764/251): board and tabby house. — This tabulation shows the difference in names of materials from one period to another:

162

# GLOSSARY

| NUMBER OF APPARENT CARRY-THROUGH BUILDINGS | DATE 1764 | 1788 |
|---|---|---|
| 12 | *ripio* | *mampostería* |
| 3 | *ripio* | *mampostería y madera* |
| 1 | *ripio y tablas* | *mampostería* |
| 6 | *ripio* | *ostión* |
| 2 | *ripio* | *ostión y madera* |
| 2 | *ripio* | *ostión y mampostería* |
| 2 | *ripio* | *ostión, madera y mampostería* |

Figs. 31-32.

**roof.**
*Techo.*—"Flat roofed Spanish kitchen (1780/117-118).—Spanish ruin "had a flat roof upon it, which he repaired and made into a pitch roof" (1780/20). — "Mended the roof of an old Spanish house" (1780/196). See *azotea, cáscara de ciprés,* clapboard, *guano,* shingle, *tabla, tablazón, techo, teja,* thatch, tile. Figs. 46-47, 58-71.

**rubble wall.**
A wall built of stones irregular in shape and size and coarsely jointed.—Random r.: walling built with irregular pieces of stone usually less than 8" thick, loosely packed without regard to courses.—Coursed r.: walling that is leveled up in courses 12" or 18" deep, the depth varying in different courses according to the sizes of the stones. Stones are dressed before use to obtain a level bed and perpendicular face.—Coursed squared r.: walling in which the stone is squared and roughly faced up. The stone is set in courses, the depth of each course being made up of one or more stones. This is the technique most used in St. Augustine.—Regular coursed r.: walling in which all stones in one course are of the same height. Fig. 30.

**sabino, savino, savina.**
Bald cypress, *Taxodium Distichum* (L.) L. C. Rich; or pond cypress, *Taxodium Ascendens* Brongn.—*Savino:* cypress post for house wall construction (1595), and for shingles. — *Savina:* savin, red cedar, which was used extensively for fence posts. See fence, shingle. Figs. 22B-C, 60, 68.

**sala.**
Main hall; parlor, drawing room.—*Un travesaño principal de la sala y aposento de arriba* (1688): a principal cross-beam of the main hall and upper bedroom.—*Cielos rasos de la sala y quartos altos* (1763A: Rodríguez-Salas): flat ceilings of the parlor and upper rooms. (The phraseology suggests that the *sala* is on the second floor.) Fig. 40.

**shake.**
A short board, rived from a block, crudely dressed, and used in overlapping rows to cover the roofs and sides of buildings; *rajón.* See *rajón.* Fig. 60A.

**shingle.**
A thin board, dressed, jointed, and with one end thicker than the other, used in overlapping rows to cover the roofs and sides of buildings; *rajón.*—"Laying shingles on the roof" (1780/31). — Cypress shingles (1780/64, 157).—In 1778 Watson sent a crew to his 20-acre tract up North River to cut lumber and make shingles (1780/157). — Watson built "a wooden framed house, short shingled"; a store "shingled in the same manner" (1780/158). See *tejamaní.* Fig. 60B, 68.

**shutter.**
A hinged wooden cover for a window.—The *rejas* had "strong shutters within side, many of which had a little one in each" (1765A). Outside shutters replaced them as glazed sash were introduced. Fig. 44.

**solar.**
Lot, plot of land. — *Solar del rey* (1790/192): lot belonging to the crown. See *terreno.*

163

# GLOSSARY

**sotea.**
See *azotea*.
**soberado, soverado.**
Story, floor. — *Segundo s.* (1763B: Governor's House): second floor.—*Sobrerado* (1763A: León): same. See *piso, suelo*.
**suelo.**
Floor, flooring, pavement, story, ground. — *Suelos bajos* (1763A: Blanco): ground floors. — "Mended floors of old Spanish house" (1780/196). See *piso, soverado*. Figs. 72-74.
**tabby.**
A concrete composed of approximately equal parts of lime, sand, and shell aggregate; (Spanish:) *tapia, ostión, ripio*. It was used for walls, floors, roofs, walks, fences and benches, being poured into the formed space and compacted. The size of the aggregate was varied to suit the work; *i.e.*, coarse oyster shell was used for rough work such as walls, relatively fine coquina shell to produce the dense mortar needed for finished floors.—Many houses built of stone and tabby (1715). — Tabby is "a mixture of shell, lime, sand and water in equal proportion by measure and not weight" (1844). See *ostión, ripio, tabique*, terrace. Figs. 14, 31-32.
**tabique.**
Partition, thin wall, wall. — *T. de alfardas, rajones y enlucido* (1788/65): stud-framed partition, split-lathed and plastered.—*T. de ostión* (1788/45): house wall of tabby (oyster-shell concrete).—*T. de mampostería con 4 varas de largo y 4 de alto* (1790/38): masonry wall 4 varas long and 4 high.—*T. de raja* (1788/121): wall of rived boards.—*T. maestro:* main partition.—*Una pared con 4 varas de alto; otro tabique con 4 varas* (1790/38): a wall 4 varas high; another wall (synonym) 4 varas high. See *atajadiso, cerca, muro, pared*. Fig. 32.
**tabla.**
Board, *madera;* plank. The board used for walling structures since early times (1595).—64 of 239 houses are *tablas y guano* (1759): board and thatch.—*Casa de t.* (1764/42, casa de tablas (1764/43): board (clapboard ?). — *Casa de ripio y tablas* (1764/23): tabby and board house.—In the 1788 plan, *madera* is a synonym for *t.* (1764/43, 98, 113; 1788/28, 79, 126).—*Techada de t.* (1759): board (or plank) roof.—*Tablas de la azotea* (1763B: Governor's House): flat roof planking. — *Tablas de cañón* (1763A: Blanco): gutter (?) boards. — *Cercas de tablas* (1788 nota): board fences. See board, clapboard, *madera*, plank, *rajón*. Figs. 4, 25D-E, 29, 61-62, 79.
**tablazón.**
Boards, planks, lumber, flooring.—23 of 303 houses had *techadas de taxamani u t. de la misma materia* (1759): shingle or board roofs of the same material. The reference occurs as part of an enumeration of roof materials *(sotea, paja, guano)* and probably may be interpreted as "cypress shingle and cypress clapboard roofs." Figs. 61-62.
**tablón.**
Plank.—*Tablones de varia y pino de quatro dedos de grueso* (1686): random width pine planks 4 fingers (2¾") thick (used as sheathing under a tabby slab roof).
**tapia.**
See tabby.
**techado, tejado**
Roof; ceiling; shed; roofed. (1759.)
**techo.**
Roof; ceiling. — *Techos de azoteas* (1788/5): flat roofs. — *Carpintería de puertas, ventanas, piso y techo* (1790/45): carpentry of doors, windows, floor and roof. See roof. Figs. 46-47, 58-71.
**teja.**
Baked clay roof tile. Specifically, a tile of semicircular section about 17" long, having a diameter of about 6" at one end and about 7" at the other, and about ½" thick. Examples of these c.1760 are in the Castillo ravelin, fragments c.1675 were recovered from Castillo courtyard ruins, and enough sherds have been found on town homesites to indicate limited use.—The reference to 9 vitrified spouts (1790/89) may have been *tejas* used in pairs to form a pipe through the parapet (as in the Castillo ravelin). See *azotea, ladrillo*, tile. Figs. 62, 69.

164

# GLOSSARY

**tejamaní.**
Shingle, shake, *rajón—Techadas de taxamaní u tablazón de la misma materia* (1759): [cypress] shingle roofs or board roofs of the same material. — In Michoacan, Mexico, *t.* signifies a shake or long shingle (about 8" x 48"); probably the St. Augustine product was similar. See *rajón, shingle.* Fig. 60.
**tercia.**
One third of a *vara;* about 11 inches. —*Dos chimeneas de tercia de grueso* (1790/112): 2 chimneys 11" thick.
**terrace, terrass.**
Tabby. — Terraced walk, seats, flat roof, chamber (upstairs) floor (1765A): tabby walk, etc. Figs. 13, 14, 31-32, 62, 73.
**terraplén.**
Platform; flat roof; terreplein. (1763-A: Porras.)
**terreno.**
Land, field, plot, lot.—*Casa con su t.* (1790/202-203): house with its lot. See *solar.*
**terrero.**
Shack; humble, 1-story; having its floor at ground level (Arana).—*Dos terreros con 11 varas de largo y 4 de alto* (1790/45): two shacks [barns?] 11 *varas* long and 4 high. —*Casa terrera de madera* (1790/2): wooden shack.—*Casa terrera de mampostería* (1790/3: masonry hut.
**thatch.**
A covering for walls or roof made of palm fronds, straw, reeds, or the like; *palma, guano, paja.*—"A small stone house and only thatched" (1780/152). See *guano, paja, palma.* Figs. 58-59.
**tienda.**
Store.—*Tienda mostrador* (1763A: Porras): store counter.
**tile.**
A thin slab of baked clay, used in overlapping rows to cover a roof.— "David Yeats tiled the house" (1780/22).—"A new stable built of wood and covered with tiles" (1780/21). See especially *teja;* also *azotea, ladrillo.* Figs. 63, 69.
**torta.**
Solid matter, fill; slab. — *Tortas de las azoteas* (1763B: Guardhouse): concrete (tabby) slabs of the flat roofs. Figs. 62.

**traspatio.**
A second patio. (1763B: Governor's House.)
**travesaño.**
Beam, cross-piece.—*Un t. principal de la sala y aposento de arriba* (1688): a principal beam of the main hall and the bedroom above.
**Tuscan.**
In architecture, pertaining to a classical (Roman) order, distinguished by a plain column and the absence of decorative detail.
**vara.**
Measurement of length. In St. Augustine, the *vara Castellana* (32.9") was used; hence for practical purposes, 33" or about 1 yard. See *tercia, dedo.*
**varanda.**
Railing; handrail (of a balustrade). —*Varandas de azoteas y escaleras* (1763A: Rodríguez-Salas): railings of flat roofs and stairways. Fig. 54.
**ventana.**
Window.—*Carpintería de ventanas* (1790/45): carpentry of the windows. See *window.* Figs. 41-45.
**vidriera.**
Glass; glass window.—*Armario con vidrieras:* wardrobe with glass panes. —*10 ventanas con sus puertas y vidrieras de mismo tamaño:* 10 windows with their shutters and glazed casements the same size.—*Un balcón con sus puertas y vidrieras:* a balcony with its shutters and glazed windows. (1763A: Rodríguez-Salas).
**viga.**
Beam, rafter, joist—*Vigas para los quarteles son de una tercia de alto media vara de ancho* (1686): rafters for the quarters are 11" high by 16" wide [the span was about 19'].— *Vigas y tablas de la azotea del cuerpo de guardia:* rafters and boards for the flat roof of the guardhouse.— *vigas de la cosina y tablas de su azotea:* rafters and boards for the flat roof of the kitchen. — 38 *vigas del soverado principal y 54 tablas para el mismo:* 38 joists in the main floor and 54 boards for it. (1763B: Governor's House.)
**vivienda.**
Living quarters.—*V. vaja* [*baja*] (1763A: Porras): lower quarters.— *V. alta interior* (1763A: Blanco): upper interior quarters.

165

# GLOSSARY

**wainscot.**
A lining or facing of wood on interior walls.

**wattle and daub.**
See *cuje*. Fig. 34.

**weatherboard.**
A board used to form the outside protective covering of a wall, especially a board shaped to shed water by forming lapped joints with the boards above and below; a clapboard.—"A wooden framed and weather boarded house built about 1770" (1780/120). See clapboard, *rajón*, *tabla*. Figs. 28E-29.

**whitewash.**
Lime in water, sometimes with other ingredients, for painting wood or masonry surfaces, to improve weather resistance and appearance. To whitewash a house inside and out was not uncommon practice in colonial times on the frontiers (Peterson, 23).— *Encaladas por fuera y dentro* (1580): [half of the 60 houses at Santa Elena were] whitewashed outside and inside.—Whitewash is evident on most historic St. Augustine structures.— "He made an addition . . . floored, plaistered and white washed on the inside" ( 1780/118 ). — "A large framed wooden house . . . glazed, plaistered and whitewashed" (1780/118).

**window.**
An opening in the side of a building to let in light and air; the framework that fills such a space; *ventana*.—Glazed windows (1764A: Salas; 1765A).—Large windows on the street were masked by *rejas*. Many had half lattices. "Little bannistered and latticed windows" were also on common houses. East window *rejas* projected up to 18″ into the street, were "very wide and proportionately high." West windows were small. (1763A.) See *ventana*. Figs. 41-45.

**wall.**
A structure of stone or other materials, raised to some height as an enclosure or for security or defense; one of the upright enclosing parts of a building or room. Figs. 28-34, 36, 79-80.

**yucca.**
Specifically *Y. aloifolia*, the Spanish bayonet, an American plant (family Liliaceae) having long, thorn-pointed, rigid, fibrous leaves on a woody caudex. It bears a large pannicle of white blossoms. It was much used as a hedge and as a barrier. Fig. 79.

# Index

Accountant's House, 20, 21, 23, 83-85
Anastasia Island, 17, 20, 28, 67
Apalache, 108, 116, 117
Arana, Eugenia, 3
Arana, Luis R., 3
Arcade, 58, 59, 74, 91, 92, 93
Arch, 28, 31, 61, 73, 74, 88, 91, 92, 93, 131
Architecture, 7, 8, 10, 12, 18, 36, 47, 79, 92
Architecture of St. Augustine:
    description of structures 10, 11, 12, 15, 16, 19, 20, 22, 23, 26, 27, 28-33, 34, 35, 36, 37, 38-40, 41, 43, 45, 47, 48*ff*., 105, 122
    influences on, 8, 9, 10, 20, 22, 23, 27, 34, 35, 36, 43, 45, 47, 61, 64, 65, 73, 74, 79, 93, 108, 109, 111, 115, 121, 127, 128
    orientation to:
        climate: 8, 9, 11, 20, 27, 29, 55
        site, 11, 55, 61, 86, 92
*Argamasa*, 105
Arnade, Charles W., 3
Arris, 93, 121
Avero, 44
*Azotea*, 17, 99, 102, 104, 105, 107, 108, 109, 120
    See also *roof*.

Bahamas, 39, 101
Bakery, 13
Balcony 12, 22, 26, 28, 29, 31, 35, 39, 52, 55, 74, 83, 85, 93-96, **115-116**, 131
Balk, Bruce, 4
Baluster, 31, 33, 74, 87, 95, 96-97
Balustrade, 95-98
Bannister: see *baluster*.
Bannister, Turpin C., 4
Barge, 66
Barracks, 28, 36, 73, 129
    of St. Francis, 13, 40
    dragoon, 92
Barrel, 125
Bartram, John, 31, 32, 34, 44, 61, 68, 80, 87, 88, 95, 97, 101, 106, 108, 113, 120, 122, 124, 126, 131
Battlement, 31, 90
    See also *parapet*.
Beam, 31, 95, 105, 106, 107, 121
Bedroom, 26, 27, 31, 33, 38, 51, 61, 95, 97, 110, 123, 127
Bench, 124
Benedit Horruytiner, Joseph, 26
Board, 15, 16, 20, 25, 34, 36, 38, 39, 40, 44, 62, 63, 65, 66, 81, 84, 104, 105, 107, 117, 118, 127, 129, 130
    deal, 117, 118, 130
    feather-edge, 40, 65, 104
    form, 32, 69
    tongue-and-groove, 81, 110, 117, 118
Board-and-thatch, 17, 20, 23, 25
Bracket, 95
Brasier, 33, 81
Brick, 17, 36, 39, 62, 73, 98, 120, 124, 133
Brick kiln, 73

# INDEX

Brick masonry, 62, 73
Brickyard, 73
Bryant, William Cullen, 47
Bull, Governor, 36

*Caballeriza*: see *stable*.
*Cal*, 62, 66, 67, 99
Calderón, Bishop, 20
Cameron, Ann, 34
Cameron, James, 34, 35
Canvas, 27, 39, 121
Carolina: see *origins*.
Carolina house, 36
Carriage, 47
Carry-over, 58, 60, 83, 108, 115
Castillo de San Marcos: see *fortification*.
Cedar, 64, 66, 82, 131
Ceiling, 95, 105, 115, 120, 121
Cellar, 29, 38, 61, 127
Cement, 17
Cendoya, Manuel de, 20
Chamber: see *bedroom*.
Chamfer, 93, 95
Chapel, 22
Charcoal, 33, 71, 81, 123
Charleston, 4, 35, 36, 37, 61, 93
Chickee, 100, 101
Chicken, 15, 128, 130
 house, 127
Chimney, 12, 29, 31, 33, 34, 38, 39, 40, 73, 74, 98-99, 124
Church, 28
 Cathedral, 13, 45
 parish, 8, 22, 23, 45, 109
 Trinity Episcopal, 13
Claims, 24, 41
Clapboard, 35, 38, 39, 40, 62, 65, 99, 103, 104, 124, 129, 130, 133
Clay, 63, 64, 71, 73, 79, 113
Closet, 38, 120
Column, 74, 91, 92, 131
"Common freeholders' house," 36, 118
Concrete, 17, 28, 62, 69, 119
Construction:
 details, 38-40, 44, 62*ff*.
  balustrade, 95-98
  floor (tabby), 118-119
  roof:
   masonry, 68
   thatch, 101-102
  wall, 68
Convent of St. Francis: see *friary*.
Coping, 90
Coquina, 28, 62, 67, 118, 120
 discovery of (1580), 17, 21, 67
Córcoles, Francisco de, 26
Cornice, 74, 89-90, 115
Courtyard, 31, 95, 105, 113, 124
Crichlow Jr., Bartolo, 3

# INDEX

Crown property, 21, 26, 67, 102
  See also *Accountant's House, Customs-and-Counting House, Governor's House, Guardhouse, Treasurer's House.*
Cuba, 9, 20, 27, 28, 34, 73
*Cujes y barro*, 71, 73
Cupola, 37
Curtis, William (shop-keeper), 37
Customs-and-Counting House, 45, 83-85, 89, 95, 109, 111, 113, 124, 127, 130
Cypress, 15, 36, 40, 62, 63, 64, 66, 82, 101, 102, 113, 125
  bark, 99, 108

De Brahm, William Gerard, 28, 92, 124
Design, 48*ff.*
  plans, 48-61
  façades, 74-99
    height, 79-80
    openings, 80-89
    cornices, 89-90
    posts, columns, arches, porches, 91-93
    balconies, 93-96
    stairways, 95-98
    chimneys, 98-99
  roofs, 99-116
    slopes, 109-112
    spouts and gutters, 113
    balcony, 114-115
    dormer, 115-116
  interiors, 116-124
  floors, 116-120
    walls and ceilings, 120-121
  kitchens, 122-124
Dickinson, Jonathan, 21
Dining room, 34, 38, 61
Door, 12, 31, 37, 38, 39, 61, 74, 80-85, 124, 131
  frame, 81, 82, 83
Drake, Sir Francis, 8, 15
Dunham, David R., 4

Eave, 74, 89, 90, 112, 115
Economics, 7, 9, 26, 27, 33, 35, 41, 43, 44, 110, 118
  agriculture, 9, 14, 15, 18, 41, 42, 43, 44
  commerce, 9, 43, 45, 66, 118
  construction, 43, 44, 66
  fishing, 15, 43
  Indian trade, 43
  industry, 9
  ranching, 9, 44
Edison Home, The, 3
Edwards, Henry C., 4
Elixio de la Puente, Juan Joseph, 58, 71
England (Great Britain), 8, 9, 15, 22, 35, 36, 37
Entrance, 12, 29, 31, 74, 80, 89
*Escalera:* see *stairway.*
*Espinos:* see *yucca.*
*Estaca:* see *stake.*
Expansion of structures, 24, 53, 54, 58, 68, 72, 117, 121, 123

Façades, 12, 28, 29, 60, 74-99, 131

# INDEX

Fascia Board, 89, 90
Fatio, 46
  See also *houses*.
Fence (and fence wall), 12, 26, 32, 35, 38, 39, 40, 47, 48, 66, 68, 70, 80, 84, 104, 124, 128-131
Fire, 8, 9, 11, 12, 15, 16, 17, 19, 20, 21, 22, 23, 25, 43, 64, 65, 105, 106, 107
  cooking, 22
Fireplace, 29, 33, 34, 61, 81, 98, 99, 122, 123, 124
Firewood, 33, 34, 69
Floor, 17, 33, 34, 35, 36, 38, 39, 67, 68, 116-120
  earth, 116
  masonry, 118-120
  terrazo, 118
  wood, 116
Floor plans, 48-61
Florida, 9, 17, 20, 22, 26, 36, 37, 41, 43, 44, 45, 47, 64, 101, 102, 104, 109, 111
Florida Rangers, 34
Florida State University, 3
Food, 15, 18, 33, 43, 122, 123
Fort George Island, 73
Fortification, 15, 16, 17, 25, 28, 42, 79, 118, 119
  Castillo de San Marcos, 8, 9, 11, 13, 19, 20
  (construction began), 21, 22, 23, 25, 35, 67, 73, 105, 113, 120, 133
  City Gate, 13, 45
  first fort, 14
  palisade, 25
Foundations, 17, 21, 27, 68, 120
Fowl house, 39, 127
Frame construction, 62
  See also *timber frame*.
France, 22, 45
Franciscan friars, 26
Freebooters, 8, 19-20
Friary of St. Francis, 16, 17, 23, 26, 40
  See also *barracks*.

Gable, 38, 72, 89, 90, 99, 109, 110, 111, 112, 115, 116
Gallery, 29, 58, 59, 61, 84, 92, 93, 98
Garret, 34, 38, 39
*Gallinero*: see *chicken house*.
Garden, 9, 15, 18, 32, 33, 34, 38, 40, 41, 47, 61, 124, 128, 129, 130
Garrison, 14, 15, 22, 25, 28, 31, 33, 34, 35, 41, 43, 45, 69, 92, 116
Gate, 12, 80, 129, 131-133
Genovar, Juan, 73
Georgia, 28, 34, 35, 36, 108, 129
Gjessing, Frederik C., 3
Glass, 12, 31, 35, 38, 39, 40, 74, 89, 128
Goggin, John M., 4
Gordon, Peter, 36
Governor's House, 13, 20, 21, 23, 25, 26, 89, 93, 98, 110, 111, 127, 131
Grape arbors, 29, 124-125
Grating, 74, 86, 87, 89
Great Britain: see *England*.
Great Smoky Mountains, 129
Griffen, William B., 3
Griffin, John W., 3

170

# INDEX

*Guano,* 64, 71, 99, 102
Guardhouse, 25, 90, 105
Guardroom, 84
Gutiérrez, Nicolás, 73
Gutter, 112, 113, 115

Halgrim, Robert, 3
Hall, 31, 61
Hardware, 44
  hinge, 82, 88, 127
  holdback, 89
  hook, 87
  lock, 38, 82
  sash weight, 89
Harrington, Jean C., 3, 120
Harris, J. Carver, 3, 105
Hartridge, Walter, 4
Havana: see *Cuba.*
Hearth, 50, 122
Height of structures, 39, 58, 74, 79-80, 92, 95, 108, 112
  1-story, 12, 40, 67, 69, 74, 75, 80, 120, 128
  1½-story, 12, 37, 38, 40, 74, 75, 80, 116
  2-story, 12, 28, 34, 35, 38, 39, 61, 67, 71, 74, 76-77, 80, 93, 108, 116, 120, 121, 128
  tall 2-story, 77-78
  3-story, 36
  "highest," 22
  fence, 128, 131
Historic American Building Survey, 3
Hog house, 39, 127
Horse, 18, 25, 26, 35, 39, 127
Hospital, 18, 22, 23
Houses:
  42 Avenida Menéndez, 13
  46 Avenida Menéndez, 13, 77
  12 Avilés, 13, 78, 111
  20 Avilés, 13, 46, 78, 83, 96, 98, 111
  32 Avilés, 13, 77, 111
  36 Avilés, 13
  46 Bridge, 13, 75
  20 Charlotte, 13, 78, 111
  101 Charlotte, 13
  257 Charlotte, 75
  16 Marine, 13, 78
  43 Marine, 13, 76
  45 Marine, 13, 76
  56 Marine, 13, 77
  14 St. Francis (Oldest House), 13, 53, 65, 76, 111, 133
  22 St. Francis, 13, 76, 111
  31 St. Francis, 13, 53, 54
  14 St. George, 13, 75, 111
  39 St. George, 13
  43 St. George, 13, 77
  46 St. George, 13, 24, 53, 106
  52 St. George, 13
  54 St. George, 13, 75
  65 St. George, 13

# INDEX

  105 St. George, 13, 77, 111
  143 St. George (Treasurer's House [which see]), 13, 75
  214 St. George, 13, 77, 131
  224 St. George, 13, 76
  250 St. George, 13, 75
  279 St. George, 13
  42 Spanish, 13, 76
  62 Spanish, 13, 76
  57 Treasury, 13, 75
Hollingsworth, F. A., 4
Housing, history of:
  to 1763, 14-33
  British period, 34-40
  to 1821, 41-47
Hrawbouski, Ann, 125
Hrawbouski, Samuel (storekeeper), 125
Huts, 14, 17, 26, 35, 37, 43, 46, 50, 58, 64, 73, 122

Indian, 17, 18, 19, 25, 79, 108, 109, 122
  Seminole, 100, 101
  Timucua, 14, 15, 22, 63, 64, 101
Infirmary, 22
Inn: see *tavern*.

Jamestown, Va., 18
Joist, 95, 106, 121
  ceiling, 25, 107, 110, 121
  floor, 99, 117, 118

Kitchen, 22, 26, 27, 31, 34, 35, 38, 39, 50, 51, 52, 61, 80, 84, 98, 122-124, 128
Kubler, George, 4

*Ladrillo*, 62
  See also *brick*.
Lamb's tongue, 95
Lath, 44, 101, 102, 103, 110, 120, 121
Lattice:
  window, 31, 33, 74, 87
  gate, 132
*Lavadero*: see *wash house*.
Leslie, John, 43
Lime, 17, 20, 28, 44, 62, 66, 67, 71, 73, 118, 120
  "lime-shell," 32
Lime kilns, 20, 26
Limestone, 17
Linseed oil, 119
Livestock, 15
Living room, 26, 34, 38, 61, 98
Lock, 38, 82
Loft, 50, 110, 111
Log house, 39, 66
Loggia, 11, 12, 55, 56, 59, 61, 74, 80, 91, 92, 95, 97
Lookout, 38
Lord, Benjamin (surveyor), 35, 130
Lumber, 27, 37, 44, 66, 118, 130
  yard, 66

172

# INDEX

*Madera*, 15, 33, 46, 62, 64, 71
  See also *wood*.
*Mampostería*, 46, 62, 71, 72, 73, 120, 131
  see also *masonry*.
Man, Spencer, 61
Mangus, Harry, 4
Manucy, Adolphus N., 4
Manucy, Clara, 4
Manucy House, 42
Map: see *sources*.
Market, 13, 18
Marran, David, 66
Masonry, 17, 20, 21, 25, 28, 29, 33, 34, 46, 55, 58, 60, 61, 62, 64, 65, 66, 69, 71, 72, 79, 80, 83, 86, 88, 91, 99, 102, 104-108, 117, 124, 127, 128, 131, 133
  first recorded masonry construction, 17
Masters, Karl, 4
Matanzas Bay, 14, 15, 61
Materials, 8, 9, 12, 19, 25, 27, 48*ff*.
  wall, 62-73
    thatch, 64
    wood, 64-66
    masonry, 66-73
    lime, 66-67
    stone, 67-68, 70
    tabby, 68-71
    plaster, 70-71
  combinations, 71-73
  brick, 73
  roof, 99-116
    thatch, 99-102
    wood, 102-104
    masonry, 104-108
    other, 108-109
  interior, 116-124
    floor, 116
      earth, 116
      wood, 116-118
      masonry, 118-120
    partitions, walls, ceilings, 120-121
    kitchen, 122-124
  See also names of materials.
Méndez Canzo, Gonzalo, 17, 18
Menéndez de Avilés, Pedro, 14, 91
Menéndez Marqués, Pedro, 17
Merlon, 90
Mexico, 9, 20, 27, 101
Mill for corn-grinding, 18
Mills, John, 35, 36
Molding, 65, 81, 89, 93, 98, 99, 121
Moore, Dorothy, 34
Moore, John, 34, 35
Mortar, 17, 32, 44, 66, 68, 69, 71, 73, 106, 118, 119, 131
Moultrie Creek, 66
Mud, 63, 64

Nails, 44, 66, 101, 120, 131
Napoleon, 8

# INDEX

National Park Service, 3
National Geographic Society, 3
Necessary: see *privy*.
Negro, 10, 22, 43
  carpenter, 37
  slave, 9, 10, 19, 37, 39, 43, 44, 45, 66, 67
New England, 9, 65
New Smyrna, 4, 43, 44
New Spain: see Mexico
New York, 36
Newton, Earle W., 4
Nombre de Dios (mission), 21-22, 23
North River, 37, 66
Nuestra Señora de la Leche (hermitage), 23
Nuestra Señora de la Soledad (hermitage), 22, 25
  see also *church*.

Oak, 14, 64
Oglethorpe, James, 36
Origins of colonists and others:
  Canary Islands, 9, 43
  Carolina, 8, 9, 22, 25, 35, 37, 60
  Cuba, 9, 20
  England, 9, 28, 37, 40, 41, 43, 72
  Florida, 43
  Ireland, 9
  Mediterranean (Balearic Islands, Italy, Greece), 10, 41, 42, 43, 44
  Mexico, 9
  Spain, 9, 41, 43, 45
  United States, 10, 45, 47
  Other, 9
  See also *Negro*.
*Ostión*, 46, 62, 71, 72, 73, 120
  *ostión y postes*, 69
  *piedra de ostión*, 28, 68
Outbuildings, 35, 38, 39, 48, 65, 84, 123, 127
Oven, 34, 38, 84, 124

Paint, 121, 131, 133
  blue, 127, 133
  yellow, 42, 106, 133
  red, 35, 133
  other, 133
*Paja*, 62, 64, 99, 102
Pale, 129, 130
Palisado, 64
Palmetto, 14, 28, 33, 101
Palm:
  thatch, 15, 17, 18, 20, 26, 28, 33, 37, 43, 62, 63, 64, 71, 99, 101
  wood, 64
*Palma*, 15, 62, 64, 99, 102
Panton, Leslie and Company, 43
Pantry, 29, 61
Parapet, 74, 80, 90, 105, 113
  castellated, 74, 90, 105
Parlor: see *living room*.
Partition, 51, 71, 72, 80, 90, 120
Patio, 26, 58, 80, 124

# INDEX

Pebbles, 17
Peterson, Charles E., 3
Piazza, 29, 38, 61, 92, 93, 112
Picket, 103, 129, 131
*Piedra*, 33, 62, 67, 71, 73
   see also *stone*.
Pier, 93
Pigeon loft, 127
Pilaster, 92
Pillar, 31, 61, 91, 92, 93
Pine, 14, 64, 66, 106, 118, 129, 130
Plan, 8, 27, 28, 34, 38, 39, 40, 48-61, 83-85, 89
   American center-hall, 60
   city, 47
   common, 49-54, 58, 60, 108
   St. Augustine, 11, 12, 49, 51, 54, 55-61, 108
   wing, 49, 58-60, 108
Plank, 105, 108, 130
   see also *board*.
Planters, 34, 44, 45
Plaster, 12, 17, 20, 28, 34, 35, 38, 39, 63, 64, 67, 68, 70, 71, 93, 98, 110, 120, 121, 131, 133
   ashlar-marked, 70, 71
Plaza, 18, 25, 28, 47, 84
Ponze, Mathias, 73
Population, 9, 10, 15, 16, 22, 26, 27, 28, 31, 34, 35, 37, 41, 43, 45, 47, 93, 117
Porch, 11, 12, 37, 51, 52, 55, 56, 61, 74, 80, 84-85, 90, 91, 92, 93, 96, 110
Portico, 28, 61, 91
**Portón,** 131
Post, 61, 62, 63, 64, 66, 69, 74, 91, 92, 93, 95, 106, 130, 131
   wall construction, 64, 65
   Post-and-tabby, 69
Powder magazine, 17, 20, 21, 45, 67
Privy, 35, 39, 40, 84, 127, 133
Property:
   crown, 21, 26, 67, 102
      see also *Accountant's House, Custom-and-Counting House, Governor's House, Guardhouse, Treasurer's House.*
   private, 41, 42, 43, 44, 48, 61, 124
Puente: see Elixio de la Puente.
Puerto Rico, 97
Puncheon, 64, 116, 117

Quarry, 19, 20, 21, 26, 28, 44, 67, 68, 118
Quiroga, Diego de, 20, 21

Rafter, 105, 106, 110, 111, 112
*Raja*, 65
*Rajón*, 66, 71, 99, 103, 129
"Red House," 35, 39, 133
Reeves, Blair, 4
*Reja*, 12, 29, 31, 74, 86, 87
*Ripio*, 33, 62, 68, 71, 73
Robinson, Robert (butcher), 37
Rocque, Mariano de la, 45, 48, 69, 72, 83, 103, 129
Rodríguez Meléndez, Joseph, 22, 24

175

# INDEX

Roof, 12, 15, 17, 20, 21, 26, 28, 31, 33, 34, 35, 36, 38, 39, 40, 50, 53, 64, 66, 69, 74, 80, 89, 90, 92, 95, 97, 99-116, 120, 121, 122, 123. 124, 127
  beehive, 109
  bell-cast, 112
  dormer, 115-116
  hip, 109, 111, 112, 115
  pitch, 108
  "St. Augustine kick," 112
  shed, 115, 116
  tar, 108

Sabal palmetto, 64, 101
St. Augustine:
  description, 14, 15, 16, 20, 26, 28-33, 37, 40, 47
  history, 8, 9, 14, 15-47, 60, 61
    See also *housing, history of*.
St. Augustine Historical Restoration and Preservation Commission, 4
St. Augustine Historical Society, 3, 4
St. Johns River, 66
Salazar, Governor, 20
Sánchez, William F., 4
Sand, 17, 28, 32, 71, 108, 118
Santa Elena, 17, 64, 104, 133
Sash, 12, 37, 39, 74, 81, 86, 87, 89
Savannah, 4, 36, 118
*Savino*, 15, 62, 64
  See also *cypress*.
Sawmill, 18, 66, 118
Sawmill Creek, 66
Scotland, James (carpenter), 37, 130
Seats, 30, 31
Seloy (Indian village), 14
Sentry box, 63
Shake, 66, 71, 99, 102, 103
Shed, 35, 38, 39, 127
Shell, 17, 20, 28, 31, 32, 47, 62, 66, 68, 70, 71, 72, 104, 118, 131
Shingle, 12, 21, 25, 31, 34, 36, 37, 38, 39, 40, 44, 62, 66, 92, 99, 102, 103, 110, 112, 124, 127, 128
Shipwreck, 18
Shop, 128
Shutter, 12, 31, 37, 74, 79, 81, 86, 87, 88, 89
Siege of 1702, 8, 11, 22-25, 37, 64, 65, 107
Siege of 1740, 8, 21, 28
Six Mile Creek, 66
Slat, 106
Slate, 109
Slaughterhouse, 38
Smith, Hale G., 3, 120
Smoke hole, 33, 101, 122, 123, 124
Solana, Father, 105
Sources, 104, 107, 109, 122, 134*ff*.
  archeology, 11, 68, 73, 79, 106, 108, 118
  archives, 10, 11, 17, 46, 83, 93, 127
  maps, 10, 111
    1593: 16, 65, 109
    1764: 33, 58, 71, 111

# INDEX

1788: 46, 48, 49, 50, 51, 55, 58, 60, 61, 66, 71, 72, 111, 124, 129
  photographs, 10, 89, 90, 93, 95, 98, 112, 115, 116, 131
  prints, 10
  sketches, 36, 89, 90, 105, 110
  sites, 10
  structures, 10, 11, 79
  tax appraisals, 7, 61, 79, 124, 126, 131
Spain, 8, 9, 11, 22, 25, 27, 28, 45, 47, 102
Spouts, 31, 90, 113
Stable, 35, 37, 38, 39, 40, 60, 109, 127
Stairway, 31, 50, 61, 74, 84-85, 95-98
Stake (fence), 129
Stewart, Richard H., 3
Stewart, William, 4
Stirling, Mrs. Matthew W., 3
Stone, 10, 12, 17, 20, 21, 24, 25, 26, 28, 31, 33, 34, 38, 39, 44, 46, 47, 62, 67, 68, 70, 71, 72, 73, 91, 93, 98, 108, 120, 122, 123, 125, 127, 130, 131
  discovery (1580), 17, 67
  "Stone and lime," 38, 62, 72, 125
  stone cutting, 68
Stone, Fred, 4
Stoney, Samuel G., 4
Store, 34, 35, 38, 39, 80, 128
Storehouse, 38, 116, 127
Storeroom, 61
Stork, William, 28, 61, 91, 107
Stove, 84, 123, 124
Straw, 25, 26, 62, 64, 99, 102
Street, 12, 15, 23, 26, 31, 33, 40, 41, 47, 51, 55, 56, 59, 61, 74, 80, 83, 86, 92, 93, 94, 112, 113, 131, 132, 133
  Bridge, 25
  Charlotte, 10-11, 34, 46, 84, 98, 105
  Cuna, 23, 42
  Green Lane, 25
  St. George, 23, 25, 29, 42, 44, 109
  Treasury, 46, 98, 105

Tabby, 10, 12, 17, 20, 24, 26, 28, 30, 32, 33, 46, 62, 66, 67, 68, 69, 70, 71, 72, 73, 92, 95, 99, 101, 104, 105, 106, 107, 118, 119, 120, 122, 124, 131
*Tabique*, 69, 72
*Tabla*, 15, 62, 65, 71, 99, 104, 105, 120, 130
  *tablazón*, 99
  See also *board.*
Tanner, Helen H., 4
*Tapia*, 17, 62
Tar, 129
Tavern, 31, 34, 35, 38, 39, 40, 61, 133
  bar, 40
*Tejamani*, 99, 102, 103
Terrace (tabby), 31, 33, 120, 122
Thatch, 8, 10, 12, 16, 17, 27, 33, 34, 62, 63, 64, 71, 79, 89, 99, 100, 101-102, 107, 109, 120, 124
  prohibited (1783), 102
Tile, 73, 99, 105, 106, 107, 127
  "barrel," 20, 21, 38, 99, 109, 113
  glazed fireplace (*azulejo*), 98

177

# INDEX

Timber, 25, 44
Timber-frame, 8, 10, 20, 36, 39, 40, 46, 62, 63, 65, 66, 71, 80, 82, 117, 120, 121, 124, 127, 128
*Torta,* 105
Transom, 74, 81, 83
Transport of structures, 36, 37, 39
Treasurer's House, 20, 21, 23, 58, 90, 91, 108, 113
Trees:
  cherry, 129
  citron, 18
  citrus, 129
  fig, 18, 47, 129
  fruit, 9, 18, 124, 128
  lemon, 40
  lime, 34
  orange, 18, 34, 38, 40, 47
  peach, 129
  pomegranate, 18, 47, 129
  quince, 129
Trout Creek, 66
Tully, John (mason), 37

United States, 8, 41, 45, 47
University of Florida, 4

Van Campen, J. Tyler, 3
Vinten, C. Ray, 3
Virginia, 9

Walks, 30, 31, 92, 95, 124
Wall paper, 39, 121
Walls, 15, 16, 17, 20, 21, 26, 29, 31, 46, 47, 50, 55, 61, 62*ff.*
  materials for, 62-73
  See also *fence.*
Wash house, 127
Waterproofing, 12, 70-71, 98, 120
Watson, George, 4
Watson, William (builder), 37, 60, 66, 80, 120, 127, 128
Wattle-and-daub, 17, 71, 72, 73
Weatherboard, 39, 62, 63, 65, 89, 104
Weathercock, 37
Weights and measures, 18
Well, 31, 38, 84, 124, 125-126
West Indies, 11, 15, 36, 37, 81, 105, 106
Wicket, 87, 88
Wildlife, 15, 128
Wiles, Doris, C., 3
Window, 29, 31, 33, 35, 38, 40, 61, 74, 79, 81, 84-85, 86-89, 95, 124
  frame, 86, 88
  dormer, 111, 112, 115-116
Winter, W. J., 4
Whitewash, 17, 34, 38, 39, 64, 66, 70, 121, 133
Wood, 8, 12, 15, 17, 19, 20, 21, 22, 23, 25, 26, 28, 33, 38, 46, 60, 61, 62, 63, 64-66, 71, 72, 79, 93, 99, 123, 124, 125, 127, 129, 131, 133
  partitions, 120
  roofs, 102-104
Woodcutters' Creek, 66

# INDEX

Workmen, 9, 20, 25, 26, 27, 35, 37, 43, 44, 47, 68, 110, 118
  architect, 58
  carpenter, 36, 37, 66, 80, 90, 102, 111, 127
  engineer, 20, 27, 41, 45, 48, 92, 103
  farmer, 41, 43
  Indian, 19
  limeburner, 20
  logger, 18
  mason, 20, 21, 37
  overseer, 26, 27
  sawyer, 18
  slave, 19
  stonecutter, 19, 21
  surveyor, 28, 35, 92, 124, 130
  tiler, 37, 109
  See also *Negro.*

Yale University, 4
Yard, 11, 12, 31, 33, 34, 40, 55, 61, 74, 80, 84, 92, 93, 124-125, 128-131
  structures, 124-133
    privies, 127
    stables, etc., 127-128
    walls, fences, 128-133
    wells, 125-126
Yeats, David (tiler), 37, 109
Yucca, 128, 130